GALLIPOLI

The Battlefield Guide

ALSO BY MAT MCLACHLAN

Walking with the Anzacs:
A Guide to Australian Battlefields on the Western Front

GALLIPOLI
The Battlefield Guide

MAT McLACHLAN

hachette
AUSTRALIA

Published in Australia and New Zealand in 2010
by Hachette Australia
(an imprint of Hachette Australia Pty Limited)
Level 17, 207 Kent Street, Sydney NSW 2000
www.hachette.com.au

1 3 5 7 9 10 8 6 4 2

National Library of Australia
Cataloguing-in-Publication data

McLachlan, Mat.
Gallipoli / Mat McLachlan.

978 0 7336 2385 1 (pbk.)

Includes index.
Bibliography.

World War, 1914-1918 – Battlefields – Turkey – Gallipoli Peninsula – Guidebooks.
Gallipoli Peninsula (Turkey) – Description and travel.
Gallipoli Peninsula (Turkey) – Guidebooks.

940.426

Cover design and text design by Darian Causby/Highway 51
Cover photographs courtesy of Mat McLachlan
Internal photographs by Mat McLachlan unless otherwise attributed
Maps by KYSO Design
Text design by Bookhouse, Sydney
Typeset in 11.5/15 ITC Berkeley Oldstyle Pro
Printed in Australia by Griffin Press, Adelaide

Hachette Australia's policy is to use papers that are natural,
renewable and recyclable products and made from wood
grown in sustainable forests. The logging and manufacturing
processes are expected to conform to the environmental
regulations of the country of origin.

For Brooke and Heath

Contents

Acknowledgements

This book was a collaborative effort – it would not exist without the dedication of a large and diverse group of people.

I'd firstly like to thank my publisher, Matthew Kelly, who humoured me when my concepts for this book were somewhat sketchy, and then supported me as it came to fruition. I would also like to thank Kenan Çelik, the man who knows the Gallipoli battlefields better than anyone, and who joined me to explore them on two very important occasions: when I first visited Gallipoli as an eager but ill-informed traveller, and on my final research trip for this book, almost a decade later. His advice was invaluable in shaping the itineraries that appear in this book. All mistakes, however, are mine and not his.

No student of the Gallipoli campaign can get by without referring to the works of the official historians: Charles Bean

(Australia), Fred Waite (New Zealand) and Cecil Aspinall (Britain). Although their interpretations may sometimes be questioned, their thoroughness and dedication to making sense of a complicated campaign cannot be overlooked. Their hard work in decades past has made my job in writing this book so much easier, and I am grateful to them.

My thanks also goes to several leading historians, whose input was invaluable in gaining a deeper knowledge of this often-confusing period of history. I had many enjoyable conversations with Peter Stanley, and his perspective on the fighting around Quinn's Post in particular was extremely helpful. Peter Hart also provided insight into the campaign from the British perspective, and I am grateful to him and Nigel Steel for allowing me to reproduce quotes from their excellent work *Defeat at Gallipoli*. I would also like to thank Bill Gammage for extending me the same courtesy with his important book *The Broken Years*, an Australian classic that has brought the campaign to life for thousands of readers, and will do so for many years to come.

It would have been impossible to write this book without returning to Gallipoli several times to walk the ground and fine-tune the tours, and many people helped make these journeys a success. Thanks to Peter Douglas at Emirates and Nicholas Zaferis at Hertz, and also to Eric Goossens and his wife Özlem, proprietors of The Gallipoli Houses – in my opinion the best place to stay at Gallipoli. Eric is a keen student of the campaign, and his enthusiasm for the topic is boundless. I'd also like to thank my good mate Todd Prees who joined me on my last research trip and, like many an Anzac before him, temporarily abandoned a young family to explore a foreign land. My father Gil also joined me on an earlier trip, and took many of the photographs that appear in this book.

My thanks also goes to Peter Reynolds and Kate Hopkinson at KYSO Design, whose outstanding work on the maps in this book brought the tours to life. I also appreciate the hard work of the team at the Australian War Memorial, including Mary-Lou Pooley, Jeremy Richter, Krissy Kraljevic, Ashley Ekins and Anne Bennie. Thanks also to Adeline Dias for her assistance with French translations and Michael Molkentin for his input into the character and motivations of the original Anzacs.

To my family, I'd like to extend my eternal gratitude. Your support has been unconditional and unwavering. And to my tireless wife Merryn, who was by my side that first time I scaled Plugge's, gazed across Monash Valley and instantly fell in love with the place: your limitless encouragement gave me the confidence to start work on this book and to stick with it when it was all too hard. It wouldn't have happened without you.

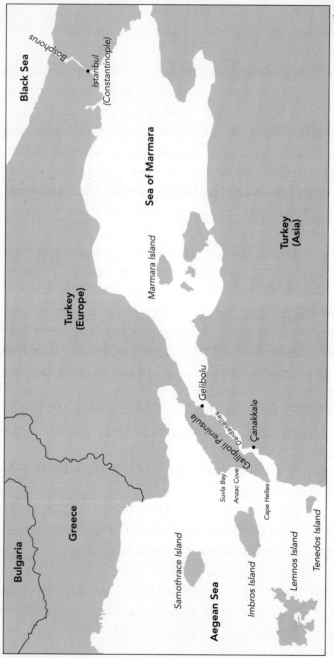

N

Black Sea

Bosphorus

Istanbul
(Constantinople)

Sea of Marmara

Turkey
(Europe)

Marmara Island

Turkey
(Asia)

Gelibolu

Gallipoli Peninsula

Çanakkale

Dardanelles

Suvla Bay

Anzac Cove

Cape Helles

Greece

Bulgaria

Samothrace Island

Aegean Sea

Imbros Island

Lemnos Island

Tenedos Island

75km

Turkey

The Gallipoli Campaign

The plan

The Gallipoli peninsula is strategically important only because it commands the Dardanelles, the narrow straits that separate Europe from Asia and control access to the Black Sea. At their head stands Constantinople (today's Istanbul), the ancient capital that has tempted invading armies since it was founded in 600BC.

By 1914 the Dardanelles had been fought over for thousands of years, and when Turkey joined the First World War on Germany's side, the Allies set their sights on the straits. While the Dardanelles remained in Turkish hands, Britain and France's key ally, Russia, was cut off. If the Dardanelles could be captured, Russia could be resupplied by sea, Turkey would be isolated from her European allies and the Germans might decide that their lofty territorial ambitions weren't such a great idea after all.

The Allied plan for capturing the Dardanelles wasn't subtle, and it wasn't particularly effective either. It was the brainchild of a young Winston Churchill, then First Lord of the Admiralty, whose basic idea was to send a fleet of battleships into the Dardanelles, blow the hell out of the forts that guarded the straits and steam on to Constantinople and glory. With Constantinople in Allied hands, Turkey's ability and will to fight would be shattered, and its brief involvement in the war would reach a sudden end. What Churchill didn't realise was that the job of capturing the Dardanelles was harder than it looked and that the Turks weren't going to give up their homeland without a fight.

The naval battle

On 18 March 1915, a fleet of 18 British and French battle-ships barged their way into the entrance of the Dardanelles and began blasting away at the forts on both sides of the straits. The Turks had heavily mined the waterway and dotted the shoreline with mobile artillery batteries, which could fire quickly and accurately and were almost impossible to spot from the deck of a ship. The attack started well and the forts were soon being pounded by Allied naval fire. But things started to go wrong when the unarmoured British minesweepers failed to clear the mines under a storm of Turkish fire. And they got worse when the battleships started running into mines that they didn't even know were there.

In the days before the battle the Turks had watched the Allied ships manoeuvring in the wide expanse of Erenköy Bay, and in response the stout-hearted Turkish minelayer *Nusrat*

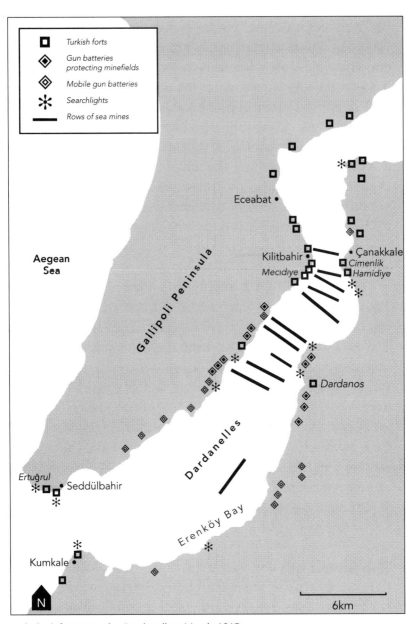

Turkish defences at the Dardanelles, March 1915

had laid a line of mines parallel to the shore. The French battleship *Bouvet* was the *Nusrat's* first victim, hitting a mine and sinking in a few minutes. Next the British battlecruiser *Inflexible* hit a mine near where the *Bouvet* had gone down and, crippled, floated impotently out of the straits. HMS *Irresistible* soon suffered the same fate. After her crew was rescued she was abandoned on the shoreline and was blasted by the Turkish guns until she sank. Late in the day HMS *Ocean* hit another mine and drifted helplessly until she sank in nearby Morto Bay later that night. Several other ships in the fleet were seriously damaged, and the Royal Navy refused to take on the forts again unless the army supported them with a landing.

And so the plot for a landing at Gallipoli was hatched. The theory was that the army would land, cross the peninsula and capture the forts and batteries that guarded the straits. The navy would then clear the minefields and capture the Dardanelles, steaming on to Constantinople and knocking Turkey out of the war. The landings were planned for two main sectors: the Australian and New Zealand Army Corps would land midway along the western coast of the peninsula, push quickly inland to secure the high ground and cut the peninsula in two. At the same time, British troops would land on the toe of the peninsula at Cape Helles and drive straight up the peninsula.

The landings

In the murky dawn of 25 April 1915, a small armada of open row boats approached the shore in the Anzac sector.

The plan called for them to land in several waves on a wide frontage and push inland, capturing the three rough ridges that hemmed in the sector. But vague instructions, poor navigation and confusion during the approach to the beach resulted in the boats bunching up and landing in a muddled jumble on a narrow beach that came to be known as Anzac Cove. Their plans to advance quickly inland were soon in tatters, as battalions became intermixed and lost the ability to fight as a cohesive force.

Turkish reinforcements under the command of Mustafa Kemal (who would later lead the Turkish revolution and be remembered as Kemal Atatürk, 'Father of the Turks'), began streaming into the sector, blocking the progress of the Anzacs. The fighting was reduced to a series of violent close encounters on the heights of Second Ridge. The Anzacs dug in well short of their objective, the Turks dug in opposite them and the front line would move little for the next eight months.

At Helles, the British fared little better. They came ashore at five beaches and, in spite of greatly outnumbering the Turkish defenders, were mown down in waves. In three days of bloody fighting they won 15 Victoria Crosses but advanced only a few kilometres inland. French troops also landed on the Asian side of the Dardanelles as a diversion from the main landings, but withdrew after a series of violent encounters with the Turks.

For the next three months the British and French threw themselves against the Turkish defenders at Helles in a series of major attacks that inched the line forward, but resulted in appalling casualties. By July both sides were exhausted and Helles had become a siege. At Anzac both the Allies

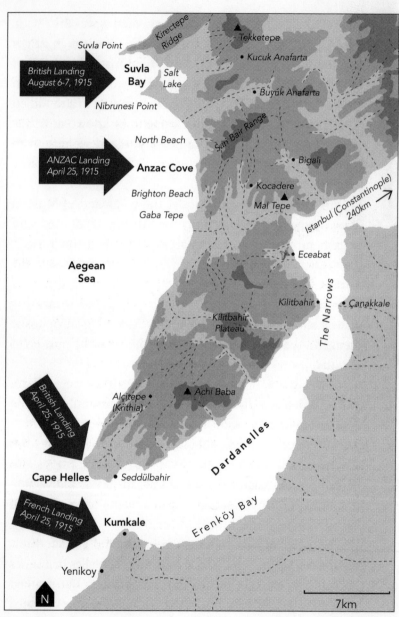

The Gallipoli peninsula, 1915

and Turks launched frontal assaults in an attempt to drive through their enemy's lines, but with little result. The largest of these was a huge Turkish assault on 19 May, which failed to capture the Anzac trenches but resulted in more than 10,000 Turkish casualties. The thousands of bodies in no-man's-land began to putrefy, until a truce on 24 May enabled the battleground to be cleared and for soldiers from both sides to briefly fraternise.

The August Offensive

By August the Allied commanders at Gallipoli were desperate. What had begun as a naval battle had turned into a land war, and a decidedly costly one at that. Their final plan to capture the peninsula involved a surge in troop numbers and a bold attack at Anzac that would outflank the Turks and open up the advance to the Dardanelles.

The August Offensive began on the evening of 6 August, when Australian troops launched a diversionary attack on Turkish positions at Lone Pine. The attack was intended to hold Turkish reserves in the area and prevent them from defending more critical parts of the line. The Australians succeeded in capturing the Turkish trenches, and also in drawing Turkish reserves on them. For four days some of the bloodiest hand-to-hand fighting of the campaign raged in the claustrophobic trenches and tunnels at Lone Pine. Seven Australians were awarded the Victoria Cross. By 10 August both sides were exhausted and the Turks gave up trying to retake their old positions. Even though the attack was a success, little of strategic value had been gained.

While the Battle of Lone Pine was raging, the key attack of the August Offensive was launched. On the night of 6 August, New Zealand troops cleared the foothills north of Anzac, and then a combined Anzac and British force advanced in two columns, with orders to capture Chunuk Bair, Hill Q and Hill 971, the three highest points in the Anzac sector. Most of the attacking troops were ill with dysentery, they were advancing in the dark through unfamiliar country, and the plan was impossibly complicated. Delays were inevitable and units became lost in the tangle of gullies and ravines.

At Chunuk Bair the New Zealanders attacked repeatedly and eventually captured the summit, but were stretched to hold it against ferocious Turkish counterattacks. On 10 August they were relieved by British troops, who came into the line just in time to face a murderous Turkish attack. Thousands of Turks swarmed over the summit, slaughtering the British troops without mercy and pushing the Allied line off the heights of Chunuk Bair.

At Hill Q, a battalion of Gurkhas under Major Cecil Allanson charged the summit and set the Turks to flight, before a salvo of shells from an Allied gun landed among them and broke up the advance. They were forced to retreat.

Meanwhile, the Australian 4th Brigade under the command of Colonel John Monash was struggling in its efforts to capture Hill 971. A disastrous shortcut during its advance had delayed it by hours, and a wrong turn during the advance meant that it was now hopelessly lost. Over the next few days the Australians tried in vain to advance on the high ground, but were forced to retreat after heavy casualties.

As part of the plan to capture the high ground, Australian light horse troops had been ordered to launch an attack on the strong Turkish positions at the Nek in the early hours of 7 August. The attack was intended to be supported by the New Zealanders after they had captured Chunuk Bair – the New Zealanders would attack the Turkish trenches from behind as the light horsemen charged across no-man's-land. The New Zealanders, of course, were nowhere near securing Chunuk Bair, so the light horsemen were ordered to advance on their own. In one of the most hopeless attacks of the war, four waves of Australians threw themselves at the massed Turkish machine guns and rifles at the Nek. They were annihilated. After the war, the remains of more than 250 men were found in an area the size of three tennis courts.

While these attacks at Anzac were raging, the British unleashed the surprise element of their offensive plan. On the night of 6 August, the British IX Corps landed at Suvla Bay, 8 kilometres north of Anzac. Originally the plan called for the troops to advance inland, swing south and assist the Anzacs in their advance on Hill 971, but the plans were watered down. The British landed with vague instructions about securing a northern base and capturing a smattering of strategically unimportant hills. By morning on 7 August, almost 20,000 British troops were ashore at Suvla and the high ground in front of them lay open. But the British commanders on the spot dithered. For two days troops were marched around on the flat Suvla plain, and little attempt was made to advance on the heights. Eventually the British ordered an assault on the high ground, but Turkish reinforcements beat them there by 30 minutes. Like Anzac and Helles, Suvla became a siege.

So ended the August Offensive, and with it the last real chance of Allied success at Gallipoli. Attacks were launched at Suvla in late August on Hill 60 and Scimitar Hill, but these only succeeded in linking the lines at Anzac and Suvla.

On 16 October, General Sir Ian Hamilton, the commander of the British forces at Gallipoli, was sacked and shortly after the British War Cabinet began drafting plans for the evacuation of the peninsula. The decision to abandon Gallipoli was made in November after winter storms lashed the peninsula and hundreds of soldiers died of exposure. On 19 December the last troops left Anzac and Suvla. Helles was evacuated in early January. The Gallipoli campaign was over.

Getting Started

How to use this book

The Gallipoli battlefield area is surprisingly small and, because the Allies failed in their attempts to capture the peninsula, the front lines remained fairly fixed for the entire campaign. This means that, compared to the big, wheeling actions on the Western Front, a huge amount happened in a very small space at Gallipoli. Every gully and ridge could tell a thousand stories, and getting your head around exactly what went on here can be a challenge.

The story of the Gallipoli campaign is so riven with intrigue and misadventure that it can be difficult to follow. As soon as you feel you have a handle on one attack and the reasons it went so badly wrong, you find that another one took place over the same ground soon after, usually with the same disastrous results.

In an effort to simplify things, the Gallipoli battle area has been divided into six main tours: Anzac Cove and the Landing

Beaches; Second Ridge; Chunuk Bair and Gun Ridge; Helles and Krithia; Suvla and North of Anzac; and The Asian Shore. Each tour has a brief introduction explaining what went on there, and a comprehensive tour that visits the key sites at each location and explains why they are important. Many of the stories are told in the words of those who were there.

Before visiting Gallipoli, study the maps in this book and familiarise yourself with the history of the campaign in the Gallipoli Timeline (page 347). Every action at Gallipoli was linked with the actions before and after it, and a good understanding of the motives and outcomes of each stage of the campaign will make things much easier to appreciate on the ground.

The tours in the Anzac sector (Anzac Cove and the Landing Beaches; Second Ridge and Chunuk Bair and Gun Ridge) can be walked if you are fit and have the time. One of the main enemies at Gallipoli was the terrain, so following in the footsteps of the soldiers and getting a feel for the land allows a better understanding of events. All the tours follow roads, however, and can be driven. The tours of Helles and Krithia, Suvla and North of Anzac and The Asian Shore are all long and can only be completed by car.

Planning your trip

In spite of its geographic isolation, Gallipoli is an accessible destination. Many Australian and New Zealand visitors to Turkey consider it an essential stop, and it fits neatly into any itinerary that visits the western part of the country.

The Anzac area is surprisingly compact – especially considering how much blood was spilled to gain the ground. It can be visited in one day, although you will also need to allow a day's travelling either side from Istanbul and on to your next destination. The main Anzac walking tours in this book (Anzac Cove and the Landing Beaches, Second Ridge, and Chunuk Bair and Gun Ridge) may be completed in a day and will give you a good overview of the main sites in the Australian sector. For Australians, these tours cover the essential sites. They fit in neatly with the schedule of memorial services on Anzac Day, or can be completed back-to-back at any time of the year.

For a more thorough tour and to see more than just the key Australian sites, three days on the peninsula (plus travelling time) is really the bare minimum. Break up a trip of this length by spending a day walking in the Anzac sector, and then drive the Helles and Krithia, and Suvla and North of Anzac tours over the next two days.

All the tours in this book can be completed in five days on the peninsula (plus travelling time), although you may not have much time left over to take in additional sites outside the main tours. For a trip of this length, spend two days in the Anzac sector and then a day each driving the Helles, Suvla and The Asian Shore tours. This will give you a complete overview of the entire Gallipoli campaign and take you to most of the important sites in the region.

If you would also like to visit Ancient Troy – and you really should while you are in the area – either allocate an extra day or spend the afternoon there after completing The Asian Shore tour.

Travelling in Turkey

Turkey is an intriguing blend of the modern and the traditional. As per Kemal Atatürk's design, it is a secular state, but its roots grow deeply in Islam. Gallipoli locals are used to seeing tourists and are very tolerant of them, but don't abuse their hospitality by failing to respect their customs and sensitivities.

Women should not display too much bare skin. Shorts and T-shirts are fine, but swimwear should only be worn on the beach. When visiting a mosque, both men and women should dress conservatively and remove their shoes, and women may need to wear a headscarf.

Unless you are keen to experience some of the same maladies as the Anzacs, drink bottled water and be careful when ordering food. Only eat fruit and vegetables that have been cooked or that you have peeled. Cooked-to-order meals are better options than buffets, where food might not be kept hot enough to kill bacteria. Even with the best precautions, many travellers still suffer from the 'Sultan's Revenge' in Turkey, so it's a good idea to carry anti-diarrhoea medication.

Be conscious of personal safety. Turkey isn't a particularly dangerous country to visit, but pickpockets can be a problem in Istanbul and tourists are sometimes robbed. Use common sense, make sure your vaccinations are up-to-date, take out adequate travel insurance and visit your government's travel advisory website (www.smarttraveller.gov.au or www.safetravel.govt.nz) before you travel.

When to go

Gallipoli has a tough climate, hot in summer and bitterly cold in winter. So unless you are a very hardy traveller, it's not really a year-round destination. Most Australian visitors come here during the warmer months, from April until about October.

The busiest time is of course April – half the Australian tourists who visit Gallipoli in any given year come for Anzac Day. The Dawn Service at Gallipoli must rate as Australia's most important regular overseas event, and the moving commemorations will be well remembered by those who attend. However, the sheer volume of visitors makes the Anzac Day period the most difficult time of the year to visit the peninsula. Accommodation is relatively expensive and hard to find, and some sites are closed or inaccessible during preparations for the service. Traffic slows to a crawl on the peninsula's narrow roads. Something important is also lost during Anzac Day: the sense of tranquillity that pervades the peninsula at any other time of the year. Gallipoli is a place of pilgrimage and reflection, and standing alone at a cemetery or on a jagged ridge and trying to make sense of what went on there is an important aspect of a journey to Gallipoli. If you have the luxury, go to Gallipoli for Anzac Day and then come back at another time of the year for a more thorough visit.

The best times to visit are when the climate is suitable – May/June and September/October are probably the best. Many Australians visit in high summer (July/August), but be prepared for searing heat at this time of year. Gallipoli can also be visited in winter (November to January) but be prepared for rain and snow. The Anzacs were forced to endure the peninsula in all seasons, and a winter visit certainly gives you a new insight into the hardships faced by the troops in the period just before the evacuation – an aspect of the Gallipoli saga that is often overlooked.

Getting there

In Turkey the name 'Gallipoli' (Gelibolu in Turkish) applies almost universally to a small town that is more than 50 kilometres from the battlefield area, rather than the Gallipoli peninsula. Don't make the mistake of organising transport only as far as Gelibolu. When booking tickets or getting driving directions, be sure to ask for one of the towns in the battlefield area: Eceabat (pronounced *Eh-cha-bet*) or Çanakkale (pronounced *Chun-uk-ah-lee*).

The difficulty in getting to Gallipoli was once part of its appeal, but the huge growth in visitor numbers since the 1990s and improving tourism infrastructure throughout Turkey mean that Gallipoli is now on the tourist circuit.

Most visitors to the area stay in Çanakkale, a lively university town of about 80,000 people, which has an excellent range of accommodation and restaurants. The drawback to staying in Çanakkale is that it is situated on the Asian side of the Narrows, which means you must take a 30-minute ferry ride across the Dardanelles to reach the battlefields.

Another option is the small town of Eceabat on the European side of the Narrows. Known as Maidos during the war, Eceabat is the port town on the peninsula where the ferries from Çanakkale dock. Its convenience to the battlefields is somewhat diluted by its lack of tourism facilities. The town really only consists of a couple of basic hotels and a small selection of restaurants and shops but it is a good option for the visitor who can only spare a day or two to visit Gallipoli, and isn't too concerned with nightlife.

The Gallipoli peninsula is just over 300 kilometres from Istanbul and the most convenient (and cheapest) way to get there is by bus. Inter-city bus services in Turkey are some of the best in the world, with clean, modern coaches (usually with toilets), air-conditioning and even cabin attendants offering refreshments and a squirt of rose-water hand cleanser during the journey. Buses from Istanbul leave for Çanakkale (via Eceabat) as frequently as hourly. The journey takes just under six hours to Çanakkale (including the ferry ride) and about five hours to Eceabat. Onward bus services from Çanakkale run to a range of destinations throughout western Turkey. Hotels and travel agents in Istanbul can book coach tickets, with many companies offering hotel pick-ups.

Another option is to hire a car in Istanbul and drive to the peninsula. The journey takes about four hours on good roads, but the locals tend to drive fast and observance of road rules can be a bit casual. Always drive defensively and never drive at night. Hire a car at Istanbul airport rather than in the city itself. The drive will be adventure enough without having to also negotiate Istanbul's maze of congested streets.

While the convenience of having your own car on the peninsula is compelling, another option is to travel by bus or plane to Çanakkale and hire a car there. Be warned that car hire companies on the peninsula usually offer older cars and their employees often don't speak English. Car hire in Turkey is also relatively expensive.

Çanakkale has a basic but modern airport, but air services have been irregular in the past. At the time of writing, Turkish Airlines offered flights several days a week between Istanbul and Çanakkale. A shuttle bus operates from the airport to the centre of Çanakkale, and taxis are cheap and plentiful.

A large number of local businesses offer short tours of the battlefields, either departing from and returning to Istanbul or operating out of Çanakkale or Eceabat. Once again, travel agents and hotels in Istanbul can make bookings for you. Most hotels in Çanakkale and Eceabat can organise a guided tour for you. Extended tours booked from Australia and New Zealand are also popular. A growing number of companies offer tours, particularly for Anzac Day. The Australian War Memorial operates an extensive tour, and Mat McLachlan Battlefield Tours (www.battlefields.com.au) has regular departures.

Getting around

Many visitors to Gallipoli join an organised tour. This is by far the easiest way to see the battlefields but the downside is the loss of the independence and solitude possible with self-touring. Short organised tours will only show you the bare minimum key battlefield sites, and you won't have the opportunity to explore further afield or do the tours in this book.

The best way of touring the battlefields is with your own hire car. The major hire car companies have outlets at Istanbul airport, and a number of small local companies operate in Çanakkale and Eceabat. With your own car you have the freedom to explore the Anzac sector by car or on foot, and also complete driving tours of Suvla, Helles and the Asian side of the Dardanelles.

If you plan on just visiting the Anzac sector and don't mind walking, catch a taxi to Anzac Cove from the ferry port in Eceabat and arrange for the driver to pick you up at the end of the day. Taxi fares are cheap, and the drivers are generally reliable.

A more expensive option is to hire a car with a private driver. Your hotel will be able to arrange this. The car and driver will stay with you throughout the day while you tour the battlefields. Some drivers double as tour guides, and can help you plan the best route to make the most of your stay.

Public buses operate between the villages on the peninsula, but there is no public transport that services the battlefield areas.

Where to stay

Çanakkale offers the widest range of accommodation and best tourist facilities, but is located on the Asian side of the Dardanelles, so daily ferry rides become part of your touring experience. Çanakkale is the only major town in the region, so it's one of the few places that offers anything worth visiting that isn't connected to the battlefields. The movie *Troy* was filmed near Çanakkale in 2004, and the giant wooden horse that was the movie's main prop stands proudly in the town.

While the village of Eceabat is on the European side of the Dardanelles, and is more convenient for battlefield visits, it offers only basic tourist facilities. Staying in Eceabat saves up to a couple of hours travelling each day, but there is only budget accommodation.

Hotels in Turkey are cheap by Australian standards, so even budget travellers should consider staying at a hotel rather than a hostel. Breakfast is almost always included in the tariff. Following are my favourite accommodation options (star ratings are based on Australian standards).

The Gallipoli Houses
Kocadere Village
Eceabat/Çanakkale 17900
Turkey
Phone: +90 (286) 814 2650
Fax: +90 (286) 814 1617
email: talk2us@gallipoli.com.tr
Web: www.gallipoli.com.tr
A European-style B&B located in the tiny village of Kocadere, only 10 minutes from the Anzac battlefield and overlooking the rear of the Turkish line at Anzac. Rooms are spacious and very well equipped, the location can't be bettered and owners Eric Goossens and his wife Özlem are charming and helpful hosts.

Canak Hotel
Cumhuriyet Cad. Dibek Sok. No. 1 (Dibek Street)
Çanakkale, Turkey
Phone: +90 (286) 214 1582

Fax: +90 (286) 214 0906
email: sales@canakhotel.com
Web: www.canakhotel.com
A clean and comfortable 3-star hotel in the heart of Çanakkale.
Rooms are spacious and staff are friendly. The hotel has a
good restaurant and bar.

Anzac Hotel

Saat Kulesi Meydani No. 8
(Clock Tower Square)
Çanakkale 17100, Turkey
Phone: +90 (286) 217 7777
Fax: +90 (286) 217 2018
email: info@anzachotel.com
Web: www.anzachotel.com
A Gallipoli institution, this basic 2-star hotel has hosted
thousands of Gallipoli visitors and is one of the most popular
places to stay in Çanakkale. Located in the centre of town,
the hotel is clean, welcoming and has lots of character, but
if you are looking for a bit more luxury, you'll do better
elsewhere.

Anzac House International Youth Hostel

Cumhuriyet Meydani No. 59
Çanakkale 17100, Turkey
Phone: +90 (286) 213 5969
Fax: +90 (286) 217 2906
email: hasslefree@anzachouse.com
Web: www.anzachouse.com

The most popular accommodation choice for backpackers and budget travellers in Çanakkale. The hostel is central, clean and friendly and has single, twin and dormitory rooms. It offers a few nice touches that will be welcomed by backpackers, including Vegemite on toast and barbecues in summer.

Tusan Hotel
Güzelyali
Çanakkale 17001, Turkey
Phone: +90 (286) 232 8747
Fax: +90 (286) 232 8226
email: info@tusanhotel.com
Web: www.tusanhotel.com
A popular family-run 3-star hotel located 14 kilometres south of Çanakkale on the shore of the Dardanelles. A picturesque location and a good option if you would like more tranquillity than you will find in town. You will need your own transport to make the most of your stay. Hotel facilities include a pool, bar and restaurant with water views. A nice oasis after a hectic day touring the battlefields.

Kolin Hotel
Kepez
Çanakkale 17001, Turkey
Phone: +90 (286) 218 0808
Fax: +90 (286) 218 0800
email: info@kolinhotel.com
Web: www.kolinhotel.com

The Kolin is Çanakkale's most luxurious property. It has spacious, modern rooms with good service, but could be considered a little soulless compared to other accommodation in the area. It is located on the outskirts of town, so is not as convenient to the ferry port and restaurants as some of Çanakkale's other hotels.

Maydos Hotel

Yali Caddesi No. 12
Çanakkale 17100, Turkey
Phone: +90 (286) 213 5970
Fax: +90 (286) 217 4090
email: info@maydos.com.tr
Web: www.maydos.com.tr
A welcoming 2.5-star hotel. The hotel is well located on the Çanakkale waterfront, so ask for a waterfront room. A good option for travellers who want clean and basic accommodation at a very good price, or budget travellers who are looking for more comfort and privacy than a hostel.

TJ's Hostel/Eceabat Hotel

Cumhuriyet Meydani 20A
Eceabat 17900, Turkey
Phone: +90 (286) 814 3121
Fax: +90 (286) 814 3122
email: enquiries@anzacgallipolitours.com
Web: www.anzacgallipolitours.com
Another Gallipoli institution. TJ's Hostel has been the stopping point for thousands of backpackers over the years and it is valued for its convenience to the battlefields. TJ is a well-

respected Gallipoli guide and has been running his battlefield tour company for over a decade. With his Australian wife Bernina, they operate a clean and comfortable hostel and a 3-star hotel. TJ leads small group tours of the battlefields most days of the year.

Guiding services

Gallipoli has become a busy tourist destination and there are hundreds of guides offering their services to show visitors around the battlefield. It's certainly not essential to hire a guide when visiting the battlefield but, for small groups in particular, a guide can add a new dimension to your Gallipoli visit. The number one guide to the Gallipoli battlefields is Kenan Çelik, a former lecturer at the university in Çanakkale and now a full-time battlefield guide. When presidents and prime ministers visit Gallipoli, this is who they hire to show them around. In 2000 Kenan was presented with the Order of Australia for his decades of dedication to preserving the memory of the Anzacs.

Kenan Çelik, OAM
İsmet Paşa Mah. Öğretmenler Sitesi 2 Utku Apt. D:2
17100 Çanakkale, Turkey
Phone: +90 286 217 74 68
Mobile: +90 532 738 66 75
Email: info@kcelik.com or kcelik@ttmail.com
Web: www.kcelik.com

Research

Countless histories of the Gallipoli campaign have been written, so there is a wealth of resources for researchers. Charles (C. E. W.) Bean's Volumes I and II of the *Official History of Australia in the War of 1914–18* are comprehensive. From the first days of the Gallipoli campaign, Bean saw himself as the standard-bearer of the Anzac legend, and his dedication to his 'boys' in the First AIF comes through on every page. Bean, who was official historian, had the mind of a journalist but the pen of a lawyer, and he sometimes leaves the reader drowning in a sea of parentheses and footnotes. Bean's obsession for detail makes it particularly useful for learning about the movements of individual battalions and companies at specific points during the campaign. The volumes can be found in the research sections of major libraries, or can be downloaded free from the Australian War Memorial website (www.awm.gov.au).

Three other works associated with Charles Bean are also worth seeking out. *Anzac to Amiens* is a one-volume summary of Australia's involvement in the First World War, drawn from the same sources as the *Official History*. *Gallipoli Mission* describes Bean's return to Gallipoli in 1919 as head of the Australian Historical Mission. It's an engaging read and paints a picture of a Gallipoli eerily similar to the one that can be visited today. *Gallipoli Correspondent* is a selection of entries from Bean's diaries edited by Kevin Fewster, which tells of the glory and frustrations of the campaign first-hand.

A good general overview of the campaign is Les Carlyon's *Gallipoli* (2001). Carlyon often delivers a phrase so delicious that you reread it aloud.

Another excellent summary of the campaign is *Defeat at Gallipoli* by Nigel Steel and Peter Hart. For a combination of historical accuracy, thoughtful analysis and a view of the campaign through the eyes of the men who fought it, this book is hard to beat. It is available from online bookshops.

For a different perspective of the campaign, read Tom Frame's *The Shores of Gallipoli: Naval Aspects of the Anzac Campaign*. Frame is a thorough researcher and his focus on the oft-ignored role of the war at sea sheds new light on many aspects of Gallipoli that we take for granted.

As an insight into the campaign from the men who were there, Bill Gammage's *The Broken Years* has been a classic since it was first published in 1971. Gammage has assembled a heart-wrenching collection of diary entries and letters and does a better job of telling the story of the Anzacs in their own words than anyone.

Gallipoli: The Turkish Story by Kevin Fewster, Vecihi Basarin and Hatice Basarin was somewhat revolutionary when it was published in 2003. Accounts of the campaign from the Turkish point of view have been scant, and this book gives an excellent insight into the men who faced the Anzacs.

A recent addition to the stable of Gallipoli books is Robin Prior's *Gallipoli: The End of the Myth*. Prior has a great military mind, and his new approach to some of the entrenched myths about the campaign is refreshing.

For an absorbing account of the fighting at the Anzacs' most dangerous position, read *Quinn's Post* by Peter Stanley. Formerly with the Australian War Memorial and now with the National Museum of Australia, Stanley is one of Australia's leading war historians and his book offers new insight into the Anzac participation in the campaign.

For more recommended reading, see the bibliography on page 374.

For information about researching an individual soldier who fought at Gallipoli, see Researching an Australian Soldier on page 31.

What to wear

Turkish weather can be unkind to the unprepared visitor, so pack appropriately for the season. In the warmer months that means sun protection, so hats, sunscreen and lots of drinking water are essential. In winter the weather turns very cold, and snow is common, so dress accordingly. In all seasons, a pair of stout walking boots is vital for conquering the rough terrain, and long sleeves and trousers are essential if you intend venturing off well-established paths – head-high scrub with vicious thorns clogs many of the peninsula's gullies. Also keep an eye out for snakes during warmer weather. A compass and a pair of binoculars are both handy tools to carry on the tours.

Souvenirs

The fighting in Gallipoli was intense, and relics from the battle still litter the battlefields. It can be tempting to take home souvenirs, but use care. While not as big a problem as on some other battlefields, such as the Western Front in France, unexploded ammunition can still be found at Gallipoli, and it's still dangerous. For safety's sake, leave any bullets, shells or grenades you find well alone.

The sheer volume of visitors to Gallipoli also means that many of the key sites have been picked clean by souvenir hunters. On the main paths and at the main memorials you will be lucky to find any relics from the battles at all. Gallipoli is one of the world's best-preserved battlefields and the detritus of war is as important a part of the landscape as the cemeteries and memorials. At the risk of sounding idealistic, consider whether that cartridge case or coat button belongs more in the baked earth of a Gallipoli gully than it does on your mantelpiece at home.

Human bones are also a common find at Gallipoli, particularly in the gullies behind the Turkish lines. In most cases these bones are from Turkish soldiers – after the campaign the Turks honoured their martyrs by leaving the remains where they fell. Isolated human bones should be left alone, but more substantial remains should be reported to the war graves authorities for appropriate reburial. Ask at your hotel for contact details.

Cemeteries

More than 8,000 Australians and 2,000 New Zealanders were killed during the Gallipoli campaign and the majority of their remains, along with those of more than 20,000 of their British comrades, now lie in 31 Commonwealth cemeteries on the peninsula. The cemeteries were established soon after the war, either on the site of existing cemeteries that were greatly enlarged when remains from the surrounding area were reburied there, or were new cemeteries that were started from scratch. The cemeteries were built and are maintained by the Commonwealth War Graves Commission (CWGC).

Men killed at Helles and Suvla were mostly brought together in a small number of large cemeteries, while men killed at Anzac were buried in smaller, often isolated, battlefield cemeteries, close to where they died.

The Gallipoli cemeteries are similar to Commonwealth military cemeteries on battlefields all over the world, but they have a number of individual characteristics. Out of respect to Turkey's Islamic roots, Christian symbolism is more subdued in the cemeteries of Gallipoli than in other parts of the world. Each cemetery features a large cross but, unlike the grand, freestanding Cross of Sacrifice found in other Commonwealth war cemeteries, at Gallipoli the cross is built subtly into the back wall, and some cemeteries feature a high front wall so that the cross is not conspicuously displayed. Some Gallipoli cemeteries feature a Stone of Remembrance inscribed with the stirring sentiment 'Their name liveth for evermore', but often the phrase is simply inscribed on the rear wall.

Rather than the standard CWGC headstone, Gallipoli graves feature a small headstone, almost a plaque, set close to the ground. When these replaced temporary wooden grave markers in the 1920s, the CWGC decided on a standard design. Each gravestone displays the soldier's regimental number (except for officers), rank, name, unit, date of death and age (unless withheld by the family). A standard Christian cross was included with the permission of the family. The only other religious symbol allowed was the Star of David for Jewish burials. At the bottom of the headstone, the family was allowed to add a personal inscription. These inscriptions make poignant reading and are a personal link with each buried soldier. Some families chose not to include an inscription (or could not afford it – the CWGC charged three-and-a-half pence per letter) and New Zealand did not allow personal inscriptions at all.

The men who built the cemeteries at Gallipoli were faced with a problem: the huge number of unidentified bodies. Only 20 per cent of the Commonwealth men killed at Gallipoli are buried with a headstone that bears their name. The rest are either buried in unidentified graves or still lie beneath the battlefield waiting to be discovered. On other battlefields the unknown soldiers typically have headstones inscribed with 'A soldier of the Great War, known unto God' but at Gallipoli very few of the unknown graves are marked. This means that many cemeteries feature hundreds of burials but few headstones. Bear in mind that when you visit them, as you walk across the large expanses of grass, there are hundreds of men lying beneath your feet.

The cemetery builders also had to deal with the fact that, as the losing party in the campaign, the Allies had been forced to abandon the cemeteries to the enemy for more than three years after the evacuation. When they returned, they found that, even though they had lists of the men buried in the cemeteries, most of the wooden crosses that marked the graves had been removed or lost. It was therefore extremely difficult to determine which soldier lay in which grave. The Gallipoli cemeteries therefore feature a disproportionately high number of Special Memorials, which record the names of men known or believed to be buried in the cemetery. Special Memorials are often inscribed with the poignant epitaph suggested by Rudyard Kipling (who had lost a son on the Western Front): 'Their glory shall not be blotted out.'

Memorials at Lone Pine, Helles, Twelve Tree Copse, Hill 60 and Chunuk Bair record the names of all men killed in the fighting who have no known grave.

Military cemeteries are organised into plots (indicated by a Roman numeral) and rows (indicated by a letter); to find a particular grave, first find the plot, then the row, then count along the graves. For example, a grave located at II.B.24 is the 24th grave in row B of plot II. Smaller cemeteries may not be separated into plots – in these, graves will simply be indicated by row and number (e.g. A.7).

Take your time when visiting a military cemetery. Wander the rows and look for unusual inscriptions. The cemeteries at Gallipoli are a tangible connection with the carnage that occurred there, and visiting them will be the most moving aspect of your journey to Gallipoli.

Researching an Australian soldier

One of the most rewarding aspects of a trip to the battlefields is to trace the footsteps of a relative who fought there. Wartime place names take on special significance if you know that a family member or friend trod this ground before you. Australia's heavy sacrifice during the war also means that many of the soldiers who fought here never left, and today lie in one of the picturesque military cemeteries that dot the landscape.

It used to be a challenge to research the military career of an Australian soldier but, thanks to the internet, times have changed. In a few mouse-clicks you can paint a fairly detailed picture of the military service of an individual soldier and plan which areas of the battlefield are most significant for your visit.

The first stop for any First World War researcher should be the Australian War Memorial (AWM). The memorial's website (www.awm.gov.au) has probably more information available online than any other museum of its type in the world. Available information on the AWM website includes:

- Roll of Honour: Details of the final resting place of all Australians killed in war.
- Nominal Roll: Basic information about the military service of every First World War solider including date of enlistment, fate, service number and more.
- Honours and Awards: Details of tens of thousands of Australians who received medals or awards in the First World War (excluding campaign and service medals).
- Red Cross Wounded and Missing Enquiry Bureau files: Details the circumstances of death of more than 30,000 Australian servicemen.
- Commemorative Roll: Details of Australians who died on active service with other allied countries.

The AWM also has a comprehensive Research Centre that can be visited at the museum. They can also answer basic research questions over the phone.

For the most detailed record of an Australian soldier's war service, contact the National Archives of Australia. The National Archives holds the service records of all Australian First World War soldiers – this is a personal record of a soldier's entire military career and sometimes stretches to hundreds of pages. The NAA's website (www.naa.gov.au) has an online search facility for service records (as well as other historic documents). The complete service record of every Australian soldier who served in the First World War can be downloaded for free.

Useful websites

Mat McLachlan Battlefield Tours (www.battlefields.com.au): The author's website. Contains detailed information about books, television appearances and tours.

Australian War Memorial (www.awm.gov.au): The essential site for researching Australia's involvement in war.

National Archives of Australia (www.naa.gov.au): Stores Australian historic documents and service records of Australian soldiers.

Google Maps (www.maps.google.com.au): Useful for planning driving routes in the battlefield areas.

Commonwealth War Graves Commission (www.cwgc.org): Custodian of all Commonwealth war graves throughout the world. Online database of cemeteries and casualties.

Imperial War Museum (www.iwm.org.uk): Britain's venerable museum of warfare.

Gallipoli and the Anzacs (www.anzacsite.gov.au): A comprehensive resource for learning about Australians at Gallipoli.

New Zealand History Online (www.nzhistory.net.nz): An excellent resource about New Zealand history, featuring comprehensive information about the New Zealanders at Gallipoli.

Department of Veterans Affairs (www.dva.gov.au): Administers Australian war graves and memorials overseas. Provides useful information about cemeteries and memorials.

Australian Bronze Commemorative Plaques (www.plaques. satlink.com.au): Since 1990 Melbourne sculptor Dr Ross Bastiaan has placed bronze plaques commemorating Australia's wartime heritage at battlefields all over the world. His website gives details about the 10 plaques at key sites at Gallipoli.

British military organisation

Unit	Size (full strength)	Commanded by
Army	150,000+ men	General
Corps	75,000+ men	Lieutenant-General
Division	18,000 men	Major-General
Brigade	4,000 men	Brigadier-General
Battalion	1,000 men	Lieutenant-Colonel
Company	250 men	Major or Captain
Platoon	60 men	Lieutenant
Section	15 men	Sergeant

Unit sizes are approximate and are for 1915.

Military abbreviations

ADS	Advanced Dressing Station
AFA	Australian Field Artillery
AFC	Australian Flying Corps
AIF	Australian Imperial Force
ANZAC	Australian and New Zealand Army Corps
BEF	British Expeditionary Force
CCS	Casualty Clearing Station
CO	Commanding Officer
CSM	Company Sergeant-Major
CWGC	Commonwealth War Graves Commission
GSW	Gun Shot Wound
HE	High Explosive
HQ	Headquarters
KIA	Killed in Action
MEF	Mediterranean Expeditionary Force
MO	Medical Officer
NCO	Non-Commissioned Officer
OC	Officer Commanding
RAP	Regimental Aid Post
RFA	Royal Field Artillery
RFC	Royal Flying Corps
RSM	Regimental Sergeant-Major

Common decorations

VC	Victoria Cross
DSO	Distinguished Service Order (officers only)
DCM	Distinguished Conduct Medal (other ranks only)

MC	Military Cross (officers only)
MM	Military Medal (other ranks only)
MID	Mention in Despatches

Notes

'Bar' indicates a decoration was awarded twice (e.g. MM & Bar)

During the First World War the only posthumous decorations that could be awarded were the Victoria Cross or Mention in Despatches. This explains why many men who were killed during a gallant act were seemingly overlooked for a bravery award (only receiving an MID) and why some men received a posthumous VC for actions that would have warranted a lesser award had they survived.

The Tours

Anzac Cove and the Landing Beaches

The Heart of Gallipoli – North Beach to Brighton Beach

There are few chapters in Australian and New Zealand history more celebrated than the landing at Gallipoli. Something fundamental changed when those boats first touched the shore – suddenly Australia and New Zealand had a national identity, and nothing would ever be the same again.

There are also few chapters in our history that have generated as much misunderstanding. Most people know the story of the landing without knowing why the Anzacs were really there. Others become so enraptured with the Gallipoli myth that the real story – often more heroic and tragic than the myth – gets pushed to the background.

The plan for the Anzac landings was complicated. The Australian 3rd Brigade would land first as a covering force, on the wide beach north of the prominent headland known as Gaba Tepe, and push inland as far as the chain of hills known as Third Ridge (and later, Gun Ridge). There they would dig in and cover the landing of the main force of Australians and New Zealanders, which would then push inland for about 5 kilometres to their first-day objective near the hill of Mal Tepe. With the high ground secure, the Anzacs could then advance towards the Dardanelles.

The covering force would come ashore in two waves. The first wave consisted of men from the 9th, 10th and 11th Battalions who would speed towards the shore in three battleships, and then transfer into 12 'tows', each made up of a steamboat pulling three lifeboats. When the tows were close to shore, the lifeboats would cast off and the men would row in, hitting the beach at about 4.30 a.m. The second wave of 2,500 men would steam towards the shore in seven destroyers, then transfer to lifeboats and land soon after the first wave. Each battalion had a precise objective on Third Ridge, and they would fan out from the beach to secure them as quickly as possible. Later in the morning the main body of Australians and New Zealanders would land from transports.

The plan began well. The first wave of the covering force boarded their correct boats on time and the tows chugged towards the shore. But then things started to go wrong. The first troops ashore didn't arrive on a wide front on the beach north of Gaba Tepe; they landed in a bunched mass about 2 kilometres further north, in a narrow cove flanked by prominent headlands. The rest of the force landed behind

SPECIAL NOTE FOR ANZAC DAY: The two most important tours in this book for Australian and New Zealand visitors, Anzac Cove and the Landing Beaches, and Second Ridge, have been designed to fit in with the schedule of memorial services held on Anzac Day. The Anzac Cove tour begins at the Anzac Commemorative Site at North Beach, and can be walked at the conclusion of the Dawn Service. The Second Ridge tour begins at Artillery Road, which is the main route followed to reach Lone Pine Cemetery for the memorial service later in the morning. A good schedule to follow on Anzac Day is to attend the Dawn Service at North Beach, walk the Anzac Cove and the Landing Beaches tour, begin the Second Ridge tour at Artillery Road and follow it to Lone Pine, attend the Lone Pine service, and then complete the Second Ridge tour from Lone Pine. At other times of the year, the two tours can also be completed back-to-back.

them, and from that day onwards, the narrow beach where they came ashore would be known as Anzac Cove.

What had gone wrong? In the last 90 years a whole host of explanations has been suggested, from the cunning Turks moving the marker buoys used to help the battleships navigate, to a mysterious current that sprang up from nowhere and pushed the boats northwards. It has also been suggested that the landing at Anzac Cove wasn't an accident at all – that a last minute (and completely undocumented) change in plans altered the landing point from Gaba Tepe to Anzac Cove.

The reality is somewhat less exciting than the conspiracies. The most likely explanation is that a whole host of small factors came into play that affected the landing point. Firstly, and most importantly, the plans for the landing weren't particularly specific, so it is difficult to say exactly where the 'correct' landing place was supposed to be. The orders simply called for a landing between Fisherman's Hut (on North Beach) and Gaba Tepe (the prominent headland south of Brighton Beach). The most specific they get is to specify a landing point 'about 800 yards north of Gaba Tepe'. Considering that the troops were supposed to land on a front 1,600 yards wide, this places them all along Brighton Beach and into Anzac Cove. It seems likely that the Anzac commanders weren't too concerned where the troops came ashore, as long as they pushed forward quickly and secured their objectives on Gun Ridge. Secondly, the ships that carried the troops from their base on the island of Lemnos had to travel almost 25 kilometres in the dark without any visible landmarks and using dead reckoning to determine when they'd reached the right point from which to launch the landing. Naval navigation wasn't nearly as accurate in 1915 as it is today, and the ships most likely anchored north of the intended position. Thirdly, the night was inky and the tows that landed the first wave could not see each other when separated by the 135 metres specified in the orders. They were forced to close to a distance of only 45 metres, meaning that the first wave was spread out on a front of only 500 metres, not the 1,500 metres originally planned. Finally, the navy crews responsible for bringing the troops to shore made several spontaneous adjustments as they steamed towards the beach. One midshipman reported that he was

Australian officers coming ashore at about 10 a.m. on 25 April 1915. Their relaxed attitudes and the lack of battle debris on the beach indicates that the landing at Anzac Cove was not as violent as is commonly believed.
AWM A01000

concerned the troops in his tow would be exposed to heavy enfilading fire as they hit the beach, so deliberately steered northwards. The other tows, being bunched up much more than intended, had no choice but to follow him.

The result was that the tows began to cross paths as they neared the shore. By the time they cast off their boats, the three battalions were hopelessly intermixed and they landed in a chaotic jumble at the base of Ari Burnu, the northern headland of Anzac Cove. Even then, all was not lost. The hills above the cove were only lightly defended, and the covering force's objectives were actually closer than they would have been had they come ashore further south. The terrain, as devilish as it was, shouldn't have caused too many problems if the troops had come ashore as a cohesive fighting force. But the battalions were so badly mixed up that it took much of the day to sort them out, and the landing plans fell into disarray. It was this disorganisation, rather than the location where the men came ashore, that was most responsible for the failure of the landing.

Once ashore, the Australians found themselves facing a rugged landscape that climbed from the beach in three ridges. They scaled the First Ridge quickly, encountering only light resistance from the hopelessly outnumbered Turkish defenders. But as they climbed the Second Ridge, Turkish reinforcements began to arrive. Some Australians managed to push inland towards their objectives, but most dug in on the crest of Second Ridge as waves of Turkish infantry descended on them. The fighting was incessant and bloody, but the Australians held their ground. By the end of that first day, the Anzac line was fairly secure, although hopelessly short of its intended position. It changed little for the rest of the campaign.

The beach where the Anzacs had come ashore became their operational base, and from the first day the legend was born. The Anzacs hadn't achieved what they had set out to do, but they hadn't given up either, and were hanging on in places where others wouldn't. Anzac Cove became an icon to the original Anzacs, as it still is to Australians and New Zealanders today.

Anzac Cove and the Landing Beaches Tour

This tour takes in the beaches around Anzac Cove – the place where the Anzacs came ashore on 25 April 1915, and the place where they left from eight months later. The tour is about 2.5 kilometres long, with an extra kilometre on a very rough track on the optional climb to Plugge's Plateau Cemetery. It can be driven in about two hours, and walked in about four, not including driving time to reach the tour area or the optional walk to Plugge's Plateau. At each stop, park your car and explore the area on foot. It is a rewarding journey, taking in the iconic sites where the Anzacs lived for eight months, and four of the cemeteries where many of them are buried.

The tour begins at the Anzac Commemorative Site, where the Anzac Day Dawn Service is held. To reach the site from Eceabat, follow the road to Bigali north out of town and then turn left at the major intersection after 2 kilometres. Follow this road for about 8 kilometres as it heads into the Gallipoli Peace Park, past the Gaba Tepe Museum. Ignore the road leading right to Chunuk Bair (Conkbayiri) and carry on with the sea on your left. Three kilometres after the Chunuk Bair turnoff you will reach Anzac Cove. Drive on for another kilometre and park at the Anzac Commemorative Site at North Beach [1].

North Beach sweeps north for 8 kilometres and joins the Anzac sector to Suvla Bay. In Australian folklore North Beach is Anzac Cove's poor cousin and barely rates a mention, but in reality North Beach was a vital operational base for the Anzac forces at Gallipoli.

Its most curious geographic feature is the Sphinx, a craggy outcrop of eroded sand that looms over the southern end of the beach. The Anzacs had trained in Egypt, and the pyramids at Giza and the nearby Sphinx were subjects of fascination for the troops, many of whom had never seen anything more exotic than the suburbs of Brisbane or

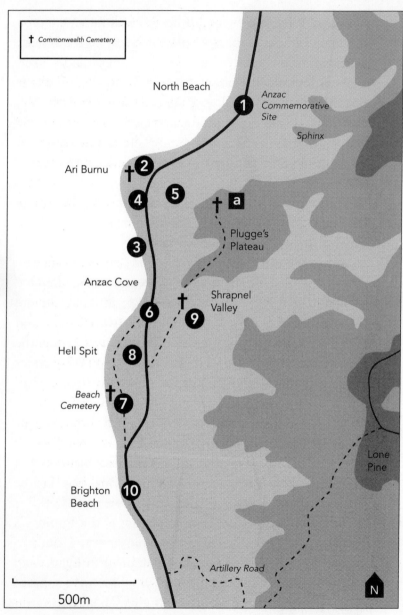

North Beach

Anzac Commemorative Site

Sphinx

Ari Burnu

Plugge's Plateau

Anzac Cove

Shrapnel Valley

Hell Spit

Beach Cemetery

Lone Pine

Brighton Beach

Artillery Road

N

500m

Anzac Cove and the Landing Beaches tour

Auckland. When they arrived at North Beach the comparison was irresistible, and the Sphinx was christened on the first morning.

Anzac troops first came ashore at North Beach on the morning of the landing, but unlike at Anzac Cove, there was no headland here to protect them from Turkish fire. Several boats landed on the beach in front of the Commemorative Site and were hit by heavy fire from Fisherman's Hut, a shack about a kilometre north. The highest casualties of the landing occurred at this spot on North Beach. The *Official History* describes the scene:

> The Turks on this northern flank had been thoroughly awakened by the arrival of the battleship tows further south on Ari Burnu [Anzac Cove] a quarter of an hour before. The northward Turks had not been embarrassed by any attack, and were fully prepared and in their trenches. Before the boats left the destroyers, bullets were rattling against the high bows of the warships. The rowing boats were under heavy fire all the way to the shore; and as the foremost of them reached the land, the first Turkish shells came singing over from Gaba Tepe . . . Bullet after bullet went home amongst the men in the crowded boats . . . [In one], six were hit before reaching the shore, and two more as they clambered from the boat. (Bean, Vol. I, p. 268)

The Anzac front line was established on the ridges above North Beach and for several months the beach was exposed to heavy Turkish fire. Dugouts were built in protected corners of the gullies behind the beach and engineers excavated a wide trench, called the Big Sap, that provided a measure of protection on the exposed shoreline but, for the most part, North Beach was a dangerous place to be. In August, however, the huge Allied thrust pushed the Turkish front line back. The attack failed to reach its objectives, but it cleared the foothills overlooking North Beach and established a new Allied presence at Suvla Bay and, from then on, North Beach became relatively safe. For the first time the Anzacs were freed from the claustrophobic confines of Anzac Cove, and North Beach soon became the sector's most important operational base. Hospital tents were erected on the flat ground below the Sphinx, dugouts dotted the slopes, piles of stores lined the water's edge and transports chugged into wooden piers day and night. An Australian soldier returning to Gallipoli after a hospital stay described his surprise at landing at North Beach instead of Anzac Cove:

Once more on old Anzac. What a change! Why, when we left there was hardly anything round this side of the Cove. It was not safe. Now there are tents and a Y.M.C.A. and what is this great sandbag mansion going up directly in front of us? A Post Office, eh. Eighty feet long, twelve feet high and twenty-four feet wide. Some building! Windows, doors and a counter, too. Crikey, they are coming on in these parts. (Sergeant Cyril Laurence, in East, 1981, p. 111)

In December 1915, North Beach was also the place where the last Anzac troops left Gallipoli, silently streaming down Walker's Ridge and boarding transports from the flimsy wooden piers. Their last view of Anzac was the Sphinx standing sentinel over the deserted beach. It was hard for many to leave:

> All that sacrifice, all that labour, all that suffering for nothing at all. No advantage gained and the flower of Australia's manhood lies on and below the earth which is not even in our own hands. Wandering parties of Turks in search of loot will trample over them . . . I feel bitter about it. (Captain George Mitchell, 10th Battalion, diary entry 21/12/1915, Australian War Memorial, 2DRL/0928)

Another officer expressed the commonly held feeling of disbelief that after eight months of struggle, the Anzacs were simply packing up and leaving:

> The Turks have beaten us . . . Tonight's . . . the last night at Anzac . . . it hurts to have to leave that place. I . . . was undoubtedly sick of it and needed a rest, but . . . to absolutely chuck the whole thing cuts right in. And I'm damned if they can say the Australians failed to do what was asked of them. They did everything . . . more than they were asked. We feel it very much believe me. We haven't had a fair chance. (Lieutenant Harry Moody, 3rd Field Artillery Battery, died 27/8/16, in Gammage, 1974, p. 111).

Today North Beach is home to the Anzac Commemorative Site – the Dawn Service was traditionally held at Anzac Cove but, as in 1915, the huge number of people crammed into the small space soon made the cove impractical. The Commemorative Site was a joint initiative of the Australian and New Zealand governments and was dedicated by the prime ministers of the two countries on Anzac Day 2000. The site's sensitive design utilises native plants and stone, and is complementary to the local environment. Its principal design element is a path leading towards the beach between two walls – a low 'commemorative' wall on the seaside emblazoned with the word 'ANZAC', and a higher 'interpretive' wall beside the road that features panels detailing the campaign. The stone path aligns to the Sphinx and leads down to the water, linking the two most important topographical features of Gallipoli – the high ground and the beach. On Anzac Day officials sit on chairs on the lower level between the two walls and members of the public cram into the grassed area below the Sphinx. This space is supposed to hold up to 15,000 people, but the usual 10–12,000 people pack in fairly tightly.

By standing beside the road above the interpretive wall with your back to the sea, you can take in much of the Anzac sector in one sweep. From right to left you can see the hump of Ari Burnu (the northern knoll of Anzac Cove), Plugge's Plateau (the first height scaled by the troops on the morning of the landing), the Razor Edge (the narrow saddle joining Plugge's to Russell's Top), Reserve Gully below it (a sheltered area for troops in reserve), the Sphinx, Mule Gully, Walker's Ridge (the main thoroughfare to the front line from North Beach), No. 1 Outpost (the bare yellow slope), Maori Hill (the last hill before the water), No. 2 Outpost (the high ridge behind) and No. 3 Outpost (the pointy hill on the left). Walker's Ridge formed the Anzac front line in the days after the landing, but during late April and May New Zealand troops captured the low hills that overlooked North Beach and designated them as the outposts listed above. In fact, much of this steep ground was the domain of the fierce fighters from the New Zealand infantry and mounted rifles throughout the campaign.

Leave the Commemorative Site and walk south, with the water on your right, for 400 metres to Ari Burnu Cemetery [2]. The cemetery is located on Ari Burnu point, the northern headland of Anzac Cove (Ari Burnu translates to 'Bee Point' in Turkish). In the early days of the campaign the headland was known as Cairo Point, but its Turkish name was adopted by the Anzacs soon after. The beach in front of the cemetery is where the first Australians set foot on Gallipoli on the morning of 25 April 1915. We'll never know for certain the identity of the first man ashore, but Charles Bean writing in the *Official History* says that it was probably Lieutenant Duncan Chapman of the 9th Battalion,

Ari Burnu Cemetery

a 26-year-old clerk from Maryborough in Queensland. After Gallipoli, Chapman was promoted to Major and served with the 45th Battalion on the Western Front. He was killed at Pozieres on 6 August 1916.

Sergeant William Turnley described the suspense of approaching the beach as part of the first wave.

How we wish they would fire – or that we could land . . . ! The suspense is nerve-wracking . . . Crash! Swish! Ping! At last we breathe a sigh of relief, the suspense is over! . . . some get ashore safely, some are hit slightly, others are drowned in only a couple of feet of water because in the excitement no one notices their plight . . . [One] fellow remains in the boat after all the others have disembarked . . . he . . . looks at us dazedly, leaning forward on his rifle. A sailor . . . touches him on the arm, and the soldier falls forward in to the bottom of the boat, dead. (Gammage, p. 54)

Lance-Corporal George Mitchell was still more than 100 metres from the shore when the first shots rang out:

'Good!' I remember saying 'the . . . s will give us a go after all.' 'Klock-klock-klock. Wee-wee-wee' came the little messengers of death. Then it opened up into a terrific chorus . . . The key was being turned in the lock in the lid of hell. Some men crouched in the crowded boat. Some sat up nonchalantly, some laughed and joked, while others cursed with ferocious delight . . . Fear was not at home. (Diary entry 25/4/1915, Australian War Memorial, 2DRL/0928)

Ari Burnu Cemetery was started immediately after the landing, and became the main burial ground for soldiers killed in the northern sector of the Anzac line. Most of the men buried here either died of wounds in the hospitals at North Beach or Anzac Cove, or were carried here for burial from front-line positions such as Walker's Ridge, the Nek, Russell's Top, Pope's Hill and Baby 700.

There are now 252 burials in the cemetery, of which 42 are unidentified. Australian identified graves number 149, including 82 men of the light horse – not surprising, considering the northern sector of the line was the stomping ground of the light horse for much of the campaign. Look out for light horse graves from 7 August 1915. These men were all killed in the tragic charge at the Nek, made famous by Peter Weir's 1981 film *Gallipoli*. The attack was one of the most futile in the history of the AIF and resulted in a slaughter as four waves of men from the 8th and 10th Light Horse threw themselves against a barrage of Turkish machine-gun and rifle fire. Relatively speaking, the men buried here were the lucky ones – the remains of most of the light horsemen killed in the charge laid out in no-man's-land until 1919 and now lie unidentified in the cemetery at the Nek. Lieutenant-Colonel Albert Miell was the commander of the 9th Light Horse Regiment, which provided supporting fire during the attack from trenches behind the Nek on Russell's Top. During the height of the fighting he was directing fire from the parapet of his trench when he was shot dead (grave A.17). Other notable graves from the attack include Lance Corporal Lindsay and Trooper Ross Chipper, two brothers from York in Western Australia who lie close together in graves E.19 and E.15. Officers killed in the attack and buried here are 2nd Lieutenants Leopold Roskams (grave F.44) and Alexander Turnbull (grave E.16), Lieutenants Leo Anderson (grave G.11) and Edward Henty (grave A.14) and Captain Andrew Rowan (grave E.18).

Visitors to Ari Burnu Cemetery are often puzzled by the late dates of death on some of the graves: 1918, 1919 and even 1922. These men were part of the British force that occupied Turkey after the war and died of illness. They were originally buried at Kilitbahir or Gelibolu, on distant parts of the peninsula, and were moved here to be closer to their comrades in the 1920s. There are also special memorials to several men believed to be buried in the cemetery, including three Muslim men from the Indian Mule Corps, whose headstones face Mecca. Trooper Bertie Lyon was an Australian who served with the Auckland Mounted Rifles. He was killed on 31 May (grave C.19).

A final noteworthy grave is that of labourer Giuseppe Camilleri of the Maltese Labour Corps (grave J.4). After the August campaign, Egyptian and Maltese labourers arrived on the peninsula to help in the construction of roads and other engineering works, thereby relieving the burden of this work from the Anzac troops. Most of them left in November 1915, but Labourer Camilleri was unfortunate not to be among them. He was killed on 7 December, less than two weeks before the last troops left Anzac for good.

The Anzac Day Dawn Service was traditionally held at Ari Burnu Cemetery until the increase in visitors in the 1990s raised concerns for the welfare of the cemetery. The last service held here before the move to the new Anzac Commemorative Site was in 1999 and was attended by 8,500 visitors. In 1990 Ari Burnu Cemetery also hosted a contingent of about 100 Gallipoli veterans, the first trip for most of them to the peninsula since 1915, and the last large gathering of the old soldiers.

Climb down the steps on the ocean side of the cemetery and walk south along the beach for 100 metres. This is Anzac Cove [3], probably the most iconic 'piece of Australia' not actually in Australia. This 600-metre curved strip of sand, ridiculously small when you stand on it, was the base of the entire Anzac operation. The landings here, although unplanned, were in some ways a blessing. The prominent Hell Spit and Ari Burnu headlands screened the Anzacs from Turkish fire and observation, and made Anzac Cove the only place on this entire stretch of coast that was safe enough to

Anzac Cove, 1915. AWM A03632

form a beachhead. It's also worth remembering that some troops were always intended to land at Anzac Cove – just not the entire force!

For the eight months of the campaign Anzac Cove, or simply 'the Beach' to the troops, was a hive of activity. Charles Bean describes the cove in the *Official History:*

> When the struggle of the Landing had subsided, the Beach on summer days reminded many onlookers of an Australian coastal holiday-place. The shoreline itself resembled rather an old-time port, with its crowded barges (often beached to prevent being sunk), a few short piers, piles of biscuit boxes and fodder stacked behind, the smell of rope, of tar, of wet wood, of cheese and other cargo; but in the water the hundreds of bathers, and on the hillside the little tracks winding through the low scrub, irresistibly recalled the Manly of New South Wales or the Victorian Sorrento, while the sleepy 'tick-tock' of rifles from behind the hills suggested the assiduous practice of batsmen at their nets on some neighbouring cricket-field. (Vol. II, p. 346)

Within four days of the landing Anzac Cove was as busy as the 'London Strand':

> . . . General Birdwood asked that the Beach between the two knolls, being the original landing-place, should be known as 'Anzac Cove'; and the name 'Anzac', till then the code name of the Army Corps, was gradually applied to the whole area. Day and night the Cove was full of the noises and sights of a great harbour – launches with

tows moving constantly in and out, the shrill whistles of small crafts, the hoots of trawlers, the rattle of anchor-chains, the hiss of escaping steam. At either end of the Beach was the hospital – the New Zealand station at the north end, the Australian at the south. Colonels Howse and Giblin would not display the Red Cross on their station, crouched as it was among supply depots which the Turks might justifiably shell. Along the middle of the Beach were long lines of picketed mules. Even by day the strand between the growing supply stacks and the water was a crowded thoroughfare. Odd men, parties, strings of animals, jostled through it, lucky if they escaped the kick of a mule. During shell fire the casual hands would quickly disappear behind stacks of biscuit-boxes; but the working parties carried on without regarding it. (Bean, Vol. I, p. 545)

Anzac Cove was the main rest area for troops in the opening months of the campaign, but it was never safe. The Turks could see parts of the beach from observation posts both north and south, and constantly bombarded the cove with artillery fire. One gun, nicknamed 'Beachy Bill', began firing on the first day and didn't stop until the evacuation. Its accurate fire prevented transports from approaching the beach in daylight, and more than 1,000 men are said to have been killed or wounded by its fire – many while swimming in the waters off the cove.

One of their shells today hit a man in the water and took off his arm – at least it was hanging by a thread, and he came out of the water holding it. It didn't stop the bathing. I heard there were 8 casualties on the beach in all, but bathing went on as usual, except for a few minutes. Some men didn't, I think, even get out . . . When some Australian (or will it be Greek) starts a hotel here after the war, bathing will be one of the chief recreations – you'll have to walk nearly to Kaba Tepe for your golf. (Bean, in Fewster, p. 149)

Engineers built several flimsy wooden piers to service transports loading and unloading at the beach, the first of which was Watson's Pier, built about halfway along the beach. It was named after Lieutenant Stan Watson of the 1st Division Signal Company who supervised its construction and fashioned a makeshift pile driver out of a Turkish shell case.

Erosion has narrowed the beach significantly since the war – during the campaign the beach was 25 metres wide. The road around the cove was originally a rough track constructed during the campaign. It was widened by the Turks after the evacuation and made permanent after the war. In 2005, controversial works widened and strengthened the road, and permanently altered the appearance of Anzac Cove, a tragic mismanagement of the one of the world's best-preserved battlefields. Consequently, it is no longer possible to follow in the footsteps of the first Anzacs ashore by scaling the heights behind the beach. A sheer cliff prevents any attempt, and makes the entire beach inaccessible except for the steps at Ari Burnu Cemetery. The only safe access to and from the beach is via the steps at the northern end.

Today the cove would be unrecognisable to the Diggers who spent so much time here, but it is still worth strolling along the pebbly foreshore to soak up the atmosphere. Rough concrete slabs towards the southern end are the remains of the foundations of a water condensation plant built by the Anzacs, and are the only tangible links with the 1915 campaign. The concrete bunker on the point at the southern end of the beach (like all the concrete bunkers at Gallipoli) was built during the Second World War and is not associated with the 1915 campaign.

Return to the road via Ari Burnu Cemetery. Next to the cemetery entrance is a bronze plaque by Melbourne sculptor Ross Bastiaan that details the fighting at this point. There are nine other plaques like this one at other important sites in the Anzac sector.

On a lawn south of the cemetery is a memorial [4] featuring the moving words spoken by Kemal Atatürk in 1934:

> Those heroes that shed their blood and lost their lives . . . You are now lying in the soil of a friendly country. Therefore rest in peace. There is no difference between the Johnnies [Anzacs] and the Mehmets [Turks] to us, where they lie, side by side here in this country of ours . . . You, the mothers, who sent their sons from faraway countries, wipe away your tears; your sons are now lying in our bosom and are in peace. After having lost their lives on this land they have become our sons as well.

This is an appropriate sentiment because the Gallipoli campaign has forged a strong bond between Turkey and Australia. You will see many memorials in this style all over the Anzac battlefield – they are intended for Turkish visitors and are usually inscribed in Turkish with an English translation on a plaque at the base.

Stand facing the prominent hill on the other side of the road. This is the hump of Ari Burnu [5], the northern headland of Anzac Cove and the first height scaled by the Australians on the morning of the landing. It was from here that the Turkish defenders first saw a small armada of white rowing boats surging towards the shore. Sensibly, the Turks didn't linger – Ari Burnu was captured by the Australians within minutes of coming ashore. Halfway up the slope they found a wounded Turk lying in a shallow trench – he became the first prisoner of the campaign. Major Aubrey Darnell described the first charge:

> A brief pause on the beach to fix bayonets . . . much swearing and cheering and we charged up a hill so steep in places we could only just scramble up. No firing, all bayonet work. Clean over a machine gun we went, men dropped all around me, it was mad, wild, thrilling . . . Not till I was near the top of the hill did I realise that in the excitement I hadn't even drawn my revolver. (Gammage, p. 57)

If you are feeling fit, you can scramble up the slope of Ari Burnu in the footsteps of the 9th, 10th and 11th Battalions. Thousands of Australian and New Zealand feet have worn a very rough track through the scrub, but to reach the top you'll still have to haul yourself up the way the Anzacs did – by digging your feet into the slope and clutching at the scrubby undergrowth. At the top you will find an excellent view of Anzac Cove, plus the shallow remains of the Turkish trench that was lightly garrisoned on the morning of the landing.

The Australians who first scaled this height didn't hang around – they clambered straight up the western slope of Plugge's Plateau (pronounced 'Pluggey's'), which looms above you. These opening hours of the advance were a mad, chaotic dash and the stakes were high.

> I had the good fortune of trying my nice shinny [sic] bayonet on a big fat Turk. He yelled out Allah, then on again we went and I came across a sniper. When he saw me coming at him with cold steal [sic] he got up and started to run but my nimble feet caught him in two strides. I stuck it right through his back. (Private Laurie Hyder, 6th Battalion, in Gammage, p. 96)

Scramble back down to the road and head south, with the water on your right. The gullies slashing into the high ground on your left were pockmarked with dugouts in 1915 – rough bivouacs made from sandbags and tarps were home to headquarters, stores, hospitals and troop shelters for the entire campaign. It's hard to picture today, but an entire army lived and worked on these scrubby slopes for the best part of a year. The names of the gullies reflect facets of life at Anzac: Howitzer Gully, Bully Beef Gully and Shrapnel Gully. Also obvious are the sheer cliff faces scoured out of the slope by the road works in 2005.

If you had been sitting in a dugout on these slopes on the afternoon of 25 May 1915, you would have had a wonderful vista of the British fleet anchored off the Anzac shore. Just after midday, however, the sight would have suddenly become much less wonderful as the largest ship, the HMS *Triumph*, lurched to starboard and sank in less than 40 minutes. She had been hit by a torpedo fired from a German submarine and went down in 55 metres of water, taking 78 sailors with her. Several other British ships had been sunk in the previous weeks, and the Royal Navy soon turned tail and slinked off to safe harbours on the outlying islands. The Anzacs watched, dismayed, from these slopes as the Navy deserted them and disappeared over the horizon.

Continue until you reach the southern end of the cove and a white monument [6]. The beach had never had a Turkish name, but had been unofficially known as Anzac Cove since 1915. In 1985 Turkish authorities made the respectful decision to officially adopt the name, and this monument was erected to commemorate the event. A plaque below the 'Anzac Cove' sign ('Anzak Koyu' in Turkish) refers to the campaign as 'one of the most glorious wars in our history'. Bastiaan Plaque No. 2, describing Anzac Cove, is next to the monument.

The beach below the monument was the site of the 3rd Field Ambulance dressing station. From here Private John Simpson and his donkey 'Duffy' trudged up to the front line and returned carrying men with leg wounds who couldn't walk. Simpson's legacy is so enduring in Australia that it is surprising to learn how little time he actually spent at Gallipoli. He was killed in Monash Valley on 19 May, only three weeks after the landing. He now lies in Beach Cemetery (see page 65).

Medical teams at Gallipoli had an unenviable job. Bloating corpses, poor sanitation and the sheer weight of numbers in such a confined space led to illness felling as many men at Gallipoli as Turkish bullets. Flies thrived in the appalling conditions and were a constant menace, spreading dysentery and making life miserable for the troops.

> Immediately I opened the tin the flies rushed the jam. They buzzed like a swarm of bees. They swarmed that jam, all fighting among themselves. I wrapped my overcoat over the tin and gouged out the flies, then spread the biscuit, held my hand over it, and drew the biscuit out of the coat. But a lot of the flies flew into my mouth and beat about inside. Finally, I threw the tin over the parapet. I nearly howled with rage . . . Of all the bastards of places this is the greatest bastard in the world. (Trooper Ion Idriess, 5th Light Horse, in Idriess, p. 42)

Medical records tell an interesting story about the mental wellbeing of the men at Gallipoli, particularly after the failure of the August Offensive. In late August rates of sickness tripled at Anzac, indicating that men were requesting treatment for maladies they had previously endured. Morale was falling. The Anzacs were losing faith in the Gallipoli adventure.

Look back along the road above the cove. The gully above the beach is the site of a prisoner-of-war cage, where captured Turks were held before being shipped to prison camps on Lemnos Island or in Egypt. Most Anzacs spent their time at Gallipoli with their heads well below the parapet of their trench, so these were the only Turks they got to see up close. Not surprisingly, they were a source of fascination for the Diggers. Charles Bean described an incident he witnessed on 8 August:

I have just seen as caddish an act as I ever saw in my life. About 100 Turkish prisoners and two Germans were sitting in the pen built by the Australian Division opposite my dug out . . . Some chap had poured out a tin of kerosene on the ground in front of it and laid a trail of kerosene . . . Some chap put a light to the trail, it flared along and when it reached the kerosene there was a huge flare of fire uncomfortably close – if not dangerously – to the Turks. The wretched prisoners rushed to the far corner of the pen like a flock of sheep rounded up by a dog, and the fellows looking on laughed . . . I wondered someone hadn't the decency to hit the man who did it straight in the face. The same thing exactly was done yesterday . . . The treatment of these prisoners makes you blush for your own side. (Bean in Fewster, p. 149)

There is a rough coastal track behind the Anzac Cove sign. Follow it south. This is all that remains of the road built by graves units after the war to enable access to Anzac Cove. The path follows the seaward slope of Queensland Point, the southern knoll of Anzac Cove, and named by the first men to land, Queenslanders from the 9th Battalion. The track leads to Beach Cemetery [7], built on the promontory known to the Anzacs as Hell Spit. The name was appropriate – Hell Spit was directly exposed to shellfire from Beachy Bill and was pummelled daily by its fire. The exposed Beach Cemetery was begun on the day of the landing and was used until the evacuation. The random layout of the headstones conveys the urgency of burying the bodies while under fire. Most of the men buried here were killed in the vicinity of Shrapnel Gully and Monash Valley, the main thoroughfare to the front line, or

The grave of John Simpson in Beach Cemetery

died of wounds after being carried down from the trenches. The cemetery is built on steep ground that slopes towards the sea. It contains 391 graves, including 285 Australians, 50 British, 21 New Zealanders, and 21 unidentified. Unusually, three of the men buried here belonged to the Ceylon Planters Rifle Corps, which had provided 80 men to serve as the personal escort of Lieutenant-General William Birdwood, the ANZAC commander. Birdwood had served in India and admired the achievements of the unit, originally formed from European tea planters in the British colony. They were attached to ANZAC headquarters at Birdwood's request.

A notable grave in Beach Cemetery is that of Private John Simpson, the 'man with the donkey'. His real name was John Simpson Kirkpatrick and he was an enigma. In life he never really asked for much and went largely unnoticed, but in death his legend grew until he attained near-sainthood, at least in Australia. The story of Gallipoli was always complicated, but Simpson's story was easy to understand. In Simpson, Australia found its ideal Anzac – a man with qualities that Australians hoped every Digger possessed, but few actually did.

Simpson joined the AIF in 1914 as a member of the 3rd Field Ambulance. He landed at Gallipoli on the first day and in short time had sequestered a donkey, which he used to ferry men with leg wounds along Shrapnel Gully to the dressing station on the beach. On the morning of 19 May Simpson passed the cooker where he normally had his breakfast, but it wasn't ready. 'Never mind,' he called. 'Get me a good dinner when I come back.' Shortly after he was hit in the chest and died instantly. Simpson's time at Gallipoli was brief, and his story simple, but in Australia it struck a chord with a dispirited public. As the story grew, so did the legend. But like most Gallipoli legends, it isn't nearly as interesting as the truth.

Simpson is often lauded as one of the greatest Australians – a noble sentiment, except he wasn't Australian. He came from South Shields on the river Tyne in northern England, and had arrived in Australia as a ship's stoker when he was 17. He had a soft spot for his adopted country, but he was always a Geordie, and hoped that joining the AIF would give him the chance to return to Europe and see his widowed mother and younger sister. Simpson wasn't a saint – his mildly chequered past was the reason for him omitting his surname on his enlistment papers – but he was an unassuming bloke whose heart was in the right spot. Charles Bean said:

> Simpson escaped death so many times that he was completely fatalistic; the deadly sniping down the valley and the most furious shrapnel fire never stopped him. (Vol. I, p. 554)

His work at Gallipoli earned him a small measure of local fame, and many Anzacs were saddened to hear he had been killed. To the Diggers he was known as 'Scottie', because of his thick Geordie accent, and many diary accounts mention him, even when it was impossible for the writer to have ever met him. Simpson had become as much a legend to the Anzacs as he was to the people at home. His beloved donkey 'Duffy' was adopted by the Indian Mule Drivers and served with them at Gallipoli until the evacuation.

Recently a campaign has begun in Australia to have Simpson awarded a posthumous VC on the grounds that his good work went unrecognised. But this isn't the case. After his death, Simpson was Mentioned in Despatches, meaning his name and actions were detailed in an official report from the senior commanders at Gallipoli. This is a rare honour for a private soldier. Simpson was 22 at the time of his death and is buried in grave I.F.1.

There are many other notable Anzacs buried here. Among them is Captain Edward Bage, who had served on

Douglas Mawson's Antarctic expedition from 1911 to 1914 as 'astronomer, assistant magnetician and recorder of tides'. He spent two winters in Antarctica and led a dangerous 1,000-kilometre journey hauling sleds across the ice, for which he was awarded the King's Polar Medal. He served at Gallipoli as second-in-command of the 3rd Field Company of Engineers and was killed by machine-gun fire on 7 May while marking out trenches at Lone Pine (grave I.D.7).

Also buried here is Lieutenant-Colonel Lancelot Clarke, a Boer War veteran and commander of the 12th Battalion. On the day of the landing Clarke reached Second Ridge by scaling the sheer slopes near the Sphinx, quite an achievement for the 57-year-old. He led his men forward to the Nek with shouts of 'Steady, you fellows! Get into some sort of formation and clear the bush as you go.' He was shot while writing a message to his commander and fell dead with the pencil in one hand and book in the other. The inscription on his grave is in French and translates as 'Without fear and without reproach', an apt sentiment (grave I.B.13).

Another officer who lies here is Lieutenant-Colonel George Braund, commander of the 2nd Battalion. He led with skill and courage during the opening days of the campaign, and was scouting forward of the Australian lines on 4 May when he was challenged by an Australian sentry. Braund was slightly deaf and didn't hear the challenge – the sentry shot him dead (grave I.A.40).

Also here is the flamboyantly named Charles Herbert Villiers-Stuart, an Australian major who served as an intelligence officer in the Indian Army. At Gallipoli he was attached to General Birdwood's staff as Chief Intelligence Officer. He was killed by shellfire at Courtney's Post on

17 May in the lead-up to the huge Turkish attack of 19 May (grave I.H.4).

Also look for the graves of Lieutenant Brian Onslow, an Australian who served with the 11th King Edward's Own Lancers (Probyn's Horse) and was aide-de-camp to General Birdwood (grave II.F.6), and Private Albert Mummery of the 23rd Battalion, who died on 16 October aged only 17 (grave II.G.2).

Plans from the 1920s show the cemetery as being fronted by 30 yards (25 metres) of beach. Today waves lap at the sea wall directly beneath the cemetery, a good indication of how dramatically erosion has altered the landscape.

Leave the cemetery and scale the culvert on the left side of the wall inscribed with 'Their name liveth for evermore'. Follow a track to the top of the hill above the cemetery to find the remains of trenches, probably dug by the Turks and improved by the Anzacs. The Turkish garrison that occupied these trenches on the day of the landing was decimated by the Australians as they charged inland.

Follow the track to the left until you reach a Turkish monument in a clearing [8]. This memorial commemorates the Turkish platoon from the 8th Company, 27th Regiment, that faced the landing Anzacs. The inscription translates as 'A platoon from the 8th Company of the 27th Infantry Regiment faced the first 1,500-man wave of the ANZAC force, which landed on the shore near Ari Burnu in the early hours of 25 April 1915, and caused them great casualties, forcing them back to the steep slopes above the beach.'

Stand next to the memorial and look inland. The valley opposite is Shrapnel Gully, the main thoroughfare linking the beach to the front line. For the entire eight months of the campaign this valley streamed with troops heading in both directions. Columns of men marched in single file along a rough track that had been hacked through the scrub in the opening days of the fighting, recalcitrant mules grunted and kicked under their heavy burdens and stretcher-bearers ferried a seemingly endless procession of wounded men down to hospitals on the beach. Every few minutes a shrapnel shell would burst overhead, its sharp boom cracking through the gully and its deadly payload of pellets throwing up a shower of dust. The sound of rifle and machine-gun fire from the front line was ceaseless, so loud that it often shocked newcomers into thinking that the Turks would break into the Anzac lines at any minute.

Early in the campaign the Turks overlooked most of Shrapnel Gully, as well as Monash Valley at its upper end. Their snipers were always busy, and always deadly.

Shrapnel Gully. The front line was on the ridge in the distance.

A party of us volunteered for a sapping job last night. We left camp at eleven and followed the road, which is the gully bottom, meandering up to the firing line. Across the gully are built sandbag barricades which shield a man just a little from the death-traps along the road. We would bend our backs and run to a big barricade, lean against the bags until we panted back our breath, then dive around the corner and rush for the next barricade. The bullets that flew in between each barricade did not lend wings to our feet for nothing could have made us run faster. A few hundred yards ahead of us and high up is the firing line, perched precariously on a circle of frowning cliffs. The Turks have a special trench up there which commands our 'road'. This trench is filled with expert snipers, unerring shots who have killed God only knows how many of our men when coming along the road. (Idriess, p. 10)

The front line was on the skyline above the gully. The yellow memorial on the left of the ridge top is the Turkish 57th Regiment Memorial on the site of a strongpoint known as the Chessboard. In the centre, the white plinth marks the site of Quinn's Post, probably the most critical (and dangerous) spot in the Anzac line. The large hill on the right of the gully in the middle distance is Braund's Hill, named after Lieutenant-Colonel George Braund, the 2nd Battalion commander who was shot and killed by an Australian sentry (see page 68). At the base of the hill the valley turns sharply left, and from here is known as Monash Valley, named after Colonel John Monash, who commanded the 4th Brigade at Gallipoli with mixed results, but found greatness on the Western Front in the following years of the war.

Walk down to the road, turn right and then follow the track to the left, signposted to Shrapnel Valley Cemetery [9]. Bastiaan Plaque No. 3 is located next to the cemetery entrance.

Shrapnel Valley Cemetery was begun soon after the landing and was used to bury men who had been carried down the gully from the firing line. It is the largest battlefield cemetery at Anzac (Lone Pine Cemetery has more burials but was made after the war). After the evacuation the Turks used the wooden crosses that marked the graves for firewood, and Shrapnel Valley Cemetery, like many of the others, was gradually reclaimed by the scrub. In 1916 Pope Benedict XV sent an envoy to Gallipoli to ensure that Allied graves were being well maintained, and the Turks hurriedly built burial mounds surrounded by stones in Shrapnel Valley Cemetery. However, when Allied graves units returned to Gallipoli after the war, they discovered that the mounds had been randomly placed and didn't match any of the actual graves in the cemetery. By using original cemetery plans and long metal rods to probe the ground, they were able to determine the locations of the real graves and re-mark them. They also brought in a handful of isolated graves from Shrapnel Valley but, apart from this, the cemetery you see today is laid out exactly as it was when the last Anzacs left Gallipoli in 1915. Chaplain Ernest Merrington had visited the cemetery in early May:

The bullets often fell thickly around our little parties of workers on this site which has become forever sacred to Australians and New Zealanders . . . I was down there by myself at dawn, and found the fallen men laid side by side ready for internment. For hours I worked, laying the bodies in the graves, with no assistance except for a few men of a fatigue party making a track near by. I placed the identity discs and personal effects at the head of each grave. I counted 42 Australians and 10 Turks. The sun arose over the eastern hill revealing the awesome scene around me, of death, nobility, valour and sacrifice. (Diary entry 9/5/1915, Australian War Memorial, 1DRL/0496)

Today there are 683 men buried or commemorated in the cemetery and all but 85 are identified. Special memorials commemorate 23 men known or believed to be buried in the cemetery. There are 527 Australians buried here, 56 New Zealanders and 28 men from Britain. Part of the cemetery is shaded by a large Judas tree, which bursts into a profusion of purple blossoms in time for Anzac Day each spring.

Notable Australians buried here include Major Hugh Quinn of the 15th battalion, for whom Quinn's Post was named. On 29 May the Turks launched an attack against the post and managed to capture part of the front line. The Australians counterattacked and the Turks were soon surrounded in a bomb-proof chamber in the front line. When the first Australians entered the chamber they found 17 Turks cowering against the wall.

Bombs had exploded among them – twenty-three of their dead lay in the trenches and the bomb-proof, of which the floor, walls and roof were scattered with the torn remains of their comrades. The wretched survivors were terror-stricken, apprehending the fate too often reserved by their own people for any wounded enemy who fell into their hands. But the waiting Australians slapped them on the back and offered them cigarettes as they marched down the hill . . . The Turks showed their relief by seizing and kissing the hands of their opponents, one of them embracing Major Tilney on both cheeks. (Bean, Vol. II, p. 221)

Major Quinn had been shot and killed during the attack (grave III.C.21).

During the same action, the 2nd Light Horse was in reserve in the valley behind Pope's Hill. The regiment was preparing to enter the fight when a stray bullet flew over the ridge and killed one of its most popular officers, Major Allan Nash. He is buried in grave III.F.29.

There are a number of brave Australian officers here, representing a range of important actions during the fighting at Anzac:

Honorary Captain Leslie Hartland of the 8th Battalion commanded an important forward post on Lone Pine on the day of the landing. On 26 July he was buried by a shell blast at Steele's Post, and by the time his frantic men dug him out he was dead (grave II.C.30). His brother William served in the 14th Battalion and was killed on 20 August during the attack on Hill 60. He has no known grave and is commemorated on the Lone Pine Memorial.

Lieutenant Herbert Biggsley of the 6th Battalion was a hero of the Second Battle of Krithia in May. During that advance he led a small group of men further forward than just about any other Australians in the attack. He was killed on 18 July by a shell from an old Turkish howitzer that blasted Steele's Post almost daily (grave II.B.35).

An Australian officer buried nearby could be considered one of the small number of Anzacs to have been 'gassed' at Gallipoli, although not by the Turks. Poison gas was never used as a weapon at Gallipoli, but on 29 October the Australians detonated a mine beneath the Turkish lines that failed to break through the surface. Lieutenant Frederick Bowra of the 4th Field Engineers entered the tunnel to investigate and when he failed to return a rescue party was sent after him. He was found overcome by poisonous fumes from the explosion and soon died. Four men from the rescue party also died (including Lieutenant Charles Thom, who lies in grave II.B.5), and 12 others were seriously gassed (grave II.B.7).

Lieutenant William Hamilton was part of a group of men from the 14th Battalion who faced a Turkish attack at Courtney's Post on 19 May. The Turks captured part of the Australian trench and were only driven out when Corporal Albert Jacka launched a one-man offensive against them which earned him the VC (see page 128). Earlier in the action Lieutenant Hamilton had tried a similar lone attack, charging the Turks and blasting away at them with his revolver. They returned fire and he was shot dead (grave IV.A.17).

Lieutenant Herbert Hinton had held an important post in Monash Valley early in the campaign, which became known as Hinton's Post. He was killed during a diversionary attack at Quinn's Post on 7 August while providing covering fire so that wounded Australians could be rescued.

Troops on their way to the firing line from the beach passed the cemetery and headed up Shrapnel Gully. Early in the fighting they cut a track through the scrub and eventually built a wide trench that led all the way up the valley, but today's visitor will find the route heavily overgrown. Some visitors follow in the footsteps of the Anzacs by trekking through the scrubby valley and then climbing up to the front line on Second Ridge, but this is not recommended. The thorny scrub is more than head-high for most of the route, it's uphill all the way and there is an extremely steep, difficult climb to the ridge top at the end. A much better option is to follow the Second Ridge tour, beginning on page 87, and climb the ridge via the much more accommodating Artillery Road.

If you are fit and are feeling energetic, you can take an optional tour to Plugge's Plateau Cemetery – it's an important historic site and a very rewarding visit, but can only be reached via a long, rough and steep track.

OPTIONAL TOUR: Plugge's Plateau Cemetery

Plugge's Plateau was the first significant height captured by the Australians on the day of the landing. To reach it, follow the sign next to Shrapnel Valley Cemetery. Allow about an hour for the return walk. The track to Plugge's climbs MacLagan's Ridge, named after Lieutenant-Colonel Ewan Sinclair-MacLagan, commander of the 3rd Brigade, the first Australian brigade to land. Sinclair-MacLagan landed early on 25 April and strode up this hill along the route you are following to get a better perspective of the chaos unfolding around him. Later in the war he commanded the 4th Division on the Western Front.

The extremely rough nature of the track is a good example of the difference between the battlefields at Gallipoli and those on the Western Front. The cemeteries on both battlefields are under the care of the Commonwealth War Graves Commission, and visitors to France will have noted how the Western Front cemeteries have been constructed in easily accessible locations. A rocky track like the one to Plugge's Plateau would be unheard of in France.

As you follow the track, look out for wild thyme growing in the scrub. Rosemary is the herb traditionally associated with Gallipoli, and it grows thickly throughout the area, but it was the smell of thyme that commonly brought back memories for Anzac veterans. Many a young soldier who had lain pressed against the rocky ground in the opening days of the battle, as machine-gun bullets shredded the tufts of wild thyme and flung the twigs down the collar of his shirt, would forever associate the aroma with the fields of Anzac.

After following the track for about 60 metres, take a minor track to the left. In the scrub to the left of this track are the remains of a wide, deep trench, almost a sunken road. This was dug by the Anzacs to provide some protection from shell and sniper fire and became the main thoroughfare for troops heading to and from the front line. Its unusual width was to allow the passage of troops in both directions, and mules carrying full loads. Today the much-eroded trench curves behind Shrapnel Valley Cemetery before petering out further up the gully.

Return to the main track and continue for 50 metres, where a clearing on the left offers good views of Anzac

Cove. If the water is clear you can make out a dark streak extending from the shore about halfway along the beach. This is the remains of Watson's Pier.

Continue along the track for several hundred metres until you look across a wide valley with the plinth of Plugge's Plateau Cemetery on the high ground above you. This is Anzac Gully, which was lined with terraces and dotted with dugouts in 1915. General Birdwood's headquarters, where most of the operations in the Anzac sector were planned, was located approximately at the base of the ridge leading down from Plugge's Plateau Cemetery. Dark streaks in the water beneath the hump of Ari Burnu mark the sites of piers at Anzac Cove.

Continue walking uphill towards the cemetery. The remains of trenches can be found in the scrub on both

The Sphinx and the Razor Edge from Plugge's Plateau

sides of the track. A plateau on the right side of the track was the home of an Anzac artillery battery.

Continue until you reach Plugge's Plateau Cemetery [a]. The cemetery is so small, isolated and difficult to get to that it is a wonder it was built in the first place. The fact that this small collection of graves was not moved to Shrapnel Valley Cemetery after the war indicates the strategic and sentimental importance of the plateau. It also suggests that the man most responsible for the post-war designation of cemeteries, Lieutenant Cyril Hughes, an Australian Gallipoli veteran, had a soft spot for the place. Due to the inaccessibility of the cemetery, it is rarely visited.

Plugge's Plateau was the first significant height captured by the Australians on the day of the landing, and was named after Colonel Arthur Plugge, commander of the Auckland Battalion, who set up his headquarters here on the first day. It was an exposed position and many men were killed here during the chaos of the opening days of the campaign. The first Australians ashore scaled the plateau soon after landing and exchanged shots with a group of Turks who sprang from a trench in front of them.

> The first Australians clambered out on to the small plateau . . . Within a few minutes . . . the Turkish fire from its farther side began to slacken. A little to the left of Leane two of the enemy jumped up from the trench and fired down at the approaching men. [Private Thomas] Batt . . . of the 11th . . . fell

wounded. But four or five men who were reaching the summit at that moment made for the Turks, who ran across the small plateau. One was nearly caught, when an Australian stepped from behind a bush and bayoneted him in the shoulder; the other was shot on the farther edge of the summit, where he rolled down a washaway in the steep side and hung, dead, in a crevice of the gravel. (Bean, Vol. I, p. 260)

Captain William Annear of the 11th Battalion, the first Australian officer to be killed at Gallipoli, was shot on Plugge's Plateau within an hour of the landing. His body was lost and he is now remembered on the Lone Pine Memorial. Other men were killed when troops who had just landed on the beach began blasting away at the Turks on the distant heights and caught their own men with their fire. One of them was Sergeant Herbert Fowles of the 9th Battalion, who had lectured his men on the dangers of friendly fire before the landing. 'I told them,' he said as he lay dying on the top of Plugge's Plateau. 'I told them again and again not to open their magazines.' (Bean Vol. I, p. 261)

Later in the campaign the plateau was home to a field gun battery and several huge water tanks, which had to be dragged to the plateau from the beach below. The cemetery, the smallest on the peninsula, contains the graves of 21 men who were buried where they fell in the opening days of the campaign, or were killed later serving with the artillery battery. Of these, 12 are Australians, eight are New Zealanders (including three unknowns) and one soldier is unidentified. Eleven of the men buried here were killed on 25 April.

The most senior Australian buried here is Sergeant John Naghten of the 4th Battalion, a 44-year-old career soldier who had moved from Ireland to Australia when he was 22. He was killed on 30 April (grave A.7). Another soldier buried here, Gunner John Le Masurier of the 3rd Brigade Ammunition Column, was born and raised on the Channel Isle of Jersey, and had only recently arrived in Sydney when he enlisted. He was killed on 29 May (grave A.3).

Plugge's Plateau offers spectacular views of most of the Anzac sector. Walk past the cemetery to take in a sweeping panorama of Ari Burnu and North Beach. The rough outline of a sunken barge can be spotted in front of the Anzac Commemorative Site if the water is clear.

Follow a rough track inland across the plateau. The remains of trenches and other fortifications can be found in the scrub on both sides of the track. The large stones scattered in the undergrowth were hauled up here during the campaign to reinforce artillery and machine-gun emplacements. Plugge's Plateau was considered the key to the inner defences of the Anzac sector – the evacuation plan called for Plugge's to be fortified like a castle 'keep', and to form the last line of defence in the event of the Turks breaking through the Anzac lines before the evacuation was complete.

Follow the track to the eastern edge of the plateau. The front line ran along the top of the ridge directly in front of you. Important landmarks (viewed right to left) include Gaba Tepe (the distant promontory to the south, home to the Turkish gun known as 'Beachy Bill'), Lone Pine (in the grove of pine trees to the south-east), Quinn's Post (marked by the white plinth of the cemetery on the ridge top directly in front of you), the Turkish 57th Regiment Memorial (the large yellow monument on the skyline), the Nek (in the clump of trees left of the 57th Regiment Memorial) and the Sphinx to your left. There are also excellent views of the rugged country to the north, extending all the way to Suvla Bay in the distance. The ill-fated August Offensive, the Allied effort to break out of the Anzac sector, was fought in this mad tangle of gullies and ravines.

Maps used to plan the Gallipoli landings indicated that Plugge's Plateau led directly to the next height, Russell's Top. But the troops who arrived at the point where you are now standing found that the two heights are connected only by the zig-zagging, perilously narrow saddle that you can see directly in front of you. Not surprisingly, the troops christened it the Razor Edge, and many of them made the mad dash across it to reach Russell's Top on that first day. The steep valley to the left of the Razor Edge is Reserve Gully, where troops were held in support behind the front lines on Russell's Top and Walker's Ridge. The gentler valley to the right is Rest Gully, a sheltered niche on the northern slope of Monash Valley where troops rested after coming out of the line. Makeshift church services were often held here for troops about to return to the fighting.

Follow the track back down to Shrapnel Valley Cemetery.

Return to the main road and turn left. After about 250 metres the road passes from behind Queensland Point and begins following the coast south. This stretch of beach was named Brighton Beach [10] soon after the landing, in honour

A sergeant-major of the Indian Mule Transport Corps on Brighton Beach.
AWM P00229.004

of the Victorian beach of the same name. This long sweep of sand, and the gentle slopes above it, was the intended landing site for the bulk of the Anzac force on the first day. After securing the beach, the troops were supposed to head inland and secure Gun Ridge. This plan soon became irrelevant, as the force landed in a bunch at Anzac Cove to the north. Whether this was a blessing or a curse has been hotly debated ever since.

Throughout the campaign Brighton Beach was under the direct observation of Turkish forces on Gaba Tepe, the prominent headland to the south, and was constantly shelled. The Indian Mule Cart Company established a supply base below Hell Spit in the northern corner, and a high wall of biscuit boxes and storage crates was erected to provide some cover from Turkish fire, but this was never going to provide much measure of safety. On several occasions direct hits from Turkish shells resulted in a massacre among the mules stationed there, and more than 90 animals were killed in one barrage alone. The camp was moved to the gullies above the beach soon after.

On 22 May 1915 one of the most curious incidents of the campaign occurred at Brighton Beach. The Turks had launched a large attack on the entire Anzac line on 19 May, and had lost more than 10,000 men without capturing a single Anzac trench. No-man's-land was littered with corpses, which were beginning to bloat and stink under the blazing sun. On the morning of 22 May, a group of Turks approached the Anzac position at Brighton Beach to propose a truce to bury the dead. A Turkish officer was blindfolded and led into the Australian camp to discuss terms for a ceasefire. The southern perimeter of the Anzac sector was protected

Naked Australian bathers carry a Turkish envoy around a barbed wire entanglement at Brighton Beach, 22 May 1915. AWM G00988

on Brighton Beach by a sandbag wall and a barbed wire entanglement that extended into the sea, and the Australians soon discovered that leading a blindfolded man over two rows of barbed wire wasn't an easy feat. Charles Bean described the scene as follows:

They directed his feet carefully over the first one – like you do in the game where a man is blindfolded and set to step over a lot of books that aren't there – irresistibly like it. They shouted for coats to help him cross the second one; but in the meantime someone had a brainwave. There were several Australians bathing along the beach near by. Someone rushed off for a stretcher – then they called the bathers. Two of these big Australians – naked as the day they were born – took the stretcher round the larger entanglement. The Turkish colonel got on to it – the two naked men carried him into the water, round the edge, and back to the beach. And I got three photographs! (Bean, in Fewster, p. 112)

The British writer Compton Mackenzie served as a lieutenant in the Royal Naval Division at Gallipoli and described what he saw at the truce negotiations.

On Whit Monday in the company of several officers from G.H.Q. I went over to Anzac, where there was a truce of eight hours for the Turks to bury their dead. It has never been perfectly clear who really did ask for this truce. Liman von Sanders says we did; Sir Ian Hamilton says they did . . . A ludicrous incident occurred when the preliminaries were being discussed by various officers of high rank on both sides. They were gathered in a tent on the beach at Anzac, those Brass-hats and Beys, all of them probably feeling a little more anxious than usual to uphold the dignity of their respective nations, when suddenly the flap was lifted at the back and a New Zealand or Australian batman put his head through to call out in a voice of indignant contempt: 'Heh! Have any of you muckers pinched my kettle?' (Mackenzie, p. 78)

The tour of the landing beaches ends here. To take the tour of Second Ridge, continue south for another 400 metres until the junction with a dirt road on the left, signposted to Shell Green and Lone Pine. This is Artillery Road, where the Second Ridge tour begins.

Second Ridge

The Front Line – Shell Green to Baby 700

Australians and New Zealanders are so fascinated with the story of the landing at Anzac Cove that it is easy to overlook that most of the fighting took place somewhere else entirely. On the morning of the landing Anzac Cove was defended by less than 200 Turks, and they had no machine guns. The Anzacs landed quickly and their casualties were light. The beach gave the Anzacs a foothold, but it was up on Second Ridge that most of the fighting and dying occurred.

Long before the Anzacs set foot on Gallipoli their leaders needed some way to make sense of the layout of the peninsula, and christened the major geographic features at Anzac First, Second and Third Ridge. But the idea that the Anzac landscape can be broken into three distinct sectors is a little too neat, and doesn't give enough credit to the crazy terrain over which the battle ebbed and flowed for eight months.

Second Ridge is the high ground that stretches roughly from Brighton Beach, south of Anzac Cove, to Walker's Ridge in the north. On the day of the landing this ridge was an intermediate objective, but the Turks got there at about the same time as the Anzacs and it quickly became the front line. Both sides stayed there for the rest of the campaign.

There were three main phases of the battle for Second Ridge. On the day of the landing the Anzacs surged up its slopes and tussled with the Turks to dominate the high ground. Nearly all the posts that later became the front line were occupied on the first day. The second phase involved the Anzacs hanging on to the ground they had captured and stopping the Turks from driving them into the sea. This phase ran from the days immediately after the landing until early August, and then continued from mid-August until the evacuation in December. The third phase involved the bitter fighting on Second Ridge during the August Offensive, the great Allied attempt to drive the Turks from the high ground and open up the advance to the Dardanelles. The fighting during this phase on Second Ridge was brutal and tragic. The Battle of Lone Pine and the charge at the Nek, in particular, were epics of glory and pain that have become entrenched in Australian folklore.

Second Ridge Tour

This tour of Second Ridge takes in the main sites along the former front line in the Anzac sector. It begins with a moderately steep climb up Artillery Road and then follows an uphill grade for most of its length. The one-way route is about 5 kilometres long, plus an optional visit of a kilometre on a track to the Çataldere Turkish Martyrs Memorial. The tour can be driven in about four hours. Allow the best part of a day to complete it on foot. Bear in mind that if walking, the tour ends at the top of Second Ridge, and you will need to allow time to walk back down to your car, or arrange for a taxi or car to pick you up. A good compromise is to drive to Lone Pine Cemetery, leave your car there and then walk the remainder of the tour (about 7 kilometres return).

The tour takes in the places where the Anzacs fought and died for the entire campaign and includes some of the most famous battle sites in Australian military history. During this tour you will visit nine Commonwealth cemeteries, two Turkish mass graves and the sites where nine men won the VC.

The tour begins at the start of Artillery Road at Brighton Beach, 1.5 kilometres south of the Anzac Commemorative Site. To reach the tour area from Eceabat, follow the directions at the beginning of the Anzac Cove and the Landing Beaches tour, but stop 1 kilometre before Anzac Cove at a sign pointing right to Shell Green and Lone Pine. To begin the tour immediately after completing the Anzac Cove and the Landing Beaches tour, walk south along Brighton Beach until you reach the sign.

Follow the dirt road indicated by the sign. This is Artillery Road [1], which was constructed early in the campaign to transport guns and men from the beach to the front line. Originally it only extended about 500 metres to Shell Green, but in the lead-up to the August Offensive it was widened and extended to the Anzac positions just behind Lone Pine. The original hand-cut road has been improved since the war

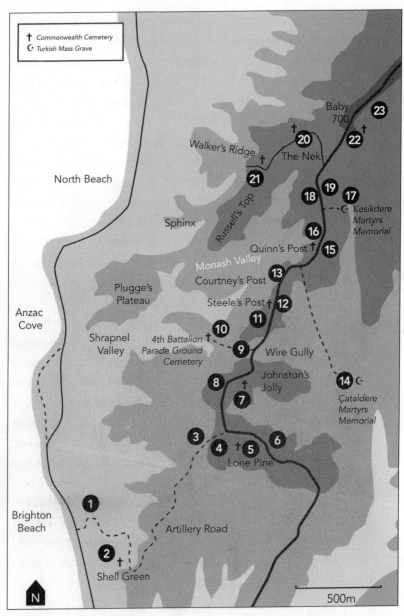

Commonwealth Cemetery
Turkish Mass Grave

Baby 700 — 23

Walker's Ridge — 20 — The Nek — 22

21 — 18 19 17 — Kesikdere Martyrs Memorial

Sphinx — 16 — Kesikdere Martyrs Memorial

North Beach

Russell's Top

Quinn's Post — 15

Monash Valley — 13

Courtney's Post

Plugge's Plateau

Steele's Post — 12

11

10

Anzac Cove

Shrapnel Valley — 4th Battalion Parade Ground Cemetery — 9 — Wire Gully

8 — Johnston's Jolly

7 — 14 — Çataldere Martyrs Memorial

3 — 4 — 5 — 6

Lone Pine

1

Brighton Beach

2 — Artillery Road

Shell Green

N

500m

Second Ridge tour

but it is still very rough. Locals often drive up it, but use caution if you attempt the drive.

Artillery Road was the main thoroughfare from the beach to the forward positions in the southern flank of the Anzac sector. As you follow this road, you are walking in the footsteps of thousands of Anzac troops who trudged up the rocky track every day. This area was relatively hidden from Turkish observers, so the surrounding hills were dotted with bivouacs and shelters. When large numbers of new troops were secretly landed before the August Offensive, this is where most of them were hidden. The Australians knew that some sections of Artillery Road could be clearly seen by the Turks, so during the evacuation in December, men were sent to deliberately loiter on the road, smoking and chatting, to give the impression that everything was normal.

After 500 metres you will reach Shell Green Cemetery [2]. Shell Green is a small plain on the seaward side of Bolton's Ridge, the high ground directly behind the green that was named after Lieutenant-Colonel William Bolton, commander of the 8th Battalion. Men from the 8th held much of this ground in the opening days of the campaign. This was a cotton field before the landing, and for the first few days of the campaign tufts of cotton littered the field like 'scattered surgical dressings', according to the *Official History*. It has even been suggested that Shell Green was named because the cotton pods were scattered like shells on a beach but, considering how exposed the green was to Turkish artillery fire, it's far more likely that it was named after a much more deadly kind of shell.

Shell Green is the site of one of the campaign's most enduring legacies, the Gallipoli cricket match. The success

Men from the Australian Light Horse playing cricket at Shell Green, 17 December 1915. The Anzac sector was evacuated two days later.
AWM G01289

of December's evacuation plan relied on the Turks believing that life was carrying on as normal in the Anzac lines. On 17 December a group of light horsemen staged a casual game of cricket on the green in full view of the Turks. Charles Bean snapped a photograph of Major George Onslow about to be caught after a dashing drive. The game didn't last long, as the Turks began shelling the Australians as soon as they saw them.

Two cemeteries were begun on Shell Green in May 1915 and were used until the evacuation. After the war they were combined and remains were concentrated here from a number of smaller cemeteries. Like many cemeteries at Gallipoli, the collection of graves tells a story about the fighting that occurred in the immediate area. Most of Plot I is made up of men from the 9th Battalion, which occupied Bolton's Ridge for much of the campaign, and the light horse who held Chatham's Post, the most southern point of the Anzac sector. Plot II contains more burials from the 9th Battalion, plus men who served with the 11th Battalion, also on Bolton's Ridge. Row G of Plot II contains the graves of 36 men from the 11th Battalion who were killed in a ferocious trench raid against Turkish positions on 1 August. Several of their comrades killed in a diversionary attack on Silt Spur on 28 June lie nearby. The third plot, known as Artillery Road Plot, includes graves of men from the 8th Battalion killed between 25 and 28 April. There are also the graves of men from various field artillery units scattered throughout the cemetery. The sheltered slope of Shell Green was home to artillery batteries throughout the campaign.

Today the cemetery contains 429 graves, of which 408 are Australian. There is one British war grave, plus the graves of 20 British sailors and soldiers killed as part of the occupation force in 1922 and 1923 that were moved here in 1927. Eleven are unidentified.

Notable Australians buried here include Private Frank Moorehead (Artillery Road Plot 19), who served with the 8th Battalion and was killed on 25 April. He was the uncle of war correspondent and Gallipoli historian Alan Moorehead. The inscription on his headstone reads, 'He did his share.'

Also buried here is Private Roy Facey (11th Battalion, died 28/6/15, grave II.G.23), brother of Albert Facey, author of *A Fortunate Life*. Both Facey brothers served in the 11th Battalion and joined in the attack on Silt Spur on 28 June. Bert came through the attack unscathed but:

. . . on arriving back I was told that Roy had been killed. He and his mate had been killed by the same shell. This was a terrible blow to me. I had lost a lot of my mates and seen a lot of men die, but Roy was my brother . . . I helped to bury Roy and fifteen of our mates who had been killed on the twenty-eighth. We put them in a grave side by side on the edge of a clearing we called Shell Green. Roy was in pieces when they found him. We put him together as best we could – I can remember carrying a leg – it was terrible. (Facey, p. 273)

The mother of Private Harold Smith, an 18-year-old fettler from Tasmania, apparently thought her son's achievements far outweighed his rank. The inscription on his headstone reads, 'Mother is proud of her hero, though he was only a private.' (12th Battalion, died 20/5/15, Artillery Road Plot 24). The grave of Major John Sergeant (8th Battalion, died 25/4/15) is inscribed with simple Australian sentiment: 'Mate o' mine.' He was killed on the first day leading a charge at Bolton's Ridge.

Bastiaan Plaque No. 4 is located on the left of the cemetery entrance.

Leave the cemetery and continue along Artillery Road for 1 kilometre. The road bends right near the top of the ridge. On the left is the site of Brown's Dip [3], a sheltered depression that was home to artillery batteries and medical aid posts. Many of the troops who would attack Lone Pine in August assembled here before the assault. Brown's Dip was most likely named after Major Alfred Bessell-Browne, the commander of the 8th Battery, 3rd Australian Field Artillery Brigade, whose guns were first stationed here in May. He was a respected officer who in 1914 commanded the 37th Battery Australian Fortress Artillery, a militia unit based in Western Australia. At the outbreak of war he called the battery to parade and asked for volunteers to join the newly formed Australian Imperial Force, and every man in the unit stepped forward.

In July Browne's battery fought a duel with Turkish artillery batteries on Battleship Hill. It was risky for the Australians to reveal the position of their guns, and Bean recorded the outcome:

The expected happened. After several high-explosive shells from the [Turkish guns] had burst on the parapet, another struck the shield of No. 1 gun and blew away its crew. Sergeant Taylor, covered with wounds, struggled to continue firing, but the relieving detachment, which had sprung at once to the gun, forced him, strongly protesting, away from it. 'See after the others,' he said, 'I'm only scratched.' Of 'the others' one gunner, Barrett-Lennard, a youngster of twenty-one, lay with an arm and a thigh shattered, but life lingered for a minute or two. 'Look after the sergeant,' he insisted. 'I'm all right – I'm done, but, by God, you see, I'm dying hard.' Another, Stanley Carter, part of whose back had been torn away, also regained a brief consciousness before he died. 'Is the gun all right, sergeant?' were his first words. Of such mettle were the men who, under the almost insuperable difficulties of Anzac, fought their guns throughout the campaign. (Bean, Vol. II, p. 344)

During the fighting at Lone Pine, the Australian dead lay so thickly that the trenches were becoming impassable.

British soldiers from the 5th Connaught Rangers were given burial duty, and spent most of 8 to 11 August dragging more than 150 bodies out of the Lone Pine trenches and burying them in two plots in Brown's Dip. These bodies were moved to Lone Pine Cemetery after the war.

Continue along Artillery Road until you reach a gravel parking area. The grove of trees to your right is well worth exploring. It contains the shallow remains of trenches and shell holes in the Australian area known as the Pimple [4].

On the day of the landing, the area now roughly occupied by the car park was a flat square of land covered in blooming poppies, dubbed the Daisy Patch by the Australians. By 26 April the front line had been established along the length of Second Ridge, except in this area, where isolated parties of the 5th Battalion were occupying some hastily dug trenches at Brown's Dip, about 200 metres behind the rest of the line. They were commanded by Major Richard Saker, a brave officer who had been wounded twice in the opening day's fighting. On 26 April, Major-General William Bridges, commander of the AIF, strode up to the position, declared the trenches 'no damn good', recklessly stood up in full view of the Turks and ordered that the men advance to the Daisy Patch to straighten the Australian line. What happened next was a picture of confusion, reckless bravery and pointless carnage that will never be fully understood. Saker began leading the men forward with the intention of digging a new line on the edge of the Daisy Patch, but was soon killed. His leaderless men carried on with no idea of their objective, crossed the Daisy Patch and kept going. Meanwhile the 4th Battalion, the only intact battalion in the whole 1st Division, saw the men advancing on its left and wrongly assumed this was the general advance on the Turkish high ground they had been waiting for since the previous day. The whole battalion left its trenches and began charging across no-man's-land. The advance then turned into a farce. Many of the leading officers were killed or wounded, and the men of the 4th Battalion somehow swung left and began advancing straight up no-man's-land, with the Australian trenches on their left and the Turkish trenches on their right. Scattered groups from other battalions joined in and in the ensuing chaos, hundreds of men were cut down by Turkish fire. One of those killed was the battalion's commander, Lieutenant-Colonel Astley Onslow Thompson, who was hit by machine-gun fire as he tried to return to the Australian line for orders. Eventually the Australians pulled back and dug in on the edge of the Daisy Patch, an odd bulge in their new front line forming the Pimple.

Next to the car park beside the entrance to Lone Pine Cemetery is a pine tree planted in 1990 by the last group of Australian veterans to visit Gallipoli. Like the tree in the centre of the cemetery, it was grown from seeds taken from a pine cone found in the Turkish lines by an Australian soldier after the Battle of Lone Pine. Trees from the same cone stand at the Australian War Memorial in Canberra, the Anzac Memorial in Hyde Park in Sydney, the Shrine of Remembrance in Melbourne and in schools and parks across Australia.

Enter Lone Pine Cemetery [5], noting Bastiaan Plaque No. 5 next to the entrance. The Battle of Lone Pine, which raged here for several days in August 1915 is one of the most famous chapters of the Gallipoli story. Lone Pine was the name given to the southern lobe of the heart-shaped

The bodies of Australians killed in the attack at Lone Pine lie in no-man's-land more than a month after the battle. This is the site of the modern Lone Pine Cemetery. AWM C01727

400 Plateau, and referred to the solitary pine tree that stood here on the day of the landing. The Turkish positions at the Pine were strong and deep, and the attack was intended as a diversion to draw Turkish reserves away from the major advance taking place against Hill 971 and Chunuk Bair north of Anzac during the August Offensive. The Australian 1st Brigade gathered in their trenches facing the Daisy Patch on the afternoon of 6 August as a furious barrage from artillery and naval guns rained down on the Turkish positions.

A 2nd Battalion man, Private Cecil McAnulty, kept one of the most remarkable diaries at Gallipoli. McAnulty scratched out the diary in pencil on the backs of envelopes and postcards – any scrap of paper he had at hand – and completed it during the fighting at Lone Pine. Whenever there was a lull in the action, McAunulty took the time to put his thoughts on paper. His entries read like a blow-by-blow account of the fighting. He described the wait before the attack:

> There [sic] artillery are replying now and shells are beginning to rain on us. They are getting the range now, shelling the support trenches. Men are beginning to drop. Howitzer shells are dropping about 30 yards from us, digging great holes where they land. The fumes are suffocating, the shrapnel is pouring all round us getting chaps everywhere. This is hell waiting here . . . Word given to get ready to charge. Must finish. Hope to get through all right. (Diary entry 6/8/1915, Australian War Memorial, 1DRL/0422)

At 5.30 p.m. the Australians charged across no-man's-land and into a storm of fire.

> Talk about shrapnel, it sounded for all the world like . . . hail . . . the bush . . . [around] the daisy patch ([in] no-man's-land) caught alight and showed us up beautifully to the Turkish machine gunners . . . The fire was simply hellish, shell, rifle and machine gun fire and I'm hanged if I know how we got across the daisy patch. Every bush seemed to be literally ripped with bullets . . . our luck was right in. (Private William Bendrey, 2nd Battalion, in Gammage, p. 69)

Most of the Turkish defenders in the front line had been killed or driven out by the ferocity of the artillery barrage, and the Australians soon reached the leading Turkish trenches.

The Turks had built a head cover of pine logs over their front line trench. This was good protection against shrapnel, but made the trench a death trap in the storm of high-explosive shells that preceded the Australian attack. Where the head cover hadn't been smashed by shelling, the Australians prised up the pine logs and leapt into the darkness below.

Within 20 minutes the Turkish front line was in Australian hands, but for the next several days Lone Pine turned into a charnel house as the Turks counterattacked relentlessly and the Australians tried to push forward in the rabbit warren of trenches and tunnels. This was probably the most horrific hand-to-hand fighting of the campaign, with the bayonet and hand grenade the weapons of choice. Grenades (or 'bombs' as they were called at Gallipoli) were primitive and dangerous. The Turks used a cast-iron grenade with a short fuse that resembled a cricket ball, while the Anzacs improvised bombs out of empty jam tins loaded with black powder and scrap metal. Lieutenant Frank Semple was on the receiving end of a Turkish bomb attack:

> They take anything from one to five seconds to explode after landing and if you are close enough the best thing to do is to throw them back . . . The other day one of our men picked up three in quick succession and threw them back to the enemy, but the fourth was one too many. It exploded in his hand blowing it off and also injured two others, one losing one eye and the other two eyes. (Gammage, p. 71)

Before long the bodies began to pile up.

The stench of the dead bodies is now simply awfull [sic], as they have been fully exposed to the sun for several days, many have swollen terribly and have burst . . . there has been no attempt up to the present to either remove or bury [them], they are stacked out of the way in any convenient place, sometimes thrown up on to the parados so as not to block up the trenches, there are more dead than living. (Sergeant Apear de Vine, 4th Battalion, in Gammage, p. 71)

The bitter fighting at Lone Pine was characterised by scores of individual acts of bravery, some officially recognised, most not. Sergeant Archie Barwick wrote in his diary that he saw:

. . . several men sacrifice themselves here, they went to certain death, one chap in particular I remember . . . we were chasing some Turks round a little sap and they reached the bend first. Everyone knew that the first man round the corner was a dead one, but this chap never hesitated, he threw himself fair at them, and the six fired together, and fairly riddled him with bullets. That was our chance and we into them, and it was all over in a few minutes. (Gammage, p. 71)

By 10 August the Turks gave up trying to take their old trenches and the Australians consolidated the newly won position into their main line. Lone Pine formed a pronounced bulge in the Australian line for the rest of the campaign, but apart from tying up some Turkish reserves the attack had

Lone Pine Cemetery

achieved little. The Australians lost more than 2,000 men and the Turks about 6,000 in the four days of bitter fighting.

At some stage during this time Private Cecil McAnulty had taken the opportunity to update his diary:

> I've pulled through alright so far, just got a few minutes to spare now. I'm all out, can hardly stand up. On Friday when we got the word to charge Frank and I were on the extreme left of the charging party. There was a clear space of 100 yards to cross without a patch of cover. I can't realise how I got across it, I seemed to be in a sort of a trance. The rifle and machine gun fire was hellish. I remember dropping down when we reached their trenches, looked round and saw Frank and 3 other men alongside me. There was a big gap between us and the rest of our men . . . behind the shelter of the Turkish

parapet . . . We were right out in the open . . . I yelled out to the other 4 chaps, 'This is suicide boys. I'm going to make a jump for it.' I thought they said alright we'll follow. I sprang to my feet in one jump– (Diary entry 6–12/8/1915, Australian War Memorial, 1DRL/0422)

The diary ends in mid-sentence, perhaps at the moment McAnulty was killed. He now lies in Lone Pine Cemetery.

Seven Victoria Crosses were awarded to Australians during the Battle of Lone Pine, the most ever awarded to Australians in a single action.

Lance-Corporal Leonard Keysor of the 1st Battalion was holding a trench on 7 August when the Turks attacked in force. For 50 hours he held the position, catching Turkish bombs in mid-air and hurling them back, and keeping up an endless bombardment with jam tin bombs. He was wounded twice but stayed until the trench was secure before seeking medical attention. After Gallipoli, Keysor served in France with the 42nd Battalion where he was promoted to lieutenant and wounded twice. After the war Keysor returned to his native London where he lived with his wife and daughter for the next three decades. He died in 1951, aged 55.

Lieutenant William Symons of the 7th Battalion led a small group in a counterattack on a sap known as Jacob's Trench on 9 August. Six officers had already been killed or wounded at the spot, yet Symons succeeded in driving out the Turks, shooting two with his revolver. During the course of the day he led several charges against Turkish positions and was responsible for the capture and consolidation of a vital part of the line. Symons was from Bendigo in Victoria and had served in the military for eight years before the start of the First World War. After Gallipoli he served in France and was gassed and Mentioned in Despatches. After the war he moved to England and became a successful businessman. He commanded a battalion of the Home Guard during the Second World War and died in London in 1948. He was 58.

Lieutenant Frederick Tubb, Corporal Alexander Burton and Corporal Bill Dunstan served in the 7th Battalion and were all awarded the VC for the same astonishing action. On 9 August Tubb was commanding a group of 10 men in a trench that came under fire from the Turks. Tubb ordered two men to stay on the floor of the trench to smother or throw back any bombs that landed there, while the rest climbed up onto the fire step and blazed away at the attacking Turks with their rifles. One of the men in the trench was killed when a bomb exploded in his face, and the other lost both his hands trying to throw a bomb back at the Turks. The men on the fire step were soon also killed or wounded by Turkish bombs. Tubb was wounded but fought on, supported only by Corporals Burton and Dunstan. The Turks launched a final attack on the position and Burton was killed and Dunstan temporarily blinded when a bomb burst between them. Tubb rallied some nearby men to drive the Turks back and successfully held the post.

Frederick Tubb was a grazier from Victoria who had served in the Essendon Rifles before the war. After Gallipoli he was promoted to major and served with his battalion in France and Belgium. On 20 September 1917 Tubb led a company of the 7th Battalion in the Battle of Menin Road, the latest phase in the larger Third Battle of Ypres. After leading a charge on a group of enemy pillboxes, Tubb and several other men were wounded by a British shell that had fallen short. He died that evening and now lies in Lijssenthoek Cemetery. He was 35.

Alexander Burton was an ironmonger from Kyneton, Victoria, before enlisting on 18 August 1914, two weeks after war was declared. He was wounded during the landing at Gallipoli, but returned to be promoted to corporal and Mentioned in Despatches. After the horrific fighting at Lone Pine his body could not be found, and he is now commemorated on the Lone Pine Memorial. He was 22.

Bill Dunstan worked as a clerk in rural Victoria before the war, and was Mentioned in Despatches twice at Gallipoli before his heroics at Lone Pine. The severe wounds he received in his VC-winning action kept him out of the rest of the war and he returned to Australia in early 1916. After the war he became a prominent newspaperman, a friend of Prime Minister Robert Menzies and indulged in a lifelong love of horseracing. He and Rupert Moon, who had won the VC at Bullecourt in 1917, owned a horse together called Maid of Money. Dunstan died in 1957, aged 61, on his way home from the Caulfield races. Seven VC winners attended his funeral.

Private John Hamilton was holding a trench with other members of the 3rd Battalion when the Turks launched a violent attack before dawn on 9 August. They succeeded in breaking into the Australian line and Private Hamilton climbed into the open and began showering the attackers with bombs. He lay out in no-man's-land for several hours, shouting out to his comrades where to best aim their bombs and sniping at the Turks. The attackers were eventually driven back with heavy loss. Hamilton was a butcher in Sydney before the war and landed with the 3rd Battalion on the first day at Gallipoli. Later in the war he served in France and was promoted to 2nd lieutenant. After the war he returned to Sydney. He rejoined the service in 1940 and served as an officer with several units in Australia, New Guinea and Bougainville. He died in Sydney in 1961, aged 67.

Captain Alfred Shout of the 1st Battalion was part of a two-man offensive that was largely responsible for securing the battalion's line on 9 August. Shout and Captain Cecil Sasse charged along a heavily occupied Turkish trench, with Shout throwing bombs and Sasse shooting. They killed eight Turks and set the rest to flight, securing the trench for the Australians. Later that day they captured another trench in a similar fashion. Shout was getting ready to launch another assault and lit three bombs at once as he charged. One exploded prematurely, blowing off his right hand and shattering the left side of his face and body. He died two days later on a hospital ship. Born and raised in New Zealand, Shout settled in Sydney in 1905. He served in the Citizen Forces before the war and distinguished himself during the opening days at Gallipoli, receiving the Military Cross and being Mentioned in Despatches for his courageous leadership. He was 33 at the time of his death and left behind a young widow in Sydney. In 2006 Shout's medals, including his VC, were sold at auction for $1.2 million. The winning bidder was billionaire Kerry Stokes, chairman of the Seven Network, who promptly donated the medals to the Australian War Memorial in Canberra. This astonishing act of generosity brought all nine Gallipoli Victoria Crosses won by Australians together in the collection of the memorial.

Lone Pine Cemetery was built on the site of the battle after the war. Considering the number of men that died here, the battle area is ridiculously small. The Australian trenches ran through the western plot of the cemetery and the Turkish trenches ran through the eastern plot, roughly where the Lone Pine Memorial stands today. The space in between was no-man's-land, and the brutal fighting that cost the lives of more than 2,000 men occurred in the tiny space now occupied by the memorial and chapel.

A small battlefield cemetery containing less than 50 bodies was begun here before the evacuation and the modern cemetery was created by bringing in bodies from the surrounding area and from two cemeteries at Brown's Dip. The original cemetery and most of the bodies that were brought in were combined to form the plot at the eastern end. The bodies from Brown's Dip were buried at the western end, now called Brown's Dip Plot. A tree, grown from the seed of a pine cone found in the Turkish trenches, marks the approximate site of the original Lone Pine.

A rough track known as Dickinson's Road used to cross the ground now occupied by the cemetery, and the original designs called for two cemeteries to be built, one on each side of the road. The plans were later abandoned but the modern cemetery still reflects the design, with a wide avenue between the Lone Pine and Brown's Dip plots. A large memorial service is held at Lone Pine Cemetery every Anzac Day following the Dawn Service at North Beach.

Like many Gallipoli cemeteries, the layout of headstones does not accurately reflect the location of graves. In spite of the u-shaped double row of headstones in the eastern plot, the graves are actually laid out in 17 neat parallel rows that run all the way from the memorial wall to the cemetery entrance in exactly the same configuration as the graves in the Brown's Dip Plot. A short row also runs along the northern wall. Visitors should be aware that even when they are strolling on the open grass expanses of the cemetery, there are graves beneath their feet. Even the pine tree has been planted on top of graves in rows J and K. Rows in the Brown's Dip Plot are accurately marked with headstones.

There are 1,167 men buried in the cemetery, but only 664 could be identified. Nearly all the identified graves belong to Australians, although two New Zealanders and 15 soldiers from Britain also lie here. The u-shaped double row commemorates 183 soldiers known or believed to be buried in the cemetery (laid out in alphabetical order), all but one of them Australians. A good indication of the horrific nature of the Lone Pine fighting is given by the large number of headstones that record a range of days as the date of death. If the best the army could do was determine that a soldier was killed at some stage between 6 and 10 August, he must have been involved in some pretty heavy and confusing fighting.

Notable burials in the cemetery include Private Benjamin Armstrong who served with the 2nd Battalion and was killed on 6–9 August. Armstrong hailed from Los Angeles, California and was one of the few Americans to serve at Gallipoli (Special Memorial C.80). Also buried here is Major Richard Saker, the 5th Battalion officer who was killed leading the attack across the Daisy Patch on 26 April (grave I.F.8). Many of the graves in the cemetery contain touching personal inscriptions, including that of Driver Walter Bergin (10th Battalion, died 6/8/15) which reads, 'A mother's thoughts often wander to this sad and lonely grave.' The headstone commemorating Private Edward Upjohn of the 2nd Battalion, who was killed on 6 August, laments, 'Oh Gallipoli, thou holdest one of God's noblest. From his loved ones' (Special Memorial C.142). Also seek out the grave of Private Cecil McAnulty, the 2nd Battalion man who may well have been killed while writing in his diary (grave II.C.14).

At the eastern end of the cemetery stands the Lone Pine Memorial, which commemorates 4,228 Australians and 708 New Zealanders who have no known grave or were buried at sea. This is the main memorial to Australians missing on the peninsula, although 233 Australians missing from the Second Battle of Krithia are recorded on the Helles Memorial (see page 228). The New Zealanders remembered here were killed in the Anzac sector before the August Offensive. Other New Zealand missing are commemorated at Chunuk Bair, Hill 60 and Twelve Tree Copse.

Behind the memorial is a stone chapel that contains the cemetery register and visitors book, but it is usually locked. The obelisk-shaped building is a prominent landmark that identifies Lone Pine, much as the stump of the original pine tree did in 1915. The names of the New Zealand missing are recorded on its north and south walls.

Notable men commemorated on the Lone Pine Memorial include Captain Alfred Shout VC (1st Battalion, died 11/8/15), a hero of the Battle of Lone Pine who died on a hospital ship and was buried at sea (see page 106). Another VC winner from Lone Pine, Corporal Alexander Burton (7th Battalion, died 8–9/8/15), is also remembered here (see page 105).

A senior officer commemorated on the memorial is Lieutenant-Colonel Alexander White, commander of the 8th

Light Horse, who was killed leading the first wave during the charge at the Nek on 7 August (see page 139). According to reports his final order was: 'Boys, you have 10 minutes to live and I am going to lead you.' The memorial is laden with the names of his comrades from the 8th and 10th Light Horse who were also killed in the attack, including brothers Gresley and Wilfred Harper from the 10th Light Horse, the inspiration for Peter Weir's *Gallipoli*.

Also look for the name of Private James Martin of the 21st Battalion, who died at sea of enteric fever on 25 October. He was only 14, the youngest Australian to die at Gallipoli.

Lieutenant Norman Greig of the 7th Battalion is also commemorated here. He was killed on 15 July leading a party of 12 men in a raid on a mine crater at German Officer's Trench and was buried by the Turks (see page 126).

Probably the most famous New Zealander commemorated on the memorial is Lieutenant-Colonel Arthur Bauchop of the Otago Mounted Rifles, who died of wounds on 10 August after leading an attack on the hill that now bears his name.

After visiting the cemetery, leave by the southern entrance and follow the fire trail that leads left towards the main road. The Lone Pine system was a rabbit warren of trenches and tunnels and their remains can be seen in the scrub on both sides of the trail. The trail skirts around the head of a shallow valley known as Coo-ee Gully to the Anzacs. In the scrub about 50 metres south-east of the chapel is the site of a memorial erected by the Turks after the campaign to commemorate the point where they stopped the Anzac attack in August. There was another one at the Nek and a third near the coast at North Beach. The memorials were still there when Charles Bean visited Gallipoli in 1919, but

Allied units who occupied the area in the following years tore the Lone Pine and North Beach memorials down and sold pieces of them to the public back in Australia. Quite rightly, this incident still rankles the Turkish people.

Follow the fire trail until it meets the main road and turn left. After 40 metres you will reach a small valley on your right running north-east away from the road [6]. This inconspicuous hollow was home to Turkish reserves and headquarters before the August Offensive and was the main route Turkish reserves followed to get to the front line at Lone Pine. It was not marked on any Allied maps and even though it was less than 20 metres from the final Australian positions at Lone Pine and was large enough to shelter a battalion, no one on the Allied side knew it was there during the campaign. Charles Bean only found out about it, and its importance to the Turks, when he returned to Gallipoli in 1919. For want of a better name, he dubbed it the Cup. During the attack at Lone Pine, Turkish reinforcements flooded into Owen's Gully (the large valley behind it) and surged into the Cup to counterattack the Australians in the captured Turkish trenches. Zeki Bey, a Turkish battalion commander, described the journey of reinforcements through the Cup in Charles Bean's *Gallipoli Mission*:

> They had to pass up the valley where the Turkish dead (brought out of the trenches) were laid out beside the track, four deep. They saw this column of dead men; at the upper end of it were some Australians, including a lieutenant or sergeant, a splendid looking fellow of very great stature, lying there – they had got well down into the position – and the sight 'knocked the stuffing' out of the incoming

troops. When they got to the top of the gully there were
the Australian periscopes looking over at them, and the
fight going on – bombs, rifle-shots. The troops were in
bad condition, and they came to a bad situation. (p. 195)

Return to Lone Pine Cemetery, leave the car park and turn
left onto the main road. This road follows the crest of Second
Ridge for most of its length and traces the line of no-man's-
land. As you follow it, imagine the Anzac trenches on your
left and the Turkish trenches on your right. Continue north
for 200 metres and park beside the cemetery on your right
[7]. This area forms the left lobe of the heart-shaped 400
Plateau. Australian troops dug in on the western side of the
lobe on the first day and didn't move for eight months. It
was christened Johnston's Jolly after Colonel George Johnston,
commander of the 2nd Field Artillery Brigade, whose guns
were stationed behind the lobe from the opening weeks of
the campaign. In Digger parlance, Johnston's guns did a
good job 'jollying up' the Turks in this area.

By May 1915 the lines at Anzac had become fairly fixed,
and the Turks planned a huge assault to drive the Anzacs
into the sea. On 18 May British aircraft and ships spotted
large numbers of Turkish troops massing opposite the Anzac
position, and in the early hours of 19 May the Australians
detected the glint of Turkish bayonets in the valley north of
Johnston's Jolly. For the next few hours, more than 40,000
Turkish troops launched suicidal head-on assaults against
most of the Anzac line. The fighting was particularly heavy
at Lone Pine, Johnston's Jolly, Courtney's Post and Quinn's
Post. The Anzacs poured almost a million rounds of rifle
and machine-gun fire into the massed Turks.

We had a gorgeous time . . . for two solid hours we blazed away . . . our rifles got too hot to hold and the bolts jammed but we got others . . . as it got lighter . . . hundreds fell in a vain endeavour to make a bolt for safety – we had them before they got 5 yards. (Captain Charles Duke, 4th Battalion, in Gammage, p. 91)

The Australians scrambled out of their trenches and sat up on the parapet to take better aim at the oncoming waves. 'Play you again next Saturday!' called one as the Turks began to retreat. By noon on 19 May more than 10,000 Turks had been killed or wounded without gaining a single metre of Allied trench. The Anzacs had lost only 600 men.

The attack demonstrated once and for all that no frontal assault would ever push the Anzacs back into the sea. The front line curved, twisted and doubled back on itself, and simply provided too many positions from which machine guns could interlock their fire and turn the narrow no-man's-land into a slaughterhouse. From May onwards, the Turks referred to this sector in sinister terms: Lone Pine became Kanlisirt (Bloody Ridge), Johnston's Jolly became Kirmizisirt (Crimson Ridge), the ground in front of the Pimple became Şehitlar Tepe (Martyr Hill) and Plugge's Plateau, from where artillery had blasted the attacking Turks, became Khain Tepe (Treacherous Hill).

In the following days the Turkish dead began to putrefy under the blazing sun, and a truce was called on 24 May to bury the bodies. Photographs taken at Johnston's Jolly show Australians and Turks mingling in no-man's-land as they undertake the gruesome task of burying the rotting corpses. The scene was awful.

We mounted over a plateau and down through gullies filled with thyme, where there lay about 4000 Turkish dead. It was indescribable. One was grateful for the rain and the grey sky. A Turkish Red Crescent man came and gave me some antiseptic wool with scent on it. The dead fill acres of ground, mostly killed in the one big attack, but some recently. They fill the myrtle-grown gullies. One saw the result of machine-gun fire very clearly; entire companies annihilated – not wounded, but killed, their heads doubled under them with the impetus of their rush and both hands clasping their bayonets. It was as if God had breathed in their faces. (Captain Aubrey Herbert, *Mons, Anzac and Kut*)

Lieutenant Compton Mackenzie, the British novelist, was standing on the parapet of the Australian trench watching the burial parties and their gruesome work, when he was advised by an Australian in the trench below him that he had his foot in an 'awkward place'.

Looking down I saw squelching up from the ground on either side of my boot like a rotten mangold [beetroot] the deliquescent green and black flesh of a Turk's head. 'This parapet's pretty well made up of dead bodies,' said our friend below, putting out his hand to help me jump back into the trench, for he saw that I had had enough of it up there. The impression which that scene from the ridge . . . made on my mind has obliterated all of the rest of the time at Anzac. I cannot recall a single incident on the way back down the valley. I only know that nothing could cleanse the smell of death from the nostrils for a fortnight afterwards. (Mackenzie, p. 83)

The Turks created several large mass graves for their dead, but also simply threw many bodies into the gullies behind their lines and covered them with a thin layer of earth, 'just enough to keep their coats from blowing in the breeze', according to one Australian witness. Their bones still litter the gullies today.

After the war Australian graves authorities decided to build a chain of cemeteries along Second Ridge that would both mark the sites of famous Anzac posts and hold the remains of men killed in or near them. (In what could be considered a final act of one-upmanship, the cemeteries were built slightly forward of the Anzac front line. In death, the Anzacs hold ground they could never take in life.)

Johnston's Jolly is the southernmost cemetery in the chain, and contains the remains of 181 men killed in the

Shallow remains of trenches at Johnston's Jolly

immediate area. Only one man could be positively identified: Lance Corporal Herbert May of the 15th Battalion, who was killed on 9–10 May. There are 36 special memorials that record the names of Australians known or believed to be buried in the cemetery. Almost all of these men were killed during fighting at Lone Pine in August, including the most senior soldier among them, Lieutenant Richard Seldon (4th Battalion, died 6–8/8/15). Seldon was made of tough stuff. On 6 August he was leading a bombing party along a captured trench at Lone Pine and was badly wounded, the remains of his eyeball hanging on his smashed cheek. He refused treatment and was leading a fresh charge against the Turks when he was shot dead. The rest of the men buried in the cemetery are unidentified, although two are known to be Australian and one a New Zealander.

Just south of the cemetery a flight of log steps leads to the opening of a tunnel, most likely part of the Turkish line. Both sides dug tunnels relentlessly during the campaign in an attempt to surreptitiously move their lines forward or to plant explosives beneath enemy trenches. During preparations for the evacuation in December, large mines were planted beneath the Turkish trenches at key positions on the Anzac front from Johnston's Jolly to the Nek. Only the northernmost charges at the Nek were detonated. The remaining explosives, neatly packed and waiting patiently to do their dirty work, still lie beneath the ridge.

Opposite the cemetery is a network of trenches [8], the best-preserved in the Anzac sector. Most of them formed the Australian front line, although it is possible that the southernmost ones were Turkish saps extending across no-man's-land. Ninety years of rain and wind has smoothed

Tunnel entrance at Johnston's Jolly

and shallowed them, and they were damaged during a fire that swept across the ridge in 1994, but they still give an excellent impression of the layout of a Gallipoli trench system. Their zig-zag shape was designed to reduce the damage caused by shell and grenade explosions, and to prevent an attacking enemy from firing along the length of the trench. Midway along the trench line, log steps lead down to another tunnel entrance, this one dug by the Anzacs.

Follow the trenches inland. A track beyond the trees leads to a lookout offering outstanding views over the Anzac sector. The northerly view across Monash Valley is dominated by the hump of Plugge's Plateau, leading via the Razor Edge to Russell's Top. The tip of the Sphinx peaks over Russell's Top, and Suvla Bay is visible in the distance. Before the campaign, a track zig-zagged down the near side of Plugge's Plateau into the valley below. In the first hour of the landing, some of the

Turkish defenders on Plugge's tried to escape down this path but were cut off by the Australians advancing inland along Monash Valley. The Turks were surrounded and killed, or, in the words sometimes used by Turkish guides, 'executed'.

Return to the main road and continue for 150 metres until you reach a sign on the left pointing to 4th Battalion Parade Ground Cemetery. At this point two gullies cut into the ridge on both sides of the road. In 1915 the gullies met and created a 'nick' in the ridgetop that was too steep to entrench. The Australians filled the gap with barbed wire, and covered its slopes with fire from machine guns on either side. Rather unsurprisingly, it was called Wire Gully [9] from then on. Construction of the road since then has mostly filled in the gully.

For the first 10 days of the campaign the Australians established posts in Wire Gully and in the ravine on its eastern side while they dug their main defensive line. The posts were tenable during the first few days, but as the Turks probed closer the battle outposts were constantly at risk of being cut off. Turkish fire made it impossible to reach them in daylight and rendered them one of the most dangerous positions at Anzac. Charles Bean referred to them as 'death traps' and they were eventually abandoned, but not before they entered Anzac folklore. On the evening of 25 April, troops were seen advancing from the Turkish side, but someone called out 'Don't shoot – Indian troops!' and the Australians held their fire. There were no Indian troops at Gallipoli at that time, and the Australians soon realised the troops were Turks and opened fire, but for the rest of the campaign an implausible rumour persisted that the shout referring to Indian troops had come from the Turks, as a cunning ruse to stop the Australians from shooting.

On the cold, rainy night of 28–29 April, the Australians were relieved from the position by British marines of the Royal Naval Division. Most of these men were young recruits with only a few months' training, and this was their first taste of action. They slogged their way through the mud of the gullies and up the slope. When they arrived:

> . . . wild and incessant fighting continued at the head of Monash Valley [on their left]. From the dark came the distant sounds of Turkish bugle calls. Close in front of them from the dense scrub flashed the occasional rifles of snipers; overhead the bullets cracked; machine-guns sent the mud of the parapets in showers upon them. (Bean, Vol. I, p. 533)

During the evening of 30 April, the Turks attacked the outposts in strength, and Lance-Corporal Walter Parker rushed across 300 metres of fire-swept ground to treat the wounded. He was wounded several times himself, but survived the action and was awarded the first VC at Anzac.

One day in May the Australians entrenched near Wire Gully were surprised to see a Turk laden with water bottles appear in the gully above them. Apparently he'd been sent to collect water and had wandered into the Australian line. He was as shocked as the Australians, and hurled himself back down the gully before the Australians had a chance to grab their rifles.

When Charles Bean returned to Gallipoli in 1919, he found Wire Gully 'full of the skeletons and uniforms of the dead – chiefly of marines in the lower part and valley-bed, and of Australians and Turks farther up. The remains, sometimes of several men together, lay in the little pits like rags poked into drawers.' (*Gallipoli Mission*, p. 146)

Follow the track towards 4th Battalion Parade Ground Cemetery. The track is good but steep, so only attempt the walk if you are fit. This track originally ran all the way to the beach and was created by the Turks before the landing. The Australians improved it and named it Bridges' Road after their commander, and the name soon came to refer to both the track and the valley. On the morning of the landing the scattered 10th Battalion regrouped near the beach and then advanced through this valley under sporadic sniper fire to join the fight on Second Ridge.

After a short distance the track will curve left, and off to the right is the opening to a dugout or tunnel. Unlike the two at Johnston's Jolly, this one is not covered by a grill but is unstable and should not be entered.

Continue descending along the track into the valley. After 150 metres you will reach 4th Battalion Parade Ground Cemetery [10]. This shelf on the southern slope of Braund's Hill (named after Lieutenant-Colonel George Braund, commander of the 2nd Battalion) was an assembly area commonly used by the 4th Battalion. Although it was close to the front line, the gully was relatively safe and several other battalions also had assembly areas in niches in the valley. Charles Bean cited the nearby 3rd Battalion Parade Ground as 'probably the only place where choral singing was heard at Anzac during the campaign'. The chaplain of the 3rd Battalion, Dean Talbot, arranged for hymn books to be sent from Egypt and formed a group of Diggers into a

4th Battalion Parade Ground Cemetery

rough and ready choir. Apparently they could carry a tune: Bean reported that the Turks didn't fire so much as a mortar round at them during their performances.

The 4th Battalion Parade Ground Cemetery was begun soon after the landing and used until June. It was enlarged after the war when smaller cemeteries in the area were closed and bodies were brought in from the surrounding area. It now contains 116 burials and, unusually for Gallipoli, all except seven are identified.

There are several notable Australians buried here including Colonel Henry MacLaurin, commander of the 1st Brigade, who was killed by a sniper on MacLaurin's Hill on 27 April (see page 124). He was buried near where he fell and his body was lost in later fighting. It was rediscovered by burial parties in 1919 with help from Charles Bean, the official historian (grave A.10). Buried beside him is another senior officer,

Lieutenant Colonel Astley Onslow Thompson, commander of the 4th Battalion, whose body was discovered during the same search. Onslow Thompson was killed in the advance across the Daisy Patch on 26 April (see page 96). Witnesses described watching the evening sunlight glint off a stream of machine-gun bullets that arced towards him as he tried to get back to the Australian line (grave A.11).

The 4th Battalion Parade Ground Cemetery is one of the most peaceful places at Gallipoli. It is tucked out of the way and rarely visited. On a warm evening it is not difficult to sit here and imagine this gully crowded with bedraggled troops, laughing, smoking and chatting as the cacophony of battle continues on the ridgetop just above their heads.

Turn right into the culvert just past the cemetery and follow a track that leads to the top of Braund's Hill. The rough track continues along the ridgetop and eventually leads back to Shrapnel Gully and the beach. It is sometimes mistakenly assumed that this is the original Bridges' Road, but a quick glance at the sweeping views from these heights demonstrates that any soldier foolhardy enough to attempt this route in 1915 would have been fodder for the Turkish guns. Bridges' Road ran along the valley floor and emerged in Shrapnel Gully. Today the thick scrub has reclaimed it and it is virtually impossible to follow back to the beach.

Braund's Hill offers sweeping views of Monash Valley and the rear of the Australian positions on Second Ridge. To your left Shrapnel Valley Cemetery is prominent, and directly across the valley is Russell's Top, leading right to the Nek in the clump of pine trees. Further to the right is the distinctive spire of the Turkish 57th Regiment Memorial on the skyline, and below it the two hills that guard the head of Monash Valley. The hill on the left is Pope's Hill, named after Lieutenant-Colonel Howard Pope, commander of the 16th Battalion, which dug in on the hill on the evening of 25 April. Pope's formed part of the Australian line for the rest of the campaign. The smaller hill to the right of Pope's was scaled by British soldiers from the Portsmouth Marines early in May. As soon as they reached the top they were caught by Turkish machine-gun fire and forced to retreat. Their dead lay for days on the hillside 'like ants shrivelled by a fire' until a soldier crept out at night and rolled the bodies into the valley. From then on the hill was known as Dead Man's Ridge, and it eventually formed part of the Turkish line. The small valley to the right of Dead Man's Ridge is the aptly named Bloody Angle, scene of costly attacks by the Anzacs in May. It was never held by either side and formed a gap in the Anzac front line that was only ever occupied by patrols operating after dark. Right of Bloody Angle the white stone of Quinn's Post Cemetery can be seen. From here it is obvious what a perilous line the Anzacs held – if the Turks had broken through at any of these posts they could have charged all the way to the beach along Monash Valley.

Almost directly below in Monash Valley was the site of the 1st Battalion dressing station early in the campaign. On 15 May General Bridges was passing the dressing station on his way to inspect the front line when a shot rang out from a sniper on Dead Man's Ridge and he fell with a huge bullet wound in his thigh. He was rushed back down the valley and onto a hospital ship but died soon after. He was buried at Duntroon, the military college in Canberra he had helped found. Until the body of Australia's Unknown Soldier was reinterred at the Australian War Memorial in 1993, Bridges was the only Australian killed in the First World War whose body was repatriated.

Return to the cemetery and follow the access track back to the main road on Second Ridge. Continue north on the road, which follows the line of no-man's-land. This section of ridge was named MacLaurin's Hill, after Colonel Henry MacLaurin, commander of the 1st Brigade. MacLaurin was killed by a sniper on 27 April while standing on the slope of the hill to your left, and now lies in 4th Battalion Parade Ground Cemetery. Ten minutes earlier his brigade major, Major Frank Irvine, was observing the fighting from an exposed position at Steele's Post. The men around him warned him that he would be sniped at while standing there. 'It's my business to be sniped at,' he barked and, true to his word, fell dead with a bullet through the head. MacLaurin and Irvine were probably killed by the same sniper.

In less than 200 metres you will reach Courtney's and Steele's Post Cemetery [11] on the left. Steele's Post was the southernmost of the three crucial positions at the head of Monash Valley occupied by the Anzacs on 25 April and held until the evacuation (the others being Courtney's and Quinn's). These three posts define the Gallipoli campaign in the terms that Australians best understand it: Anzac troops tenaciously hanging on in precarious posts on the edge of the valley, a constant shower of bombs across a narrow no-man's-land, an enemy entrenched so close in front that you can hear him cough. Steele's Post was named after Major Thomas Steel of the 14th Battalion, who occupied it on 27 April. From the outset there was confusion about the spelling of the name, and it persists today. Even the Commonwealth War Graves Commission isn't quite sure, referring to the cemetery as 'Courtney's and Steel's' on its website. During the campaign the post was officially designated 'Steele's' and this is the name inscribed on the wall of the cemetery.

Like its cousins Courtney's and Quinn's, Steele's Post was an impossible position, perched so precariously on the edge of the ridge that it defies reason that the Anzacs could have held it for eight months. Bean called it 'a steep niche, of which the top was a sheer landslide of gravel where a man could scarcely climb on hands and knees'. Early on, the Anzacs slung a rope down the hillside to help the troops drag themselves up to the post. In wet weather it was impossible to reach Steele's without it.

Steele's Post was a tough position to hold. It faced one of the strongest posts in the Turkish line and the Anzacs lived constantly with the fear of attack. In July they dug a network of shallow tunnels in no-man's-land, less than 10 centimetres below the ground, and filled them with barbed wire. The tunnels would collapse under the weight of attacking troops, hindering the assault and providing a forward position that could be occupied by the Anzacs during a counterattack. Steele's Post also suffered regularly from heavy shelling. An old howitzer on the Turkish northern flank was trained on Steele's and it killed or wounded more than 130 men in one five-day stretch alone.

Courtney's and Steele's Post Cemetery is the second in the chain of battlefield post cemeteries built on the ridgetop after the war. It occupies the southern sector of Steele's Post and contains 225 burials. The heavy fighting in the area is reflected in the fact that only seven of the bodies (six Australians and one British marine) could be identified. Special memorials commemorate 58 men known or believed to buried in the cemetery. The two most senior soldiers commemorated here were both lieutenants in the 13th Battalion killed in the opening days: Harold Watkins (died 25/4/15, Special Memorial 43) and Fred Wilson (died 26/4/15, Special Memorial 44).

Bastiaan Plaque No. 6 is in the flowerbed near the cemetery entrance.

Opposite the cemetery, on the other side of the road, are the remains of trenches that formed part of the Turkish line. In May the Australians saw two enemy officers in this area who they took to be Germans. (There were few German officers actively commanding Turkish troops at Gallipoli, so the officers were probably Turks.) From this time onwards this area was known as German Officer's Ridge [12], and the Turks turned it into a fortress. It was an exposed position – this was another spot where the Turks suffered horrendous casualties in their attack of 19 May – so both sides resorted to furious tunnelling and mining beneath the ridge. In July the Australians detonated a mine here that formed a crater opening into a heavily defended Turkish trench. In broad daylight on the morning of 15 July, 12 men from the 7th Battalion stormed the crater. They were led by Lieutenant Norman Greig, a 24-year-old Melbourne school teacher who had only recently arrived at Gallipoli. A furious bomb fight broke out and soon all the Australians had been killed or wounded. Half-a-dozen men from the 6th Battalion rushed out of the Australian trenches to reinforce them, but were mistaken for Turks by a distant Australian machine gun and mown down. Greig ordered his men to retreat and was last seen in the crater, his face covered in blood, holding off the Turks with his revolver. After the war a Turkish officer reported that he had seen a 'fine young officer – very handsome and well dressed', fighting with the Turks in the crater. 'Don't kill that man,' the Turk shouted to his troops. 'We want to capture him.' 'He will not allow himself to be taken,' they replied, and soon after Greig was killed by a grenade (Bean, Vol. II, p. 340). According to Bean, the Turks buried Greig behind their lines 'with more reverence than was generally shown to the dead of their enemies'. His body could not be found after the war and today he is commemorated on the Lone Pine Memorial.

Private Fred Muir took part in a raid against a Turkish machine-gun at German Officer's in June:

> About 60 [men] in all . . . lined up along the parapet. Suddenly a whistle blast sounded and we were over the parapet and towards the enemy's trench. We fixed bayonets as we ran tripping over our own barbed wire and other obstacles. At first not a shot was fired by the enemy but just as the first of our men reached the trench the alarm was given out and a murderous fire from rifles and machine guns broke out . . . In addition the Turks threw a number of bombs with good effect . . . we were forced to retire amid a heavy fire having however put the machine gun out of action . . . the whole affair lasted only some 10 minutes but nearly every second man was injured, the total casualties 27 wounded and 5 killed. (Gammage, p. 62)

A little-known chapter in the Gallipoli saga played out at this spot during the August Offensive. On the night of 6–7 August, the 6th Battalion was ordered to attack German

Officer's Ridge as part of a series of attacks taking place all along the Anzac line (the most famous of these being the attack at Lone Pine and the charge at the Nek). The plan called for several mines to be detonated beneath the Turkish trenches and for the 6th Battalion, made up mostly of raw recruits, to rush the Turkish line from 21 specially constructed tunnels. The result was a bloodbath – from 20 metres away the Turks opened a murderous fire from rifles and machine guns the moment the Australians left the tunnels. After two unsuccessful attempts, the Australians returned to their lines, leaving 80 of their comrades dead and 66 wounded. Most of the dead were never recovered and are commemorated on the Lone Pine Memorial, although you will see a few of their graves in the cemeteries nearby.

Continue past the cemetery for another 250 metres, until the road bends sharply right. On your left is the site of Courtney's Post [13], the centre of the three crucial posts at the head of Monash Valley. Courtney's was named after Lieutenant-Colonel Richard Courtney, commander of the 14th Battalion, whose men consolidated the position on 27 April. It was a precarious post – New Zealanders who spent time there described themselves as 'flies hanging on a wall'. Courtney's was the scene of some of the fiercest assaults during the Turkish attack of 19 May – at one stage a group of Turks bludgeoned their way into the Australian line and captured part of the post. Corporal Albert Jacka, a 22-year-old forestry worker from Bendigo in Victoria, led a small party from the 14th Battalion to drive the Turks out, but several of the men were hit and the attack failed. Jacka then ran alone along a communication trench, out into the open and dived into the main trench among the Turks. His comrades heard several shots, shouts and screams, and they ran forward to find Jacka surrounded by dead Turks, his face flushed with exertion and an unlit cigarette hanging out of his mouth. 'I managed to get the beggars, sir,' he said. He had shot five Turks, bayoneted two and set the rest to flight. He was awarded the VC, the first to an Australian in the First World War.

Albert Jacka was the archetypal Anzac: brash, tough and recklessly brave. He was an outstanding leader but disdained authority and constantly quarrelled with his commanding officers. But he was also a born soldier. General Brand, commander of the 4th Brigade, said he was 'more than a fighter. He was a genius. He had that superb quality of knowing when to act and how to act, and the sublime courage that made that which seemed impossible, possible.' (Wigmore, p. 33)

Jacka was a standout from the moment he joined the AIF and raced through early promotions. He was promoted from private to 2nd lieutenant within a year of the Gallipoli landing and was a captain by March 1917.

At Pozieres in August 1916 Jacka led a spirited attack against German troops, during which he was wounded seven times and almost died. For this action he was awarded the Military Cross, although many considered he deserved a second VC. At Bullecourt in April 1917 he reconnoitred the ground in front of the Australian lines and captured two Germans, including an officer. This earned him a bar to his MC. By late 1917 the 14th Battalion was being called Jacka's Mob after further exploits at Messines and Polygon Wood. Jacka was gassed in early 1918 and sent to England. He never rejoined his unit.

After the war Jacka was a businessman and served as the mayor of St Kilda, but he never really recovered from his war wounds. He died in 1932, aged only 39. His last words, spoken to his father, were, 'I'm still fighting, Dad.' He is buried in St Kilda Cemetery.

Continue along the road past Courtney's Post and turn right into a dirt road, signposted to Çataldere Şehitliği [14]. This is a Turkish mass grave created during the 24 May truce, and used for the rest of the campaign. It is located 500 metres along the track at the bottom of a flight of steps. As with other Turkish mass graves, the memorial tablets record the names of the dead but not their resting place. The grave itself is in the valley behind the memorial. It contains the remains of 2,835 men from the 1st, 5th, 6th, 27th and 57th Regiments. Just before the memorial is the tomb of Lieutenant-Colonel Hüseyin Avni Manastir, the 34-year-old commander of the Turkish 57th Regiment (the colonel's name was Hüseyin Avni; 'Manastir' was his hometown in Macedonia, then part of the Ottoman Empire and now called Bitola). Zeki Bey, a Turkish battalion commander, told Charles Bean in 1919 that he went to visit Avni during Ramadan on 13 August 1915.

He told me he had a letter from his home – his children were asking how long this war would last, and whether 'Father' would be with them for the feast, as he had been the year before: they all told him how dreary it was without him. Within two hours of his telling me this, the poor fellow lay dead, killed by a shell from one of your howitzers. (Bean, *Gallipoli Mission*, p. 179)

The memorial tablet next to the colonel's tomb recounts the heroic service of the 57th Regiment at Gallipoli, and the unit's numerous awards and merits. There are excellent views of the Turkish side of Johnston's Jolly and Lone Pine to the south.

Return to the main road and continue for another 100 metres until you reach a tomb on the right side of the road. This is the final resting place of the Turkish Captain (*Yüzbaşi*) Mehmet [15]. According to legend, his body was found in a trench during the 24 May truce, entwined with the body of an Australian soldier. It's an unlikely story, but touching all the same.

Cross the road to Quinn's Post Cemetery [16]. Quinn's Post was named after Major Hugh Quinn of the 15th Battalion

Australian light horsemen using a periscope rifle at Quinn's Post. AWM H10324

who was killed there on 29 May and now lies in Shrapnel Valley Cemetery. Quinn's was probably the most vital position at Anzac. It was located squarely at the head of Monash Valley and was the lynchpin of the Anzac line. The slope was so steep and the ridge so narrow that it was a miracle the Anzacs could hold it for eight hours, let alone eight months. But hold it they did, through some of the most brutal fighting of the campaign. Other places at Gallipoli like the Nek and Lone Pine became famous because of short but ferocious actions that occurred there. Quinn's Post became famous because the fighting there was incessant and murderous.

To the Turks this was Bombasirt (Bomb Ridge), and the name was well chosen. No-man's-land at Quinn's was only a few metres wide, little more than the width of the modern road, making the post a fertile ground for grenade warfare. Both sides kept up a constant stream of bombs, and the cacophony of explosions, shouts and screams was relentless. Men walking in Monash Valley would hear the din and glance up at Quinn's 'as a man looks at a haunted house' (Bean, Vol. II, p. 91). It was not uncommon for companies holding the post to throw more than 300 bombs in a day.

Early in the campaign the Turks completely dominated Quinn's Post with both rifle fire and bombs. The Turks had a plentiful supply of black 'cricket ball' bombs and made good use of them. The Anzacs on the other hand, had no experience with bombs and virtually no supply. By early May a bomb-making factory had been set up on the beach and small numbers of jam tin bombs began to arrive, but the Anzacs were still severely outgunned. By June, however, they had strengthened the position and were using periscope rifles to return fire without having to show their heads above the trench. They had also brought up machine guns to cover the post from the flanks, which gave them a large fire advantage over the Turks. There were six machine guns at Russell's Top, the long hill on the other side of Monash Valley, and nine machine guns at Courtney's Post, the prominent northern shoulder of which you can see jutting out into the valley south of the cemetery. Both sides launched attacks at Quinn's Post in the early days of the campaign, but this weight of machine-gun fire made them suicidal.

Lieutenant Richard Casey watched 30 Australians charge on 30 May:

> None of them came back and I am afraid none of them could have got out alive. It was a very sad – and wonderfully gallant – sight to see those 20 or 30 men going to certain death with all the dash imaginable. I shall never forget the last man to go into the Turk trench – he just stood upon their parapet and threw bomb after bomb into the trench – just as he was hurling the last one he was knocked down by a dozen bullets. (Diary entry, 30/5/15, Australian War Memorial, 3DRL/3267)

On 7 August the 2nd Light Horse Regiment was ordered to launch an attack from Quinn's Post to accompany the attack at the Nek, the first time the Anzacs had attempted an assault there since early June. The first wave left its trenches just before 5 a.m. and was mown down even quicker than its comrades at the Nek. Of the 60-odd men who went over in the first wave, 18 were killed and 37 wounded.

It was all over in less than a minute. In their excitement the Turks continued to expose themselves, standing shoulder-high above their parapets both opposite Quinn's and on the Chessboard, and so sustained losses which they would otherwise have escaped. (Bean, Vol. II, p. 631)

But at Quinn's, unlike at the Nek, sanity prevailed. The attack was called off before the second wave left the trenches.

Quinn's Post Cemetery is the last in the chain of battle post cemeteries and also the largest. It was originally formed after the war when 225 unidentified bodies were brought together from the surrounding area, and was enlarged in the following years. A small cemetery at the base of nearby Pope's Hill was closed and its 73 bodies were reburied in a plot in front of the Cross of Sacrifice, and isolated bodies found in the post-war years were also brought in. Today the cemetery contains 473 graves and, given the tough nature of the fighting in the area, it's unsurprising that 294 of them are unidentified. An extraordinary range of units is represented in the cemetery, a reflection of the chaotic clashes that characterised life at Quinn's. Browse the headstones and you'll see men from the 13th, 14th, 15th and 16th Battalions who held this area of the ridge in the opening days of the campaign, members of the Otago Regiment and Royal Naval Division who joined them in the first week of May and died by the score trying to take Baby 700, and troopers from the 1st and 2nd Light Horse Regiments who attacked here on 7 August. Brothers Fred and Harold Sherwood, both troopers in the 1st Light Horse, were killed in this attack and now lie side by side in graves C.5 and C.6.

The most senior officer commemorated here is Major Thomas Logan of the 2nd Light Horse, who was killed leading the first wave in the charge of 7 August, falling dead 'before he had gone five yards' (Special Memorial 14).

Another officer commemorated nearby is Captain William Hoggart of the 14th Battalion who was killed on 27 April while trying to locate a machine gun that was causing casualties among his men (Special Memorial 11).

Bastiaan Plaque No. 7 is near the cemetery entrance.

After visiting the cemetery, walk behind it and climb down into the culvert at the south-western corner. From here the view straight down Monash Valley demonstrates why Quinn's was such a vital position. If the post had been lost, the Turks could have advanced unimpeded to the beach and cut the Anzac position in two. During the campaign the slope was layered with terraces that sheltered support troops behind Quinn's. Today they are long gone. Erosion has washed the terraces and most of the post into the valley. To your right, the two hills of Dead Man's Ridge and Pope's Hill are prominent at the head of the gulley. There was a gap in the Australian line here – the posts at Pope's and Quinn's were cut off by Dead Man's, which was in Turkish hands. Crossfire from machine guns on the flanks prevented either side from breaking into the enemy lines.

The position on the other side of the road was known as Turkish Quinn's, and here there was quite an extensive network of shallow trenches that snaked through the scrub. But in 2004 a car park was built on the site to accommodate the large numbers of Turkish visitors to the nearby 57th Regiment Memorial. It's one of the great ironies of Gallipoli that constant building works to cope with growing numbers of tourists are destroying the landscape they come to see. At the far end of the car park on the right of the road, a short flight of steps leads to Kesikdere Şehitliği [17], another Turkish mass grave. This one contains 1,115 bodies and was used throughout the campaign. It contains the bodies of men from the 18th, 27th, 57th and 64th Regiments.

Return to the road and cross to the car park on the other side. At the far end stands the imposing Turkish Soldier Statue [18]. To the Turks this statue is known as Türk Askerine Saygi Aniti, which roughly translates as 'Respect to the Turkish Soldiers Memorial'. This is an appropriate name because the Anzac troops initially expected their Turkish foes to be inept fighters who would run at the first sight of a bayonet. There were also rumours that the Turks were barbarians who would mutilate any prisoners they captured. Not surprisingly, the opening encounters between the Anzacs and Turks were brutal, with virtually no prisoners taken by either side. But the Turkish attack of 19 May, unsuccessful as it was, demonstrated that the Turks possessed a courage that the Australians couldn't help but admire. From then on the Anzacs held a grudging respect, occasionally bordering on affection, for 'Johnny Turk'. During lulls in the fighting, relations between the two sides were sometimes cordial:

A note was thrown over by the Turks, evidently in answer to one from our chaps asking the distance to Constantinople . . . 'You ask how far it is to Constantinople. How long will you please be in getting there?' They used a knife as a weight when they threw the note and asked for it to be returned. It was thrown back but fell short . . . On being told where it was they asked our chaps not to fire while one of them got it . . . On another occasion there must have been a German officer approaching, for all of a sudden the Turks began signalling to our chaps to get down in their trenches. They immediately took the hint and then a machine gun began to play along the parapet from end to end. Of course, no damage was done. This shows something of the fairness with which the Turk fights. (Lieutenant Jack Price, 2nd Division Signalling Company, in Gammage, p. 92)

The statue was unveiled in 1992, and it dominates the upper reaches of Monash Valley in much the same way as the Turkish defenders did in 1915. Visitors with a keen eye will note that the sculptor slightly favoured evocative design over historical accuracy. The Turk is charging forward holding a strange hybrid of a British and Turkish rifle.

Cross the road to the towering 57th Regiment Memorial [19], built on ground known to the Anzacs as the 'Chessboard', after aerial photographs revealed a labyrinth of Turkish trenches on the site. The 57th Regiment was the first Turkish unit to arrive at Anzac after the landing. It was hopelessly outnumbered, but managed to slow the Anzac advance long enough for other Turkish reinforcements to arrive. On that first day, Mustafa Kemal ordered a suicidal attack and uttered the famous words, 'I don't order you to attack, I order you to die.' And die his men did, suffering horrendous casualties in the opening days and also during the Turkish attack of 19 May. Between June and August the 57th also did a 45-day stint in the trenches at German Officer's, one of the deadliest spots in the Turkish line. It was a tough regiment and is worthy of being honoured.

The memorial was unveiled in 1992 in response to feedback from growing numbers of Turkish visitors who were disappointed at the lack of monuments to their own soldiers on the peninsula. The recent commitment by Turkish authorities to commemorate their dead is fitting because this is the scene of a great Turkish victory. But the works have not been without controversy. When this monument was built there were concerns that the planning and construction had been too hasty, and the memorial didn't fit in with its surroundings. It is certainly prominent, with the mustard-yellow tower visible from nearly every point on the Anzac battlefield. There was also criticism that in their efforts to celebrate the legend of Turkish bravery, there were a few shortcomings in the design of the memorial. There are no burials here, and the headstones are designed to represent the sacrifice of the average Turkish soldier, rather than commemorate individual burials. While this is a noble sentiment, it seemed odd when the mass graves where the Turkish dead were actually buried remained unmarked and forgotten in the valleys behind the memorial (this inconsistency has since been redressed by the construction of memorials on the sites of the mass graves). There are also some curious inconsistencies in the memorial that may mislead visitors. Many of the plaques that describe the fighting at Gallipoli are historically inaccurate, and some of the headstones in the cemetery have been duplicated. Most tellingly, the tale recounted on the stone at the top of the cemetery of a Turkish officer found locked in a 'deadly embrace' with the British Captain L. J. Walters during the construction of the memorial is pure fantasy.

Nevertheless, the memorial stands as a fitting tribute to the bravery of the common Turkish soldier at Gallipoli, and of his sacrifice, which has been overlooked for too long. Interesting aspects of the memorial include a Turkish open mosque on the right of the entrance, and the statue of Hüseyin Kaçmaz, a Gallipoli veteran, 'telling war stories' to a young girl named Eylül. Kaçmaz was Turkey's oldest Gallipoli veteran, and the statue depicts him attending the unveiling of the memorial. He was built of tough stuff: he also served in the Balkan War of 1912–13 and the Turkish War of Independence in 1919–23. He died in 1994. Turkish services commemorating the naval battle of 18 March and Anzac Day are held here each year.

Return to the main road and continue north for 150 metres. Turn left at an intersection signposted to the Nek Cemetery and Walker's Ridge Cemetery and continue for 200 metres until you reach a memorial set among trees on your right. This is the Nek [20], the place with probably the most evil reputation on the entire Gallipoli peninsula. The origins of the name have been lost in the mists of time, but a likely explanation is that the feature formed a narrow 'neck' of land between Russell's Top and Baby 700, the hill to the east. The name was probably coined by a veteran of the Boer War, who would have been familiar with the Afrikaans word *nek*, which in this context means a narrow mountain pass.

This is the scene of the famous Australian Light Horse attack on 7 August 1915, immortalised in Peter Weir's *Gallipoli*. The plan called for about 550 men from the 8th and 10th Light Horse to launch an attack in support of New Zealand troops who would capture the high ground at Chunuk Bair and then advance towards the Nek from the

The Nek Cemetery under construction in the old no-man's-land in 1923. The Turkish memorial stands among the remains of Turkish trenches at the top of the photo. The Australian trenches, scene of the famous Light Horse charge, are at the bottom. AWM H18635

rear. No-man's-land was so narrow at the Nek that there was only space for 150 men to advance at a time, so the light horsemen would attack in four waves. The Turks were about 50 metres away and they had dug several lines of trenches, defended by multiple machine guns and the rifles of hundreds of troops.

By dawn on 7 August it was obvious that the New Zealanders had not captured Chunuk Bair and the light horsemen were on their own at the Nek. This was a bad start, but things got worse when the artillery barrage supporting the attack ended seven minutes early. Commanders on the spot made the fatal decision to stick to the timetable and at 4.30 a.m. the first wave of Victorians from the 8th Light Horse charged. A roar of machine-gun and rifle fire erupted from the Turkish lines and the light horsemen fell as if their limbs 'had become string' (Bean, Vol. II, p. 614). The few men who survived had been wounded and fell back into their own trench. Most of the dead lay within five metres of the Australian line.

Incredibly, having witnessed the massacre and knowing what their fate would be, the men in the second wave, also from the 8th Light Horse, climbed out of their trenches two minutes after the first. Like their comrades, they were cut down within metres of their own trench.

The unit's commanding officers called for the attack to be called off but the Australian brigade major, Lieutenant-Colonel John Antill, stubborn, tactless and bull-headed, was buoyed by unlikely reports that an Australian marker flag had been seen in the Turkish front line. He ordered the third wave, Western Australians from the 10th Light Horse, to advance as scheduled. The men in the third wave promptly climbed into the storm of fire and were just as promptly massacred. Private Wilfred Harper attacked alongside his brother Gresley, and was last seen 'running forward like a schoolboy in a foot-race, with all the speed he could compass' (Bean, Vol. II, p. 618). Both brothers were killed and Wilfred became the inspiration for the character of Archy Hamilton in Peter Weir's *Gallipoli*.

By now even Antill couldn't ignore evidence of the slaughter, but before the decision to cancel the attack could be made, the right flank of the fourth wave attacked without orders. The left, seeing their comrades advancing, went forward as well and the fourth wave was slaughtered as swiftly as the first three. Sergeant William Sanderson was later interviewed about his experiences of the charge:

> The Turks were two-deep in the trench ahead. There was at least one machine-gun on the left and any number in the various trenches on the Chessboard. The men who were going out were absolutely certain that they were going to be killed, and they expected to be killed right away. The thing that struck a man most was if he wasn't knocked in the first three yards. Trooper Weston, on Sanderson's right, fell beside him as they got out of the trench, knocked back into the trench. Trooper Biggs also fell next to him. Sanderson went all he could for the Turkish trench. Trooper Hill, running beside him, was shot through the stomach, spun round, and fell. Sanderson saw the Turks [close] in front and looked over his shoulder. Four men were running about ten yards behind, and they all dropped at the same moment. He tripped over a rhododendron bush and fell over a dead Turk right on the Turkish parapet . . . There were two dead men to the right towards the top of the hill, lying on the Turkish parapet – they looked like the Harper brothers. Sanderson knew how badly the show had gone. (Bean, Vol. II, p. 619)

So ended the charge of the Light Horse at the Nek. Of the 550 men who had attacked, 234 had been killed and a further 138 wounded. Four years later, with the war over, their bones still littered no-man's-land.

A light horse officer who was in hospital at the time of the charge described his feelings in a letter to his family:

You can imagine what it was like. Really too awful to write about. All your pals that had been with you for months and months blown and shot out of all recognition. There was no chance whatsoever of us gaining our point, but the roll call after was the saddest, just fancy only 47 answered their names out of close on 550 men. When I heard what the result was I simply cried like a child. (2nd Lieutenant Charles St Pinnock, letter 15/8/1915, Australian War Memorial, 1DRL/0547)

Peter Weir's *Gallipoli*, as good a tale as it was, promoted a myth about the charge at the Nek that still persists. During the film's climactic scenes the officer who orders the attack to continue in spite of the horrendous casualties has an English accent, giving the impression that it was a British commander who ordered the squandering of Australian lives. In reality, it was Lieutenant-Colonel John Antill, a native of Picton, New South Wales and a former student at Sydney Grammar School, who ordered the third wave to their deaths.

Today there are a number of interesting monuments at the Nek. The Turkish memorial surrounded by lawn and pines purportedly honours 'Sergeant Mehmet', who was said to have fought to the death here to hold back the Australians on 25 April. According to legend, his last words were, 'I die happily for my country and you, my comrades, will avenge me.' This rather improbable tale is likely a relatively recent invention. The memorial originally commemorated 70 Turks who were killed here when the Anzacs detonated a mine beneath their trenches during the evacuation. Why the memorial was later rededicated to Sergeant Mehmet has never adequately been explained. A similar memorial at Lone Pine and one at North Beach were torn down by the British after the war. The base of the memorial at the Nek is original, although the stone obelisk was added later.

The memorial also roughly marks the spot where Captain Joseph Lalor and a small group of men from the 12th Battalion dug in and held off the Turks for much of the day on 25 April. Lalor had a distinguished military pedigree and fire in his blood – he was the grandson of Peter Lalor, the leader of the rebels at the Eureka Stockade on the Ballarat goldfields in 1854. Against all regulations, he carried a family sword with him when he landed at Gallipoli but lost it during the heavy fighting at the Nek. Late in the afternoon he stood up to lead his men in a charge against the Turks and was shot dead. His body is believed to be buried in an unmarked grave at Baby 700 Cemetery (see page 151). His sword was later found by an Australian and then lost again. According to some reports it turned up on display in a Turkish museum after the war, but has not been seen since.

In the scrub on the opposite side of the road are two large water tanks which had originally supplied water to the Anzac troops in the front line. The massive iron tanks had to be dragged by hand to the top of Plugge's Plateau, and water was then pumped up from the beach. Sergeant Cyril Lawrence watched men from the New Zealand Maori Contingent drag a tank up the slope:

> I saw a party of Maoris hauling up one of these big tanks, all yelling and puffing. Great big men. Golly! That tank fairly flew up. All Australia stood still to watch and afterwards gave them a cheer. (East, p. 55)

The tanks were moved here after the war to provide water to the gardens and cemetery at the Nek.

Continue on the dirt road past the memorial until you reach the Nek Cemetery. When Charles Bean returned to Gallipoli in 1919 he found the former battlefield at the Nek virtually unchanged since the light horse attack nearly four years earlier. The men killed in the charge had not been buried, their bleached bones whitening the soil of the plain. When Bean arrived at the Nek he:

> . . . found the low scrub there literally strewn with their relics and those of earlier Turkish attacks over the same ground. When shortly after our visit Hughes [in charge of the Australian graves units] came to bury the missing in this area, he found and buried more than three hundred Australians in that strip the size of three tennis courts. Their graves today mark the site of one of the bravest actions in the history of war. (*Gallipoli Mission*, p. 109)

This cemetery occupies the old no-man's-land, and offers a visual representation of the tragedy of the famous attack. Bean's 'three tennis courts' are now grassed over and surrounded by a stone wall. There are 316 men buried here, but only five headstones. These mark the graves of four New Zealanders and one Australian who died long before the August attack. (Showing how confused the early fighting was in this part of the line, two of the New Zealanders, Privates Thomas Moloney and Walter Rouse, are listed as having been killed sometime between 1 and 23 May.) None of the 8th or 10th Light Horsemen killed in the charge and later interred here could be identified. Four of them, known to be buried here, are commemorated on special memorials, along with an Australian who was killed in the Turkish attack of 19 May. It is a sad and lonely place.

The cemetery offers spectacular views over the mad tangle of gullies and ravines that so exhausted and confused the flanking brigades in the August Offensive.

Bastiaan Plaque No. 8 is to the right of the cemetery facing the road.

Just past the cemetery are the tumble-down remains of the Australian front-line trench. It is hard to visualise now, but this is where hundreds of men from the 8th and 10th Light Horse charged into no-man's-land and certain death. The sorry state of the trench is the result of an ongoing disagreement between Turkish and Commonwealth authorities about the maintenance of historic sites at Gallipoli. The Turkish authorities cleared the scrub out of the trench and reinforced it with pine logs in the 1990s to help define and preserve it. Commonwealth authorities, however, would prefer that the trenches be left in their natural state, which has led to an unhappy compromise: the log supports will stay, but they won't be maintained, even as they collapse into the trench. Note the tunnel entrance, pointing towards the Turkish lines, about halfway along the trench.

The remains of the Anzac trench system actually extend well beyond this front line. They snake through the scrub behind the position. The scrub is thick and thorny, and the trenches open abruptly into the sheer drop of Malone's Gully at their northern end. Use extreme care if you decide to explore them.

The trenches from which the Australians attacked formed part of the defences of Russell's Top, the narrow plateau extending from Second Ridge south-west towards the coast. The Australians occupied it soon after the landing and only held it in the opening days by tenacious defence as the Turks threw wave after wave of troops at it. When it was eventually secured it formed the highest point in the Anzac perimeter, and was home to field batteries and machine-gun emplacements. Fire from here could slice along the length of Second Ridge, and the Top formed one of the key defensive positions at Anzac. It was named after Brigadier Andrew Russell, commander of the New Zealand Mounted Rifles, who established his headquarters here in early May. The Turks appreciated its significance and launched several costly attacks against it in the opening months of the campaign, but were never successful in dislodging the Anzacs.

Continue along the dirt road for 150 metres until you reach Walker's Ridge Cemetery [21]. Walker's Ridge is the long spur that runs from behind the cemetery down to North Beach. It was named after Brigadier Harold 'Hooky' Walker, commander of the Australian 1st Brigade, and was the main route used by the Anzacs to reach the trenches on Russell's Top. The light horse and the New Zealand regiments fiercely defended this vital northern sector of the Anzac line. A track follows the crest of Walker's Ridge from behind the cemetery to North Beach. The track was used by the Turks before the landing, the Anzacs for the eight months of the campaign and by visitors to the peninsula ever since.

The cemetery was begun when two plots were dug on either side of an Anzac trench during the campaign. This layout is reflected in the design of the modern cemetery, with

Walker's Ridge Cemetery, with Suvla Bay in the distance

the two plots separated by open ground. There are 92 men buried here, 40 from New Zealand, 12 from Australia and one from Britain. All but 16 of the graves are identified and there are 26 special memorials dedicated to men known or believed to be buried in the cemetery.

Buried here is Trooper Harold Rush of the 10th Light Horse, who was killed in the charge at the Nek on 7 August. His headstone records that his last words to his mates were 'Goodbye Cobber, God bless you' (grave II.C.4). Other men from the 10th Light Horse killed in the charge include Trooper Don McLean (grave II.B.9), Trooper Herbert Pope (grave II.C.5) and Trooper Clarence Sutton (grave II.B.10). Major Thomas Redford was one of the 8th Light Horse officers who led the charge of the first wave (grave II.C.9). Also buried here is Private Roy Robertson of the 20th Battalion, who was only 16 years old when he was killed on 7 November (Special Memorial 20).

Another notable grave is that of Private Hohepa Herewini who belonged to the New Zealand Maori Contingent (grave II.B.4). The Maori Contingent sailed from New Zealand in February 1915 and was initially sent to Malta for garrison duties. After the Gallipoli landings one of its members made an impassioned plea to the New Zealand commanders:

Our ancestors were a warlike people. The members of this war party would be ashamed to face their people at the conclusion of the war if they were to be confined entirely to garrison duty and not be given an opportunity of proving their mettle at the front. (www.nzhistory.net.nz)

The carnage at Gallipoli soon gave the Maori their chance, and they landed at Anzac Cove in early July. For the rest of the campaign they worked as pioneers alongside the New Zealand Mounted Rifles, and lost heavily during the fighting at Chunuk Bair and Hill 60 in August. By September less than 60 of the original 477 members of the unit were still with it. The Maori Contingent left Gallipoli in December, among the last New Zealand troops to evacuate.

Two Australians buried here served with New Zealand forces: Corporal Ernest Hawke of the Canterbury Regiment (died 1/5/1915, grave II.C.3) and Lieutenant James Nicholas of the Auckland Mounted Rifles (died 22/5/1915, grave I.C.8).

Walker's Ridge Cemetery offers magnificent views of the country north of Anzac, stretching all the way to Suvla Bay.

Opposite the cemetery on the other side of the road was the approximate site of the 3rd Light Horse Brigade headquarters during the attack at the Nek. From here, Antill gave the order for the attack to continue, even after hundreds of men had been killed. It's interesting to note that, contrary to popular perception, Antill wasn't removed from the fighting in some distant headquarters behind the line. He was right there, only 200 metres from the spot where his men were being mown down, close enough to smell the cordite and hear the screams.

Just past the cemetery, the road ends in a lookout offering the most spectacular view at Anzac. In front of you the impossibly steep Mule Gully tumbles all the way to the sea, and the Sphinx stands sentinel over Anzac Cove and North Beach. The Anzacs made Gallipoli's treacherous ravines their own, but this one was too much even for them. Apart from a few hardy souls who scaled it on the first day, Mule Gully was never used as a route to the front line. Engineers built a crude flying fox in the gully early in the campaign and used it to haul supplies from the beach to the trenches on Russell's Top.

The impossibly steep Mule Gully, overlooking North Beach

Return past the Nek to the main road and turn left. Continue along the road for 200 metres and follow a dirt track to the right. This leads to Baby 700 Cemetery [22]. While the landing was being planned, British maps showed two hills on Second Ridge both 700 feet high. The larger one to the north was christened Big 700 and its smaller cousin to the south became Baby 700. Big 700 was renamed Battleship Hill after the landing (see page 168).

Baby 700 was a crucial early objective for the Australians. It looms over Monash Valley and offered its garrison observation and fire over much of the Anzac sector. The original plan called for the 3rd Brigade to sweep across it during their charge to Gun Ridge and to destroy several Turkish gun batteries that were known to be sheltering on its inward slopes. Fierce Turkish resistance held the Australians up, however, and control of Baby 700 seesawed between the two sides for most of the first day. Some of the most brutal fighting of the landing occurred on its slopes, with the Anzacs pushing their line down the eastern side (and briefly glimpsing the shimmering waters of the Dardanelles in the process), and the Turks driving them back to the head of Monash Valley. By late afternoon the Anzacs gave up their attempts to take the hill and never occupied it again for the rest of the campaign. This wasn't for lack of trying. On 2 May the New Zealanders of the Otago Battalion launched an attack against the hill and were decimated before getting anywhere near it, and the light horse attack at the Nek on 7 August was actually intended to end on the slopes of Baby 700.

Baby 700 Cemetery was created after the war on the site where Anzac soldiers had been buried by the Turks during the 24 May truce. After the war, the cemetery was used to bury men who mostly fell in the opening days of the campaign. These men had pushed further inland than any of their comrades would for the rest of the campaign, but they paid for this achievement with their lives. As the Turks attacked, these isolated parties of Anzacs far in front of the main line were swallowed up and destroyed. Their remains were found scattered across the hills and gullies behind Second Ridge, and were concentrated here on Bay 700, the hill that many of them had died trying to capture. The graves in the cemetery reflect the chaos of the opening day at Anzac. Look out for burials from the 11th and 12th Battalions, the first units to reach Baby 700 on the morning of the landing, as well as men from the 1st and 2nd Battalions and Auckland and Canterbury Regiments who reinforced them later in the day. New Zealanders and Australians killed in the August diversionary attacks are also buried here.

Today there are 493 soldiers buried in the cemetery and, as would be expected, 450 of them are unidentified. Ten special memorials commemorate men known or believed to be buried among them. Almost certainly buried here is Captain Joseph Lalor, the sword-wielding Eureka Stockade descendant who was killed at the Nek on 25 April (Special Memorial 4).

Sergeant Adam McLachlan of the 16th Battalion (grave D.33) died of wounds on 25 April, and his burial here comes as a bit of a surprise. The 16th reinforced Pope's Hill on the first night, and it is unlikely that its men could have probed forward as far as Baby 700. McLachlan was probably buried in an isolated grave near Pope's Hill. Why he was reinterred here and not alongside his comrades at Quinn's Post Cemetery is a mystery.

Also buried here are two light horsemen killed in the charge at the Nek: Corporal Thomas Thompson (grave D.28) and Trooper James Wilkerson (grave D.29), both of the 10th Light Horse. Second Lieutenant Harold Allen was an Australian who was killed on the day of the landing while serving with the Auckland Regiment (grave D.7).

Major Blair Swannell of the 1st Battalion was originally from England and had been an outstanding rugby player before the war. In 1899 and 1904 he toured Australia with the British Lions. After his second tour he stayed in Australia playing club rugby for Northern Suburbs, and was selected to play in a test for Australia against New Zealand in 1905. The night before the landing he had a premonition of his death and told a comrade that he intended to play this game the way he had played rugby – with his whole heart. His fears were well founded. He was shot on the slopes of Baby 700 on 25 April while kneeling to show his men how to take better aim at the Turks (Special Memorial 10). One of the officers who led Swannell's company after his death was Lieutenant Alfred Shout, who would win the VC but lose his life at Lone Pine in August.

After visiting the cemetery, climb onto the rear wall and face north-east. Directly across the valley is Battleship Hill (originally Big 700), with the slopes of Chunuk Bair behind it. Battleship Hill was reached on the morning of the landing by Captain Eric Tulloch and a small group of men, one of only two Australian units to reach their objective (see page 168).

Walk behind the cemetery and follow the track that heads north-east through the scrub. (In October 2008 while researching this book I found a human skull that had been exposed by recent rain half-buried in the middle of the track.)

A human skull exposed by rain on the path to the *Mesudiye* Gun

After 35 metres the track ends at a rusted and broken artillery gun in a clearing. This is the *Mesudiye* Gun **[23]**, originally part of the armament of the Turkish ironclad *Mesudiye*, which was torpedoed in the Dardanelles by the British submarine *B-11* on 13 December 1914. The submarine's commander, Lieutenant Norman Holbrook, was awarded the first VC to a submariner soon after. In 1915 the New South Wales town of Germanton abandoned its unpatriotic name and called itself Holbrook in honour of the lieutenant. Today the town displays a replica of the *B-11* along with other submarines and memorabilia. Lieutenant Holbrook visited the town several times during his life, and his widow donated his VC to the local shire in 1982.

After the *Mesudiye* was sunk her guns were salvaged and converted to mobile batteries, which helped sink the French battleship *Bouvet* during the naval battle on 18 March 1915. It is uncertain how the gun was used during the remainder of the Gallipoli campaign but in 1919 Charles Bean noted that:

> There stood, in an open patch on the inland side of the summit of Baby 700, a solitary 6-inch gun with a few shells – the only armament then remaining at Anzac, and still guarded by three Turkish soldiers. This gun, standing out on the hillside, had, of course, been placed there by the Turks since the Evacuation – during the campaign no gun could have shown its nose except to peep from good cover. (*Gallipoli Mission*, p. 101)

The gun was badly damaged by the British occupation force after the war to prevent it being used against them by Turkish forces. The gun had come full circle – the *Mesudiye* had originally been built in England and was commissioned into the Royal Navy in 1875.

A dirt track leads to the main road. This completes the tour of Second Ridge, but the whole story of the Anzac battles will only fully be told by taking the Chunuk Bair and Gun Ridge tour. At the very least, walk or drive to Chunuk Bair and complete that section of the next tour.

Chunuk Bair and Gun Ridge

The High Ground – Battleship Hill to Scrubby Knoll

A walk along Second Ridge is a commemoration of achievement. The Anzacs might not have won the day at Gallipoli, but the fact that they clung on to their ridiculous foothold for eight months speaks volumes about their abilities as soldiers and as men. A walk from Chunuk Bair to Gun Ridge, by comparison, is an exercise in disappointment. This is the 'What if' walk – 'What if a larger force had landed at Anzac Cove on the first day?', 'What if the plan for the August Offensive had been less complicated?', 'What if the troops had pushed left instead of right, or climbed this ridge instead of that one?' Nothing about this part of the Anzac sector is particularly glorious or worth celebrating, except perhaps the courage of men asked to do the impossible.

The two important chapters of the Gallipoli saga explored on this walk are the mad dash made by the Anzacs on the first day for their objectives on Gun Ridge, and the huge assault on the high ground of Chunuk Bair and Hill 971 during the August Offensive.

On the first day the Anzacs were badly disorganised after the landing, and were held up by stronger than expected Turkish defence. But small groups of men – ridiculously small when you consider what they were trying to do – managed to break away from the main struggle on Second Ridge and push forward to their objectives on Gun Ridge. They didn't stay for long, and many of them died there, but they had advanced further than any of their comrades would for the rest of the campaign.

The plan for the attack in August was for a composite force of Anzacs and British troops to wheel north out of their 'cage' at Anzac and attack the dominant hills of the Sari Bair range: Chunuk Bair and Hill 971. They would then link up with a large British force that would stage a new landing at Suvla Bay, and together drive the Turks back across the peninsula. The attack on Sari Bair was the vital component of the August Offensive. Everything else relied on the successful capture of Chunuk Bair and Hill 971. But the plan was too ambitious. It relied too much on everything going just right and, at Gallipoli, that was never going to happen. The following condensed explanation illustrates how impossibly complicated the attack plan was. It's hard enough to follow on paper, let alone on the ground, in the dark and under attack.

The battle began with diversionary attacks at Lone Pine and Cape Helles on 6 August. The Lone Pine attack was a 'success' insofar as the Turkish trenches were captured, but it also alerted the Turks that bigger things were afoot at Anzac. The Helles attack (like all the attacks at Helles) was a costly failure.

The preliminary movement against the Sari Bair range began on the night of 6 August, when a covering force from the New Zealand Mounted Rifles performed one of the outstanding feats of the Gallipoli campaign by clearing the foothills north of Anzac. This opened up the way for two columns to advance along the valleys leading to the high ground of Sari Bair. The right column of New Zealanders under Brigadier-General Francis Johnston was tasked with capturing Chunuk Bair. Johnston was not well suited to the stresses of front-line command – historians with generous dispositions say he was 'ill' on 6 August. The less tolerant give more weight to the accounts that say he was blind drunk. Either way, the right column was in trouble. The left column was made up of Australians and Gurkhas under Brigadier-General Vaughan Cox and was tasked with capturing Hill 971 and the nearby Hill Q. The vital assault on Hill 971 would be made by the Australian 4th Brigade, commanded by Colonel John Monash. Monash would later earn fame as the engineer of Australia's finest victories on the Western Front but, at Gallipoli, his abilities as a commander left a bit to be desired.

The columns had been ordered to advance on an extremely tight schedule through some of Gallipoli's roughest terrain, and to be ready to launch a simultaneous attack on the three hills at 4.30 a.m. But they soon lost their way in the tangle of gullies and delays were inevitable. On the right the Otago, Wellington and Auckland Regiments had a difficult advance along Rhododendron Ridge but eventually reached a knob known as the Apex, which was near the summit of Chunuk Bair. The plan called for them to link up with the Canterbury Regiment and assault the summit before dawn. But the Canterburys had become hopelessly lost and Johnston made the fatal decision to wait for them before attacking. The New Zealanders sat down and ate breakfast, oblivious to the fact that the summit of Chunuk Bair, less than 500 metres away and the key to the entire peninsula, was defended by only 20 Turks.

After a delay of several hours, with the morning sun high in the sky, his men exhausted and no sign of the Canterburys, Johnston resumed the attack. Major-General Hans Kannengiesser, a German officer in command of a Turkish division at Gallipoli, raced to the summit of Chunuk Bair as soon as he heard about the advance. When he arrived, the 20 Turkish defenders were unaware they were about to be attacked and their commander was asleep.

Suddenly the enemy infantry actually appeared in front of us at about 500 yards range. The English [actually New Zealanders] approached slowly, in single file, splendidly equipped and with white bands on their left arms, apparently very tired, and were crossing a hill-side to our flank, emerging in continually increasing numbers from the valley below. I immediately sent an order to my infantry to open fire. I received this answer: 'We can only commence to fire when we receive the order of our battalion commander.' This was too much for me altogether. I ran to the spot and threw myself among the troops who were lying in a small trench. What I said I cannot recollect, but they began to open fire and almost immediately the English laid down without answering our fire or apparently moving in any other way. They gave me the impression that they were glad to be spared further climbing. (Kannengiesser, p. 207)

Before long the feeble Turkish garrison on the summit was reinforced, and the New Zealanders were mown down as they charged at the crest.

The only really shining moment for the New Zealanders came when Lance Corporal Cyril Bassett won the VC for braving the extremely heavy Turkish fire to lay and maintain telephone cables back to the New Zealand headquarters. Without his tireless efforts the attack would have fallen into a greater shambles than it already was. Cyril Basset had enlisted soon after war was declared and landed with the New Zealand Divisional Signal Company on 25 April. Soon after his VC-winning exploits he was evacuated sick and never returned to Gallipoli. He served with distinction on the Western Front, being promoted to lieutenant and wounded twice. He also served as an officer in the Royal New Zealand Corps of Signals in the Second World War. He died in Auckland in 1982, aged 91. Cyril Basset was the only New Zealander to receive the VC at Gallipoli, an outrage considering the New Zealanders' stellar achievements on the day of the landing and later at Quinn's Post, Krithia, Hill 60, Russell's Top, the Anzac outposts and, particularly, Chunuk Bair.

On 8 August the New Zealanders attacked again and this time captured the summit. For the first time since 25 April, Anzac troops glimpsed the waters of the Dardanelles. The

Wellington Regiment was commanded by Lieutenant-Colonel William Malone, a clear thinker who led his men with compassion and skill. Malone had been responsible for much of the construction work that had turned Quinn's Post into a tenable position in May, but at Chunuk Bair he made a controversial decision. When deciding where to site his trenches he followed the advice of a recently published British military pamphlet which, heavily influenced by the carnage on the Western Front, suggested that trenches should be dug on the reverse slope of hills, rather than the forward slope, to reduce casualties from shelling. That made sense in France, where every inch of ground was dominated by artillery, but it was less relevant at Gallipoli. What it did do was limit Malone's view of the battlefield, and that would prove fatal. For the rest of the day the Wellingtons, supported by the 7th Gloucesters and 8th Royal Welch Fusiliers, fought in close combat with the Turks, who could creep to within 20 metres of the New Zealand line before being seen. Malone was killed by a shell in the afternoon, most likely fired from a British ship or Anzac battery. By the time the Wellingtons were relieved after dark, fewer than 50 men remained unwounded. Private Victor Nicholson, one of the few survivors, recounted the day's fighting:

> The bayonet fighting seemed to last weeks; I suppose it was only minutes. No one likes bayonets, and the Turks seemed to like them less than us. I don't remember any charges. It was all stand and defend with the bayonet, just a mad whirl. In the back of my head I could hear the words: 'Get the bastard before he gets you. Get him or he'll get you!'. I don't remember bayonets going in.

Perhaps I shut my eyes. I don't know who I killed or who I didn't. (Shadbolt, p. 93)

On 10 August the New Zealanders were relieved by regiments from Kitchener's New Army: the 6th Loyal North Lancashires, the 5th Wiltshires, the 6th Leinsters and the 10th Hampshires. The new arrivals had just settled in when they heard the Turks charging across the summit.

Kemal Atatürk was commanding the Turks at Chunuk Bair, and he devised a plan that was both simple and brutal – a frontal assault to win back the summit. He crept forward alone and waved his whip. At the signal, the entire Turkish line charged down the hill, shouting and screaming. The British defenders were overwhelmed. The Turks were merciless, bayoneting anything that moved, and they swept across Malone's trenches and began charging towards the New Zealanders on the Apex. Ten New Zealand machine guns opened fire and cut the Turks down. They were also ordered to cut down more than 300 British troops who were walking towards the Turks with their hands up.

The Turks continued to surge down the slope, pushing the New Zealanders back and massacring 1,000 British troops at a small plateau known as the Farm. Eventually British artillery broke up the attack, but Chunuk Bair was back in Turkish hands. No Allied soldier set foot on it again for the rest of the campaign.

But at least the New Zealanders had reached their objective. The Australians in the left column spent most of the night of 6 August blundering around in the dark, stumbling from one gully to the next. When they finally began the assault on Hill 971 they were actually one ridge further north than Monash thought they were, and were slaughtered by Turkish machine guns. It would be days before Monash would realise his mistake. Over several nights of confused fighting, the 4th Brigade never got anywhere near Hill 971. The Gurkhas with them did manage to reach the heights of Hill Q, but their advance was shattered by a sudden artillery barrage, probably fired from an Allied gun. So, with the New Zealanders driven off Chunuk Bair, the Australians not even within sight of Hill 971, the Gurkhas smashed by their own artillery on Hill Q and the British going nowhere at Suvla Bay, the August Offensive, and with it the last real chance for success at Gallipoli, ground to a halt.

(For more information about the Anzac advance towards Sari Bair, see the North of Anzac and Suvla Bay tour.)

Chunuk Bair and Gun Ridge Tour

This is a tour of the ground coveted by the Allies, but always held by the Turks. It is a frustrating journey that forces the visitor to ponder what might have been. The tour visits two Commonwealth war cemeteries and numerous memorials to both Allies and Turks. The ground at Chunuk Bair is especially important to New Zealanders, whose men fell thickly on its slopes during the failed August Offensive.

The total tour length is about 7.5 kilometres, with optional visits to the Farm Cemetery and Hill 971. It is really too long to walk, and should take about two hours to complete by car, not including the optional visits.

If you have just completed the Second Ridge tour, begin this tour at point [5], just after the *Mesudiye* Gun (the last stop on the Second Ridge tour).

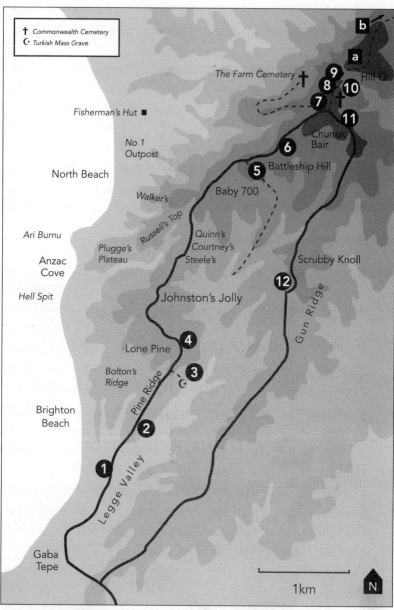

Chunuk Bair and Gun Ridge tour

If you are coming from Eceabat, follow the road to Bigali north out of town, and then turn left at the major intersection after 2 kilometres. Follow this road for about 8 kilometres as it heads into the Gallipoli Peace Park, past the Gaba Tepe Museum. Turn right at the sign to Chunuk Bair (Conkbayiri) and follow the road as it climbs towards Second Ridge (this road is one-way and completes a loop along Second and Gun Ridges).

The ridge you are following is Pine Ridge, which was captured by isolated groups of Australians on the morning of the landing. They couldn't hold it against Turkish counterattacks, however, and were either killed or forced to retreat. For the rest of the campaign Pine Ridge was in Turkish hands.

After 850 metres you will reach a flagpole (usually flying the Turkish flag) on the left side of the road [1]. During the truce of 24 May the Turks dug several large mass graves in the valleys behind their lines, and filled them with the bodies of men who had been killed in the suicidal attack of 19 May. For decades the mass graves were unmarked, effectively lost, until recent Turkish interest in the campaign prompted their rediscovery and commemoration with memorials. The valley behind the flagpole is the site of one of these mass graves, although this one is yet to be commemorated with a memorial.

Continue for another 350 metres until you reach a statue, surrounded by a small garden, on your right [2]. The statue depicts a Turkish soldier carrying a wounded Allied officer and commemorates an incident reportedly witnessed by Major Richard Casey, aide-de-camp to General Bridges, on 25 April. Casey recounted that, on the day of the landing, he saw a Turkish soldier emerge from his trench under a white flag and carry a wounded captain to safety in the Allied line. Details are sketchy and the incident may have been more fantasy than fact, but it serves as a neat reminder that for brief moments at least, respect and compassion were shown by both sides towards one another. After the war Casey had a distinguished career in politics and business and in 1965, as Lord Casey, became Governor-General of Australia. He died in 1976.

Continue driving along Pine Ridge, with the waters off the peninsula visible on your left. On the day of the landing, the Turkish 77th Regiment crossed Pine Ridge at this point and moved towards the Australians digging in on the right flank of the Australian line. British ships spotted the massing Turks and rained shells on them, causing hundreds of casualties.

When Charles Bean visited Gallipoli in 1919 he found, all along this section of the ridge, the scattered remains of Australians who had been killed on the day of the landing. In the gully on the left of the road he also found the bones of Australian men who were wounded or had been sheltering there when the Turks attacked in strength across Pine Ridge.

Follow the road for 850 metres until you reach a sign indicating the Karayörük Dere Şehitliği ('Black Tribe Valley Martyr Memorial') [3]. Black Tribe Valley was the Turkish name for the feature known to the Anzacs as Legge Valley. It sweeps roughly north–south behind the Turkish front line and was intended to be the main avenue to the heights of Chunuk Bair and Hill 971 for the attacking Anzac troops on the first morning. Scattered parties of Australians crossed Legge Valley and reached Gun Ridge (the high ground on the far side of the valley) on that first day, but they could not hold the ground and pulled back to Second Ridge.

Karayörük Dere was the site of one of the Turkish mass graves built during the truce of 24 May, and the Turks used it on and off for the rest of the campaign. The memorial on the site was built in 2006 and is reached by following a long series of steps down to rows of tablets inscribed with the names of the dead. The grave contains 1,153 bodies, and is actually located on the flat ground opposite the memorial rows. Most of the men buried here belonged to the 48th Regiment, but men from the 63rd and 77th Regiments also lie among them.

As you walk down the steps, note the small hillock to your right. When Charles Bean visited Gallipoli in 1919, he found the skeletons of four or five Australian soldiers here who had been killed on 25 April, grouped in a defensive semi-circle where they had fought to the death. A scattering of cartridge cases indicated that they had been exchanging shots with the Turks from a distance of less than 10 metres.

Return to the road and continue until you reach a Turkish memorial on the right [4]. This monument commemorates the Turkish defenders who faced the Australians during the attack on Lone Pine. Lone Pine was known to the Turks as Kanlisirt, meaning 'Bloody Ridge'. The name was adopted after the horrific Turkish attack of 19 May, but was equally appropriate in describing the brutal fighting at Lone Pine in August. The inscription translates as:

The Anzac forces attacked here on August 6/7, 1915 in order to assist the British 9th Army Corps to land in the Anafartalar region [Suvla Bay] and to hold on the

Ari Burnu front the 19th and 16th Turkish Divisions. Although the 16th Regiment suffered great losses (1520 killed and 4750 wounded), the heroic fighters successfully defended Bloody Ridge.

The valley behind the memorial was a Turkish reserve position, containing dugouts, camps and piles of stores. This was the area where Charles Bean and the other members of the Gallipoli Mission camped for the several weeks they spent exploring Anzac in the cold early months of 1919.

Continue along Second Ridge past Lone Pine and all the other stops on the Second Ridge tour until you reach the track leading to the *Mesudiye* Gun, the last stop on the Second Ridge tour. From the intersection with the track, head north on the main road for 500 metres, until a dirt fire track joins it on the right. Park your car near the track [5]. Before the landing British maps showed two adjacent hills in the Anzac sector that were roughly 700 feet high. The southern one was christened Baby 700 and the larger, northern one was called Big 700. Big 700 was a clear target for the warships anchored off Anzac on the day of the landing and for several days naval shells rained down on it in an attempt to disrupt the persistent advance of Turkish reinforcements. From then on it was known as Battleship Hill, and that is where you are now standing.

Walk along the fire track for about 400 metres, until it bends to the right. Walk through the scrub on the left of the bend until you have a clear view across the valley to the slopes of Chunuk Bair directly opposite.

On the day of the landing the 11th Battalion was supposed to advance inland and regroup on Battleship Hill. But the battalion became so mixed up and delayed by fighting on Second Ridge that it didn't get anywhere near its objective. One group of about 60 men was commanded by Captain Eric Tulloch, a Melbourne brewer and sportsman who typified the reckless bravery of the original Anzacs. He had been a champion schoolboy rower and raced with Stanley Bruce, the future prime minister. His orders after landing at Gallipoli were to advance to his objective at all costs so, in spite of only leading half a company and with the weight of the Turkish reinforcements about to descend on him, he led his men forward more than a kilometre in front of the rest of the Australians to their objective on the inland slopes of Battleship Hill. From there the Narrows were visible to their right, but it's unlikely any of the Australians noticed them, given what was about to happen. At first the hills in front of them were eerily silent, with only occasional stray bullets buzzing into the scrub. But soon the Turks spotted the Australians and opened fire, and Tulloch and his men were forced to dig shallow trenches and hold out as best they could.

Each side was well hidden in the scrub, and it was only when the Australians moved or tried to use their entrenching tools that they brought on themselves a storm of rifle-fire. The Turks had machine-guns also firing, but at very long range. While lying here Tulloch noted that on the 'northern shoulder' (apparently of a farther hill, in front) was a solitary tree, and by it stood a man, to and from whom went messengers. Tulloch fired at him, estimating the range at 800–900 yards, but the man did not stir. (Bean, *Gallipoli Mission*, p. 85)

Evidence suggests that the man may have been Kemal Atatürk, who was directing the 57th Regiment from near here at the time. How different the Gallipoli campaign would have been (and indeed the history of modern Turkey) if one of Tulloch's bullets had found its mark.

The Turks began creeping forward and picking off Tulloch's men one by one. Lieutenant Mordaunt Reid was severely wounded in the thigh but refused to be escorted back to the main Australian line, telling his comrades he would make the journey by himself. He was never seen again. After half an hour Tulloch realised his position was hopeless, and he led his men back to the Anzac line. They were one of only two units to reach their objective that day, and no Australian set foot on Battleship Hill for the rest of the campaign.

Later in the war Tulloch tore a map of Gallipoli out of *The Anzac Book* and sketched for Charles Bean the route of his advance (the map, still marked in red ink, is in the collection of the Australian War Memorial). Bean used it to trace Tulloch's advance when he returned to Gallipoli in 1919 and identified this spot where you are now standing, on the forward slope of Battleship Hill, as the point where Tulloch dug in with his men. (Bean noted that soldiers commonly overestimated how far they had advanced – Tulloch's map shows the slopes of Chunuk Bair as his final position, a point almost half a kilometre further inland than he actually reached.)

From here you share Tulloch's view of the spurs of Chunuk Bair directly in front, from where the Turks fired on the Australians. The middle clump of trees on the skyline roughly marks the spot where the Turkish officer was standing when

Tulloch fired at him. On a clear day you have a glimpse of the waters of the Dardanelles, that elusive objective that had brought the Anzacs to Gallipoli in the first place. The ground across the valley is Gun Ridge, the objective for the Anzacs after the landing, which sweeps right to Scrubby Knoll, the small hill marked by a Turkish memorial and flag.

Return along the fire track to your car. As you walk back, there are good views of Lone Pine and Second Ridge to your left, a good visual indicator of how far ahead of the rest of the Australians Tulloch's small group advanced. On each side of the main road are reconstructed trenches that formed part of the Turkish defensive line.

Drive north for 350 metres until you reach a statue on the right of the road [6]. The dramatic sculpture commemorates the heroic efforts of Talat Göktepe, Chief Director of the Çanakkale Forestry District, to fight a fierce bushfire that swept through the Anzac area in July 1994. He was killed in the attempt. The statue depicts his last moments as he desperately tries to hold back the flames.

Continue along the main road for 650 metres, turn left at the T-junction, and park at the end of the road. You are now on the summit of Chunuk Bair, the hill that loomed over the battlefield and into the nightmares of every Anzac who served there. A lot occurred here during the campaign, and today there is a complex of memorials honouring both Turks and Anzacs on the site. Allow about half an hour to visit them all, and an extra 45 minutes for the optional walk to the Farm Cemetery.

Start by exploring the reconstructed Turkish trenches west of the road. A nearby stone tomb holds the remains of a Turk that were uncovered during construction of the memorials

The grave of a Turkish soldier whose remains were uncovered at Chunuk Bair in 1985

Turkish monuments on the summit of Chunuk Bair

in 1985. Follow the trenches south-west until you emerge in a clearing that surrounds five majestic Turkish memorials [7]. The knoll that they stand on is the middle of three that form the summit of Chunuk Bair. Each of the five tablets details aspects of the Chunuk Bair fighting at various stages of the campaign. After reading the tablets, walk behind the western one (with an inscription beginning 'Mustafa Kemal . . .'). From here you have an outstanding view of the ground attacked by the New Zealanders in August 1915.

You are standing in roughly the spot where Malone controversially ordered his men to dig in on the reverse slope. The pine-covered ridge directly in front of you is the infamous Rhododendron Ridge, valiantly captured and then defended by the New Zealanders. The Apex is the prominent knoll on the far end of the ridge. The nearer knoll is the Pinnacle, which was heavily fought over during the initial advance and the Turkish counterattack.

From behind you the Turks launched their devastating attack that overwhelmed the British defenders and drove them off the summit of Chunuk Bair. From where you are standing you have a Turk's-eye view of the British and New Zealand line during their murderous advance on 10 August. Charles Bean described the scene in 1919.

The crevices and gullies leading up the side of Rhododendron contained numbers of dead and much equipment. Here and on the crest and other side of Rhododendron above The Apex, the dead lay often in groups of from three to six; in one place there were ten or twelve. But these groups were largely Turks killed in their final counter-attack on August 10th. Between The

Apex and The Pinnacle the remains lying thickly were probably those of the Auckland infantry killed on August 7th in the belated attempt to reach Chunuk. (*Gallipoli Mission*, p. 232)

A rough walking track has recently been cut through the scrub from North Beach all the way to Chunuk Bair, loosely following the advance made by the New Zealanders on 6 August. It's not possible to incorporate it into this tour, but if you are fit and keen to gain a better understanding of the tough task set for the New Zealanders, allow half a day to walk up and back. It begins on the dirt road just south of New Zealand No. 2 Outpost Cemetery, and ends on the fire trail leading to the Farm Cemetery.

OPTIONAL WALK: The Farm Cemetery

To reach the Farm Cemetery, walk back towards the car park, turn left onto a moderately steep signposted track and follow it for 540 metres. Allow about 45 minutes for the return journey.

The Farm was a small sheepfold on the slopes of Chunuk Bair that was briefly occupied by the New Zealanders during their advance to the summit. When the New Zealanders captured Chunuk Bair, the Farm became a support position and was occupied by British troops from Kitchener's New Army. The senior officer on the scene was Brigadier-General Anthony Baldwin, commander of the British 38th Brigade. The position was overrun during the Turkish counterattack of 10 August and almost the entire British garrison was slaughtered. Many men threw themselves into the steep gullies that surround the Farm to escape the onslaught and wounded men tumbled from the plateau, meeting a painful and lonely end at the bottom of the valley. When Charles Bean returned to Gallipoli in 1919 he found very few bodies at the Farm itself, but the gullies surrounding it were choked with corpses.

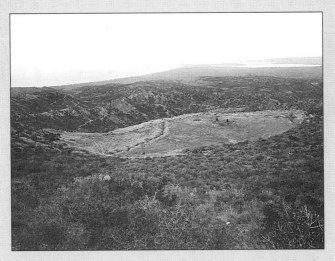

The Farm from the former Turkish positions on Chunuk Bair, 1919.
AWM G02003

We came across the remains of men, thick; all below the seaward edge of the shelf. The slope for a hundred yards down was simply covered with them. Those on the right were mostly Royal Irish Rifles; then some Wilts and Hants. As far as the northern edge of The Farm slope the bodies of Tommies were

> thick – their helmets everywhere. I have nowhere, except at The Nek, seen the dead lying so thick, I think, as on those slopes of The Farm. We searched for signs of the general [Baldwin] but could not find any. (*Gallipoli Mission*, p. 233)

Graves units created a cemetery on the plateau and buried 652 bodies in 15 long rows. None of the men interred here could be identified, and special memorials commemorate seven men who are believed to lie among them. General Baldwin was killed during the Turkish counterattack and probably lies here among his men (his name is recorded on the Helles Memorial).

As you stand at the Farm, look back up the slope of Chunuk Bair and imagine the terror of the British soldiers as the wave of Turkish attackers descended on them. Not many men who stood here on 10 August survived to tell the tale. The Farm is the least visited cemetery at Anzac, and this is a lonely spot.

Walk back up the track to Chunuk Bair.

Walk back past the car park and up the slope towards the two dominant memorials on the hilltop. This hill is the northern knoll of the Chunuk Bair summit. The third knoll is to the south-east and was not fought over during the August Offensive. At the top of the hill is the New Zealand National Memorial [8]. This is the main monument to the New Zealand forces who served at Gallipoli, and it is inscribed with the stirring words, 'In honour of the soldiers of the New

Zealand Expeditionary Force, 8th August 1915. "From the uttermost ends of the earth".' Visitors to the Western Front battlefields will recognise this from several New Zealand memorials in France and Belgium. The memorial is located about 100 metres north of the left flank held by the New Zealanders during August 1915, so is built on ground never held by the troops. Nevertheless, it's an appropriate spot, with the memorial designed to be visible from most of the Anzac sector and, even more importantly, the Dardanelles. It is the focal point for New Zealand services every Anzac Day. Designed by Samuel Hurst Seager, it is the only memorial at Gallipoli designed by a New Zealander. For decades to come, ships that plied the straits would see the memorial and remember the bravery of the New Zealanders. The explosion of tree growth in the years since the Anzac sector has been a peace park has reduced the visibility of the memorial, but it still ranks as one of the most impressive on the peninsula.

Bastiaan Plaque No. 9 is located near the memorial.

Also near the New Zealand Memorial are four large replica cannonballs, which mark the spot where Kemal Atatürk was hit in the chest by shrapnel during the fighting on 10 August. He led a blessed existence: according to his later accounts, the shrapnel ball smashed the watch he was carrying in his top pocket, saving him from almost certain death. He later gave his watch to Liman von Sanders, the German commander of the Turkish forces, as a souvenir. The watch was displayed briefly after the war but has long since disappeared. The lucky person who one day discovers it will be feted, because it was one of the most prized artefacts in modern Turkish history. Visitors who wonder why Kemal was wandering around in the open will be relieved to know that it wasn't as exposed in 1915 as it is today, and that Kemal was in a trench when he was hit.

Not far from the cannonballs is a 10-metre-high statue of Kemal, his steely glare fixed in perpetuity over the Turkish land he saved [9]. The statue commemorates the legendary order he gave to his men on 10 August. 'Soldiers!' he cried. 'There is no doubt we can defeat the enemy opposing us . . . When you see the wave of my whip, all of you rush forward together!' Kemal crept out alone, briefly surveyed the country over which the Turks would charge, and then

The New Zealand National Memorial and Atatürk statue, Chunuk Bair

gave the signal. The Turkish lines surged over the crest, completely overwhelming the British defenders and killing without mercy. The charge marked the end of the assault on Chunuk Bair. No Allied soldier would set foot on the heights again. The memorial is built slightly ahead of the spot where Kemal was most likely standing when he gave the order. The actual position was probably near the site of the preserved trench just behind the statue. The memorial was unveiled in 1992 and there was an outcry from New Zealanders who, for the previous seven decades, had felt the heights of Chunuk Bair 'belonged' to them. You can understand why their feathers were ruffled – the Kemal memorial was built less than 20 metres from the New Zealand Memorial – but only the most churlish visitor would begrudge the Turks commemorating their revered leader on the site where he so convincingly won the day.

The summit of Chunuk Bair wasn't heavily entrenched during the August Offensive, so the extensive reconstructed trenches that snake across the site today were most likely dug by the Turks at a later date, possibly after the evacuation. They are reinforced with timber and, although much shallower than they were in 1915, give a good impression of the layout of the Turkish defences. One of the trenches leads to an observation post that offers views towards Suvla Bay.

On the eastern side of the Chunuk Bair Complex is the Chunuk Bair New Zealand Memorial and Chunuk Bair Cemetery [10]. Chunuk Bair Cemetery is to New Zealanders what the Nek Cemetery is to Australians, a large cemetery with pitifully few headstones providing a tangible illustration of the pointless sacrifice that characterised much of the campaign. After Chunuk Bair had been secured on 10 August,

The court martial of Private Jack Dunn at Quinn's Post, 18 July 1915. Dunne is standing in the lower left of the photo, without a hat and with his back to the camera. The photo was taken at the moment the death sentence was read out. AWM P04250.001

the Turks buried many of the Commonwealth soldiers killed in the battle on a slope behind their lines. Chunuk Bair Cemetery was built on this spot after the war and was greatly enlarged when bodies were brought in from all over the hill. Today the cemetery contains the graves of 632 men, only 10 of whom could be identified. Most of the identified men are New Zealanders, including Private Martin Persson of the Wellington Regiment, who was only 17 when he was killed on 8 August. Before leaving the cemetery, note the shimmering waters of the Dardanelles in the distance. The men buried here are the only Commonwealth soldiers at Gallipoli who lie within view of that elusive prize.

Facing the cemetery is the Chunuk Bair New Zealand Memorial, which records the names of 852 New Zealanders missing from fighting at Chunuk Bair and at other actions up to the evacuation. (There are 856 names on the memorial, but four men recorded here have since been identified and are buried under named headstones.) Other New Zealand missing are commemorated at Lone Pine, Hill 60 and Twelve Tree Copse.

Notable men remembered here include Lieutenant-Colonel William Malone, commander of the Wellingtons and hero of Quinn's Post and Chunuk Bair (see page 161). Six sets of brothers are also commemorated here: Privates Alfred and Franklin Corlett, Trooper John and Private Kenneth McKinnon, Private Arthur and Lance Corporal Clement Mellor, Troopers Michael and Richard Murphy, Major Frank and Corporal Clive Statham and Privates James and Sydney Stokes. Second Lieutenant Thomas Grace of the Wellington Regiment had led a group of sharpshooters in a duel with Turkish snipers in Monash Valley early in the campaign. Their good work drove the Turks out of the valley and made it safe for Allied troops. Grace was killed on 8 August. The most unlucky man on the memorial must be Private Jack Dunn, also of the Wellingtons. He was sentenced to death for sleeping at his post in July, but the sentence was commuted after it was determined his relief had not arrived on time. He rejoined his regiment and was killed three days later at Chunuk Bair. He was 26.

OPTIONAL DRIVE: Hill Q and Hill 971

This drive takes you from Chunuk Bair to the next two heights in the range, Hill Q and Hill 971, also the scenes of vital actions during the August Offensive. To get to Hill

971 you must negotiate a 2-kilometre stretch of rough and winding track, but it's well worth it. From the Anzac perspective, Hill 971 was the key to the peninsula – they never got there, and few visitors today make the journey either. Allow about 30 minutes for the return trip.

From the car park, follow the road that runs between the New Zealand Memorial wall and Chunuk Bair Cemetery. The road turns into a very rough track, which existed during the campaign. After about 500 metres you will pass the twin peaks of Hill Q [a] – both hills fell within square 238Q on British maps, so became collectively known as Hill Q (occasionally contemporary documents refer to them distinctly as Hill Q North and Hill Q South). During the advance on Sari Bair, Hill Q was the objective of the 1/6th Gurkhas, under the command of Major Cecil Allanson. The Gurkhas were supposed to assault the hill alongside two British battalions but when these were late arriving on 8 August, Allanson led the Gurkhas on alone towards Hill Q. By carefully moving forward after dark, they managed to edge within 50 metres of the summit. In the early hours of the 9th they launched an attack.

> I flew up the ridge and felt a very proud man as I put my foot on it and had not lost a man practically. Below were bolting the Turks at whom our fellows fired standing up and a wonderful view which seemed to me the key to the whole peninsula: below were the Straits, Kila Nahr, the rear of Achi Baba

and the communications to their army there. And
then followed disaster which may cost us thousands
and thousands and was the most appalling sight I
ever saw. I saw a flash in the Bay. Suddenly 3 or 4
or 5 high explosive shells burst among us. The first
hit a Gurkha in the face: the place was a mass of
blood and limbs and screams though the casualties
were not really very heavy. The whole force flew
in a panic down the hill. (Major Cecil Allanson in
Steel and Hart, p. 241)

Allanson's claim that the shells that hit the Gurkhas
came from a British ship (his 'flash in the Bay') is doubtful.
It is unlikely that Allanson would have been looking behind
him as he charged up the slope, and in any case, there was
nothing behind him but the huge expanse of the Aegean
Sea. What bay was he referring to? The shells were most
likely fired by a howitzer battery at Anzac that mistook
the distant figures for Turks. Regardless, shelling your
own side is one of the surest ways to shatter the morale of
your men, and the Gurkhas, as fierce fighters as they were,
were no exception. They fled down the hill and the Turks
regained the summit. Charles Bean was so distraught by the
missed opportunities to capture Hill Q and Chunuk Bair
that almost a decade later he wrote in the *Official History*:

The occupation of the crest might have resulted in the
falling back of the already shaken Turks from Anzac,
the adherence of wavering Bulgaria, the forcing

of the Dardanelles, the fall of Constantinople, the opening of the sea route to Russia, a comparatively early victory, and a complete alteration in the course and consequences of the war. (Bean, Vol. II, p. 700)

Bean occasionally lapsed into fantasy, and this passage must rate as his most exuberant. It's hard to see how the presence of a few hundred bedraggled Gurkhas on the slopes of Hill Q was going to completely alter the course of the First World War, but the failure to capture the summit certainly was a disappointing setback.

The Dardanelles from the summit of Hill 971

Drive on for another kilometre, turn left at the track signposted to Kocaçimen Tepe (Hill of the Great Pasture) and park beside a hut. This is Hill 971 [b], the highest point on the Anzac battlefield and a tantalising objective that the Anzacs would never get close to. Climb the steps of the observation platform next to the hut, and take in one of the most spectacular views on the peninsula. To the south-west are the twin peaks of Hill Q and the heights of Chunuk Bair, with the Anzac battlefield unfolding beneath them. To the west is the tangle of spurs and valleys that so confounded the advancing columns during the August Offensive. When you consider that they attacked through these valleys in the dark, without previously surveying the lay of the land, it's little wonder they got lost. To the north-west is the Suvla battlefield, stretching out before you to the waters of Suvla Bay. Off the coast, the islands of Imbros (today known as Gökçeada) and Samothrace (Samothraki) float in the haze. Imbros was the site of General Sir Ian Hamilton's headquarters during the campaign. Samothrace was the ancient home of the Sanctuary of the Great Gods, an important ancient Greek religious site. In 1863 French archaeologists discovered a magnificent 2.5-metre marble statue of the winged goddess Nike on the site. Today the statue holds pride of place in a gallery at the Louvre in Paris.

If you arrive here in the late afternoon, you may be fortunate enough to share in one of the magnificent Aegean sunsets that so transfixed the troops at Gallipoli:

> Away on my right sparkled the Aegean, with the Isles of Greece jutting out of it, like rugged giants rising from their ocean lair. To crown all the sun was going down in a perfect blaze of colour, tipping

> the crests of Imbros and Samothrace with a glint
> of gold as it sank behind them into the sea. Never
> have I seen anything to equal the gorgeous lights
> and shades which at sundown are painted on the
> Aegean sky. If I were an artist my ambition would
> be to try to put on canvas the perfectly gorgeous
> but harmoniously blended rose, pink, scarlet,
> red, yellow, purple, green, amber and blue – a
> perfect intoxication of glorious colours which the
> imagination would be unequal to, unless they were
> absolutely thrown on the sky before one's own eyes.
> (Lieutenant-Colonel John Patterson, Zion Mule
> Corps, in Steel and Hart, p. 177)
>
> To the east the 'great pastures' from where the hill takes
> its Turkish name stretch to the waters of the Dardanelles,
> and beyond are the plains and mountains of Asian Turkey.
> Bastiaan Plaque No. 10, the most rarely visited at
> Gallipoli, is located beside the platform.
> Drive back to the car park at Chunuk Bair.

Leave the car park and continue past the intersection with
the road along Second Ridge. After 300 metres you will reach
a small memorial on the left known as the Tümen Karargahi
Su Yatağı ('8th Division Riverbed Headquarters') where Kemal
Atatürk spent the night of 9 August 1915 [11]. According
to his memoirs he had an 'uneasy and sleepless night'. Little
wonder – the Anzac assault on Chunuk Bair was raging and

the next day Kemal would head there himself to order the famous charge that would save the day.

Continue along the road. As you head south you are driving along the Third Ridge of the Anzac sector. Early in the fighting the majority of Turkish artillery batteries were dragged into position on the sheltered eastern slope and the ridge was christened Artillery Ridge by the Turks and Gun Ridge by the Allies. Gun Ridge was the objective for the Anzacs on the day of the landing. The plan was to use it as a staging point to launch the final push across the peninsula that would capture the forts on the west shore of the Dardanelles. However, the Anzacs never made it this far, and for the entire campaign Gun Ridge was little more than a distant feature on the horizon. For the Turks, however, Gun Ridge formed a wall around 'Fortress Anzac', and enabled them to keep the Anzacs locked in their 400-acre cage.

Follow the road for 2 kilometres until you reach a white Turkish memorial on a small hill on the right side of the road. This inconspicuous hill, known to the Anzacs as Scrubby Knoll [12], has an intriguing history. On the day of the landing, small groups of Australians pushed forward from the main line on Second Ridge and advanced well ahead of their comrades. Isolated and outnumbered, they were soon killed or forced to retreat, and from that moment onwards the identity of the soldier who had advanced the furthest inland was one of the great unanswered questions of the campaign.

When Charles Bean returned to Gallipoli in 1919, this was one of the key mysteries he wanted to solve, and he dedicates an entire chapter to his investigations in *Gallipoli Mission*. For a long time he was convinced that a small group of men led by Lieutenant Noel Loutit had advanced furthest – on the morning of 25 April, Loutit and his men progressed to a seaward spur of Gun Ridge, and to the slopes of Scrubby Knoll. This was the account that Bean wrote in his first volume of the *Official History*, but after it was published he received a letter from Arthur Blackburn, a private during the landing at Gallipoli who later led a distinguished career as an officer in both world wars, and won the VC in 1916. Blackburn told Bean that on the day of the landing, he and another man, Lance-Corporal Phillip Robin, had raced to Gun Ridge well before Loutit and had advanced down the inland slope of Scrubby Knoll. They faced a large group of Turks coming up the valley towards them, so they retreated to the main Australian line on Johnston's Jolly. Arthur Blackburn and Phillip Robin are therefore credited with having advanced further than any other Australian at Gallipoli, and the scene of their extraordinary feat is Scrubby Knoll. Blackburn's escapade illustrates an important failing of the landing plan. The first men ashore at Gallipoli formed a covering force that was supposed to race inland and dig in on Gun Ridge to cover the landing of the main body of troops. But even though Blackburn and Robin landed early in the morning and raced straight for Gun Ridge without being held up by the enemy along the way, they still only arrived there at the same time as the Turks. This proves that the task set for the covering force was virtually impossible: even if they had not been held up after landing there was no way they could have reached Gun Ridge and dug in before the main body of Turkish reinforcements arrived.

Scrubby Knoll was also important to the Turks. As the key feature on Gun Ridge, it was a natural observation post, and once the main line had been established on Second Ridge, Kemal Atatürk set up his headquarters here. It remained the Turkish headquarters for the Anzac sector for the rest of the campaign. When Bean visited the site in 1919, he noted that the observation post on Scrubby Knoll 'gave a perfect panorama of our line from about Quinn's to Lone Pine, as well as the chain of crests northwards to Hill 971'. The view from here was so good that when a group of Australians under Lieutenant Norman Greig attacked the Turkish trenches at German Officer's Ridge in July (see page 126), it was Turkish observers at Scrubby Knoll who first alerted their front-line troops to the attack.

To the Turks, Scrubby Knoll is Kemalyere (Kemal's Hill) and the memorial commemorates a famous order he issued from the spot in 3 May. After a week of bitter fighting his men were exhausted and there was a real danger that his army was about to break down. Kemal issued a divisional order which included the statement now inscribed on the memorial:

> All soldiers fighting with me must realise that, in order to fully carry out the honourable duty bestowed on us, we must not retreat a single step. I remind you that succumbing to the desire for sleep will lead not only to deprivation for us, but to eternal deprivation for the entire nation. (Kemal, p. 88)

They were stirring words, and the Turks took them to heart.

This is the last stop on the Gun Ridge Tour. Follow the road to the end of the ridge and turn left to Eceabat or right to Anzac Cove.

Helles and Krithia

The British Sector and the Forgotten Anzac Battlefield

When British planners first came up with the idea of staging a landing at Gallipoli they were conscious of two crucial factors. Firstly, the troops needed adequate artillery protection as they came ashore, so they needed to land in places where their assault could be covered by the guns of the Royal Navy. Secondly, they had to come ashore at a point not too far from the Dardanelles forts, their ultimate objective. Anzac was perfect. Its wide beach and prominent hills would make clear targets for the ships' guns, and it was only 7 kilometres across the peninsula from the straits, a feasible advance for a well-supported army.

Helles offered the best and worst of both worlds. The landing beaches here were more than 20 kilometres from the forts, a huge distance for an army to cover under fire, but its location on the toe of the peninsula meant that the advance could be covered by the ships' guns from three sides. The planners hoped that the Anzac landings would cut the peninsula in two, preventing Turkish reinforcements from flooding in and giving the British at Helles a clear dash to the straits. As it happened, the Anzacs' failure to reach the high ground gave the Turks ample opportunity to bring in reinforcements, and the men from the British 29th Division who landed at Helles, as well-supported by the Royal Navy as they were, soon realised that they faced a difficult task. Instead of a swift advance along the peninsula they found themselves inching forward against a dug-in and determined enemy, and the cost in lives to push their line forward would be immense.

The Helles plan called for the British to come ashore at three beaches on the toe of the peninsula, dubbed 'V', 'W' and 'X'. A small party would also land at 'S' Beach, on the eastern shore of the peninsula facing Asian Turkey. A cunning flanking landing was planned for 'Y' Beach, higher up the west coast and behind the main Turkish defences. In addition, French troops would land at Kumkale on the Asian side of the straits, in an effort to divert Turkish attention away from Helles. Once the British were ashore, the French would abandon Kumkale and join the fight at Helles.

The British objective for the first day was the village of Krithia and the prominent hill known as Achi Baba that stood nearby. But the Turks weren't going to make things easy for them. After the naval battle in March, they knew a landing was coming, but they didn't know where. The Turks were commanded by a German, Marshal Otto Liman von Sanders, a cunning tactician. Rather than spread his defensive force thinly over the entire peninsula, he lightly garrisoned the places where a landing seemed most likely, and held back the bulk of his troops to reinforce where necessary. It was a bold gamble. Had the Anzac landings worked as planned, the bulk of Liman von Sanders' army would have been cut off in the north or stranded in Asia, and the job of defending the peninsula would have been left to his garrison force of about 2,000 men. But as it happened, Liman von Sanders' troop distribution was astute. His small band of defenders was able to hold up the Australians and New Zealanders at Anzac and massacre the British at Helles, and his army of reinforcements marched straight to where they were needed.

Between the time they came ashore on 25 April and the end of June, the British and French at Helles threw themselves at the Turkish line in a series of costly and ultimately pointless attacks. In a perfect example of the phenomenon known as 'objective creep', Krithia and Achi Baba ceased to be seen as merely preliminary objectives, and became the main objective themselves, even though their capture would do little to subdue the Dardanelles forts or open up the straits for the navy. More than 30,000 British and French soldiers were killed in the fruitless attempts to capture Krithia and Achi Baba. By January 1916, when the last troops left Gallipoli, the Allied line was still 2 kilometres short of that first-day objective.

The Anzacs played their part as well when they joined the attacks on Krithia in early May. Their bravery and sacrifice at Helles is one of the forgotten chapters of the Gallipoli story.

Helles and Krithia Tour

This driving tour takes in the locations of bitter fighting in the British and French sector at Helles, and also offers a good insight into the failed naval battle of 18 March that brought the troops to Gallipoli in the first place. The route is about 75 kilometres long, so allow a full day to complete the entire tour, and a second if you intend to explore the key sites. It's also a good idea to keep an eye on your car's odometer as you drive between each stop. Many of the sites are inconspicuous and will be much easier to find if you have an accurate idea of how far you have driven.

The campaign at Helles was an epic of poor leadership, stale thinking and missed opportunities. It's only when you walk the ground that you truly appreciate the terrible sacrifice made to secure the toe of the peninsula.

The tour begins at Eceabat, although you can also catch a ferry from Çanakkale to Kilitbahir and begin the tour there. In 1915 Eceabat was known as Maidos and, as the main port on the peninsula, was a target for British naval guns. Charles Bean remembered seeing smoke streaming over the hills at Anzac from the burning town a few days after the landing. By the time he saw Maidos in 1919, 'the fires started by our battleships' guns had left only half-a-dozen houses standing' (*Gallipoli Mission*, p. 46). The town has been completely rebuilt, but not necessarily in a style that is pleasing to the eye. It offers a small assortment of restaurants and budget hotels, and is convenient to the battlefields, but there are better accommodation options elsewhere (see page 19).

Drive south out of Eceabat, following the signs to Kilitbahir. After following the coast for 2.5 kilometres you

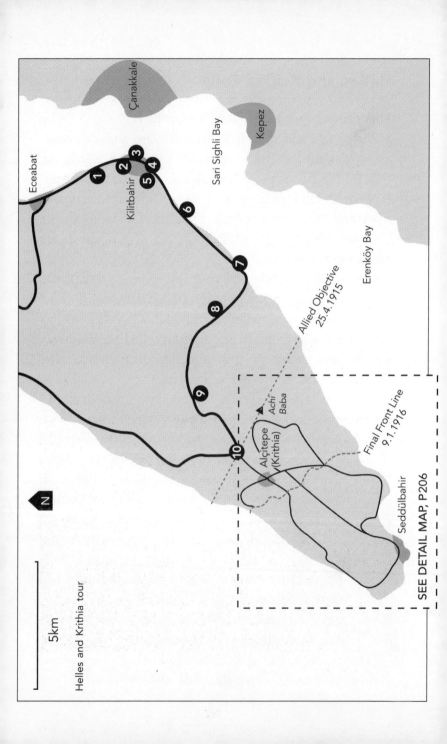

Helles and Krithia tour

5km

N

Eceabat

Çanakkale

Kilitbahir

1 2 3 4 5 6 7 8 9 10

Sari Sighli Bay

Kepez

Erenköy Bay

Allied Objective
25.4.1915

Achi Baba

Alçitepe
(Krithia)

Final Front Line
9.1.1916

Seddülbahir

SEE DETAIL MAP, P206

will pass the opening to a large valley on your right [1]. In 1915 this was the site of a Turkish field hospital, where wounded men were treated before being ferried across the straits to larger hospitals in Çanakkale. Men who could not be saved were buried in a makeshift cemetery beside the hospital, which soon had grown to more than 3,000 graves. After the campaign, the hospital was closed and the cemetery was lost. The site is currently being investigated with the intention to mark the cemetery in a similar fashion to the mass graves at Anzac.

Continue for another 1.5 kilometres, through the town of Kilitbahir and past its clover-shaped castle [2]. Kilitbahir loosely translates as 'the key to the sea', which is an apt description. The castle looms over the Narrows, the point where the shores of the Dardanelles converge. It was built in 1452 by Ottoman Emperor Mehmet II and its antiquity

Kilitbahir Castle

ensured it was not used as part of the Turkish defences in 1915, thereby saving it from damage during the naval battle. The castle is a wonderful example of Ottoman architecture, with inner and outer courtyards dominated by a soaring triangular keep. It does not hold any special significance for battlefield visitors, but is worth a brief stop if time allows.

Follow the road past the castle for another 400 metres and park in the car park opposite the Namazgah Fort [3]. The fort was built in the late 19th century and, unlike the castle at Kilitbahir, it formed an integral part of the Dardanelles defences in 1915. By the time the Royal Navy arrived on 18 March, they faced 21 guns in this fort alone, and there were 14 other forts ready to bombard the fleet, as well as dozens of mobile batteries that could fire and move before being located.

Namazgah Fort was badly damaged by British naval shelling during the campaign and stood derelict for decades, but extensive renovations in 2007 transformed it into an excellent small museum of the campaign. This is probably the best spot to gain an understanding of the ebb and flow of the naval battle in March, the drama that led directly to the Allied landings on the peninsula. A small entrance fee gives admission to the museum and the ramparts above it. After exploring the museum, climb up to the observation platform next to a beacon on the far side of the courtyard, to take in outstanding views across the Narrows and the scene of the Allied naval defeat of 18 March 1915.

From here Winston Churchill's five-point plan to force the Dardanelles is clear. To reach Constantinople by sea in 1915, the Allies first needed to destroy the forts that formed the outer defences at the entrance to the Dardanelles. They then needed to silence the inner defences of the straights before clearing the minefields that choked the narrow waterway. Once that was done, they would have to deal with the massive forts that guarded both sides of the Narrows. Finally, they could sink the Turkish fleet in the Sea of Marmara and sail triumphantly into Constantinople. As was often the case at Gallipoli, the gap between theory and reality proved vast.

The tall, modern building to the south-east on the far shore is the Hotel Kolin. It overlooks Sari Sighlar Bay, where the Turkish ironclad *Mesudiye* was sunk by the British submarine *B-11* on 13 December 1914 (see page 335). The *B-11*'s successful incursion into the straits was one of the few highlights of the Royal Navy's adventure in the Dardanelles.

Explore the rest of the ramparts before returning to your car and continuing south. After 600 metres, park next to the large statue of a Turkish soldier on the left [4]. This statue commemorates one of the most enduring Turkish legends of the campaign. During the naval battle on 18 March, Corporal Seyit was manning one of the heavy guns at the nearby Mecidiye Fort, and suffering along with the rest of the Turkish defenders under the weight of the Allied naval fire. Most of the guns in the fort were knocked out and the crane used to load shells into Seyit's gun was smashed. According to legend, in desperation Seyit picked up one of the huge shells, lugged it on his back, shoved it into the breech and fired the gun. Some even say that it was this shot that hit the rudder on HMS *Ocean* and led to her eventual sinking. Seyit became to the Turks what Simpson was to the Anzacs: a common man doing extraordinary deeds at a time when his country desperately needed heroes. And as with Simpson, the facts surrounding Seyit's actions have become cloudy as time has passed and hearts have swelled with patriotism. Once the Allied naval attack had been repulsed, Seyit became a national hero, and the press rushed to the fort to photograph him re-enacting the event. Unfortunately he was unable to reproduce the feat and the press settled for a shot of him holding a wooden replica of the shell. Seyit has become the face of the campaign for the Turkish people, and the statue is always bustling with visitors.

Directly across the road from the statue is the Mecidiye Fort [5], where Seyit performed his feat of superhuman strength. The fort was badly knocked around by the bombardment of 18 March, with much of the damage being inflicted by the heavy guns of HMS *Agamemnon*. The inclusion of this ship in the fleet must have been more than mere coincidence; in Greek mythology Agamemnon led the Greeks in the capture of Troy – in 1915 the site of the ancient city would have been visible to the ship's crew on the far side of the Dardanelles. In the fort, casualties were extremely heavy, and a white stone grave on the right near the entrance contains the bodies of 16 men killed in the bombardment. Today the fort is still partially in ruins, but you can explore its interesting network of ammunition stores and emplacements for its six heavy guns. The stone walls are still scarred from the shellfire, and the remains of trenches snake across the embankment overlooking the road.

Drive on for another 2 kilometres until you reach a brown stone monument on your left [6]. This is the Havuzlar Cemetery Memorial, which marks the burial place of 10 Turkish soldiers killed while fighting against the French at Helles in June 1915. The monument was built in 1961.

Continue along the winding coast road for another 4 kilometres and enjoy sweeping views across the Dardanelles to your left. After a sharp right-hand bend that overlooks a white shipping beacon, park carefully in the narrow lay-by on the left of the road [7]. Directly opposite on the far shore is Kephez Point, marked by a lighthouse on the water's edge. By drawing an imaginary line from here directly across the water to the near shore you have marked the furthest point reached by the British and French fleet in their quest to force their way to Constantinople. Their efforts fail to impress. The mouth of the Dardanelles, where their journey began, is less than 20 kilometres from here. Constantinople is a further 250 kilometres away.

The wide sweeping bay directly right of Kephez Point is Erenköy Bay, or 'Dark Bay' as it is known to the locals. This large feature near the mouth of the straights formed a natural turning circle for the warships of the Allied fleet, and it was here that the Turkish minelayer *Nusrat* laid her deadly line of mines parallel to the coast prior to the March naval battle. The plan worked better than the Turks could have anticipated. The *Nusrat's* mines sunk three ships and damaged several others. This hidden minefield contributed more than anything else to the abandonment of the naval campaign and the eventual landing of troops at Gallipoli. The wrecks of the three ships – *Bouvet*, HMS *Irresistible* and HMS *Ocean* – still lie at the bottom of the bay, along with several other ships and submarines sunk during the campaign.

Crewing a pre-dreadnought in 1915 was a hard and dirty job. Private William Jones was a gunner on the HMS *Prince George*.

I was a member of one of the 6 [inch] guns on the lower deck. There were eight of the crew and two by the ammunition hoist. We were in that casemate eleven hours. It was about fourteen feet wide and twelve feet deep. Inside it was very hot. Some of us were very scantily dressed. I was wearing a bathing costume and a pair of heavy boots in case a projectile dropped on your toe. Well you can just imagine being in a very hot atmosphere like that. The old fellow, a corporal in the marines with a very heavy moustache, poor old chap! We gave him the lightest job that was there, but out he went – he was right out. We went round to see him and the gunlayer sergeant said: 'Leave the old "B" alone', and we carried on. Then the old fellow came a kind of around. It was no good trying to get him outside – we were forbidden to open the casemate door. There was cocoa – it was cold – and there was biscuits. No bread. Biscuits and some corned dog, otherwise known as corned beef! We were all packed in there in the morning and we were not allowed outside. There was an officer outside with a revolver, walking up and down. What we wanted to do we had to do in the casemate, whatever it might be. When we loaded the gun it was quite a big job because the shell was about 112 pounds. You open up the breech of the gun, pulling the breech back. Up comes a No. 4. He gets a shell on top of the shell guide, gets a rammer and rams home. A No. 6 comes along with a cylinder and enters the tube, pushes it right home. A No. 2 closes the breech. 'READY'. Immediately you stand clear from the gun and it's fired by the No. 1, the gunlayer. Then open the breech again. Get the extractor on your arm, that fits around the back of the cartridge, and you fling it aside, and I can assure you it's red hot. Then the whole procedure is gone through again. (Steel and Hart, p. 24)

Directly opposite on the far shore is a white traffic tower on the top of the ridge at Kephez Point. The tower occupies the site of the Dardanos Battery, another fort that opposed the Allied fleet in March. The fleet fired more than 4,000 shells at this site alone and it was badly knocked around, but its guns still kept up a vicious fire on the exposed ships. Its commander, Lieutenant Hasan, was killed during the height of the 18 March battle, and he is buried nearby (see page 335 for the full story).

To your far right the mouth of the Dardanelles, and the Aegean beyond, can be glimpsed 20 kilometres away.

Continue along the road and after a kilometre it will sweep inland and begin following the path of a wide valley. This is the Soğanli Dere [8], one of the most prominent topographic features on the east side of the peninsula and a key logistics base for the Turks. Hospitals, camps, training grounds, cemeteries, storage depots, rest areas and more were sited here during the campaign. It was also the main route used by the Turks to stream reinforcements to Helles. The original plans for the landing called for the Soğanli Dere to be captured as the final objective on the first day. That would have been quite an achievement: the beaches where the British came ashore are more than 13 kilometres away. After much debate the objective was amended to Achi Baba hill; still a big ask considering it was 9 kilometres from the beaches. In any case, all this planning became purely theoretical. For the entire nine months they were at Helles, the British only advanced 5 kilometres.

Two kilometres into the valley you will pass the two memorials that mark Soğanli Dere Şehitliği, a Turkish cemetery used during the campaign and containing the remains of men who died while receiving treatment in hospitals in the valley.

Follow the road as it winds through the rich farming country of Helles. In the early days of the campaign the British soldiers were quite taken with the landscape and flora of Helles, and were prone to flights of prose that today seem quaint.

> You ride over fields and through gardens in which flowers abound in reckless and beautiful profusion. There are white orchids and rock roses, while mauve stock and iris abound. There are fields of poppies, white marguerites, and blue borage, intermingled with deep purple vetches, brick red pea and yellow clover, pink and white campions, and asphodel. (Ellis Ashmead-Bartlett, in Steel and Hart, p. 178)

But the constant movement of an army and its machinery of war soon changed all that.

> When we first landed the country was absolutely beautiful, all shades of green, the silver olives and a great variety of flowers. But that was soon changed. I expect it would have parched fairly rapidly anyway but what between shells, wheel tracks, men tramping about and above, and enveloping all the dust, the whole landscape took on a uniform dust colour. And not only the landscape but us

and all our belongings. Dust was all pervading. (Sapper Thomas Rowatt, RND Engineers, in Steel and Hart, p. 179)

After 5 kilometres, park on the left at the signposted Şahindere Şehitliği [9]. This was another Turkish mass grave built behind the Turkish lines and predominantly used to bury men who died of wounds in field hospitals after the battles at Helles. A flight of steps leads to a large memorial and cemetery at the top of a hill. The crescent-shaped memorial was constructed in 2005 with symbolic headstones in the shape of the enverieh, the distinctive headgear worn by Turkish troops and named after Enver Pasha, the Ottoman commander-in-chief. Each stone represents a province ruled by the old Ottomans, and the breadth of the empire as illustrated by the stones is really quite astonishing. Familiar

Şahindere Martyrs Memorial. The symbolic headstones are in the shape of enverieh, the distinctive headgear worn by Turkish soldiers at Gallipoli.

names include Kosova (Kosovo), Siraz (Shiraz), Bağdat (Baghdad), Sparta, Beyrut (Beirut) and more. The memorial commemorates 1,969 men from the 1st, 2nd, 5th, 6th, 7th, 10th and 11th Divisions who are interred on the site. As is the case with other Turkish cemeteries, the headstones are purely symbolic. The bodies themselves are buried in an unmarked mass grave on the flat ground behind the memorial and in isolated graves all over the hillside. You'll see many of them as you follow the path back down the hill, and one important grave surrounded by an iron fence. Buried here is Mustafa Efendi, a Turkish lieutenant killed on 18 September 1915. Less than a decade ago this whole site was neglected and the lieutenant's grave sat forlorn and forgotten, half-buried in the scrub. The construction of the memorial marked a turning point and the site is now popular with Turkish visitors (the whole site is often referred to as the Mustafa Efendi Memorial). The renovation of the site and the large crowds it now attracts are a credit to the Turkish people, and their growing desire to pay tribute to their countrymen who died during the campaign.

Return to your car and drive on past pretty fields for another 3 kilometres until you reach the intersection with a road on your right signposted to Kabatepe (don't turn at the intersection, simply note its location). The intersection marks the approximate line of the first-day objective for the British at Helles [10]. The objective line ran across the peninsula and included the capture of the village of Krithia and Achi Baba. Once again, this objective proved purely theoretical. The British never came close to capturing Krithia or Achi Baba, and after nine months were still more than 2 kilometres short of their first-day objective.

Continue driving into the village of Krithia (today known as Alçitepe). Turn left at the first intersection after entering the village and follow this road out into the countryside. After 500 metres take the left fork, signposted to Baki Teras (there is a small Turkish military cemetery on the right, just after the fork). After 2 kilometres the road heads uphill. Park next to a track that joins the road on the left near the top of the hill. This is Achi Baba, one of the central objectives of the land campaign at Gallipoli and a place of shattered dreams [11].

Alan Herbert described his impressions of Achi Baba in his intriguing account of the campaign, *The Secret Battle*:

> In a little the dawn began, and the grey trees took shape; and the sun came up out of Asia, and we saw at last the little sugar-loaf peak of Achi Baba, absurdly pink and diminutive in the distance. A man's first frontal impression of that great rampart, with the outlying slopes masking the summit, was that it was disappointingly small; but when he had lived under and upon it for a while, day by day, it seemed to grow in menace and in bulk, and ultimately became a hideous, overpowering monster, pervading all his life; so that it worked upon men's nerves, and almost everywhere in the Peninsula they were painfully conscious that every movement they made could be watched from somewhere on that massive hill. (Herbert, p. 21)

This description is eerily reminiscent of the sentiments expressed by Charles Carrington about the Butte de Warlencourt in France, a hill that similarly dominated the British trenches. Carrington said that the Butte 'loomed up

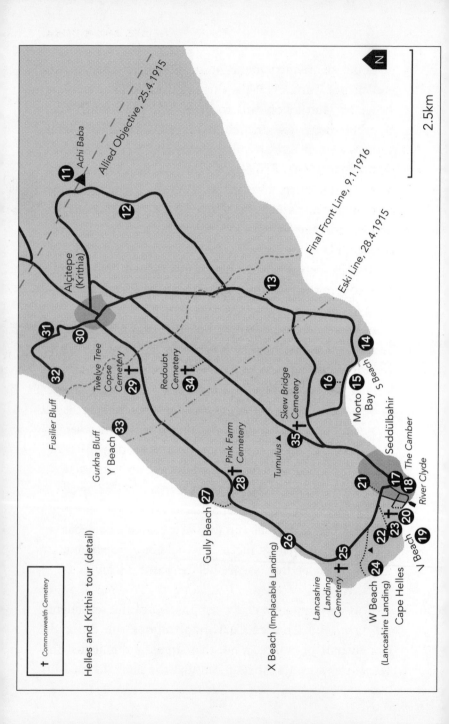

Helles and Krithia tour (detail)

† Commonwealth Cemetery

2.5km

N

Achi Baba 11

Allied Objective, 25.4.1915

12

Alçitepe (Krithia)

31

30

32

Fusilier Bluff

Gurkha Bluff

Y Beach

33

Twelve Tree Copse Cemetery 29 †

Redoubt Cemetery 34 †

Final Front Line, 9.1.1916

Eski Line, 28.4.1915

13

14

16

15 S Beach

Morto Bay

Seddülbahir

Skew Bridge Cemetery 35 †

Pink Farm Cemetery 28 †

Tumulus ▲

27

Gully Beach

26

X Beach (Implacable Landing)

25

Lancashire Landing Cemetery †

24

W Beach (Lancashire Landing)

Cape Helles

21

17

18

The Camber

River Clyde

22 23 †

20

19

V Beach

unexpectedly, peering into trenches where you thought you were safe: it haunted your dreams' (McLachlan, p. 156).

Leave your car and follow the track up the hill. After 50 metres the track bends left. Follow a rough foot track straight on towards the summit. Soon you will reach a clearing that offers sweeping views of Helles. To the south-west you can see the Dardanelles, the imposing grey Turkish memorial at Morto Bay and a vista that takes in the landing beaches and all the ground the British sacrificed so much to capture. As you pan right the view continues past the tall spire of the British Helles Memorial, to the islands of Imbros and Samothrace and all the way along the west coast of the peninsula to the Anzac and Suvla sectors in the north.

Keep following the foot track uphill past a tangle of deep Turkish trenches until you reach an antenna at the summit, and walk to the opposite edge of the clearing. The view to the north-east (towards the tallest, pointy hill on the skyline) may not look much, but it is more important to the story of Gallipoli than just about anything else you will see.

A key objective of the Helles operation from its first day had been to secure Achi Baba. General Sir Ian Hamilton, the commander-in-chief of the campaign, was an avid student of military strategy and was impressed by the tactics used at the Siege of Port Arthur in the Russo-Japanese War of 1904. The attacking Japanese secured the hills overlooking the town, and then shelled the Russian forts below them into submission. Hamilton envisaged the same result at Helles: from Achi Baba, British guns would fire directly on the Narrows forts, enabling the navy to penetrate the straits and opening up the way to Constantinople. At least, that was the plan.

In early 1919 Charles Bean rode to the top of Achi Baba, and from where you are standing made a shocking discovery: you can't see the Narrows from Achi Baba. The wide Kilitbahir Plateau completely blocks the view.

So the crusade to capture Achi Baba, a murderous nine-month slog that cost the lives of 20,000 British men, 10,000 Frenchmen and more than 40,000 Turks was a folly. In light of this, it's safe to conclude that the entire Helles operation was never a good idea from the start.

But as you saw from the clearing as you climbed the hill, there is one view that Achi Baba does offer – a sweeping panorama of the entire British and French line, laid out for the Turks 'like a raised plan', according to Bean (*Gallipoli Mission*, p. 304). And in the early hours of 9 January 1916 the Turks watched from here as the grey transports of the Royal Navy slinked away across the horizon.

Return to your car and continue for 1 kilometre until you see on the right side of the road a memorial to Field-Marshal Fevzi Çakmak, commander of the Turkish 5th Army Corps, erected in 1941 on the site of his headquarters during the campaign [12]. Çakmak was a confidant of Kemal Atatürk and after Atatürk is probably the most revered leader in modern Turkish history. After his successes at Gallipoli he fought alongside Atatürk during the War of Independence and even served briefly as prime minister before the establishment of the Turkish Republic. He and Atatürk remain the only two men in the Republic's history to have held the rank of Field Marshal. He died in 1950.

Continue driving and look out on your left for a deep valley. This is Kereves Dere, the scene of several costly attacks by the French during the battles of Krithia in April and June 1915. The French were tough troops. A British officer described watching them attack across this ground in May:

> The French general had given orders for his line to advance with drums beating and bugles blowing, and we could see their battalions streaming up the spurs leading towards the Achi Baba position. They went forward in great force and with tremendous dash, right up the spur; and, in spite of the bitter shell fire that met them as they topped the rise in front of them, they got right up to the Turkish trenches and drove the enemy out. We could see the Turks streaming away over the rise in hundreds, with the French at their heels – a most stirring sight! (Captain Guy Dawnay, GHQ, in Steel and Hart, p. 165)

Continue for another 2 kilometres and turn left at a T-junction. The hill behind the T-junction is Hill 83, also known as the Quadrilateral, a Turkish strongpoint captured by the French on 30 June.

Drive on for another 650 metres, and turn left on a minor road, signposted to Kaymakam (Yarbay) Hasan Bey Şehitliği [13]. Park beside a memorial at the end of the road. This marks the approximate spot where Lieutenant-Colonel Hasan Bey, commander of the 17th Regiment of the Turkish 5th Division, was killed on 11 July 1915. Legend has it that he was shot by a wounded French soldier and his last words were, 'Don't kill the Frenchman. He did his duty.' The memorial plinth (originally made from white painted stone, but recently refurbished with grey stone tiles) is surrounded by the remains of trenches and, unusually for Gallipoli, concrete-reinforced dugouts. The site overlooks Kereves Dere and is near the old French front line.

Return to the main road and continue driving, following the signs to 'Abide', and stop when you reach the grounds of the imposing Çanakkale Martyrs Memorial [14]. This is the main memorial to the Turkish dead of the Gallipoli campaign (the Turks refer to the Gallipoli campaign as the 'Çanakkale' campaign). It was originally intended to be built at Achi Baba, but a shortage of space led to its construction

The imposing Çanakkale Martyrs Memorial is the main monument to Turkish dead from the campaign.

here, on the southern toe of the peninsula. The memorial was originally opened in 1960, and has been constantly evolving since. In 2007 a grand symbolic cemetery was built on the site, with 1,747 futuristic glass and stone headstones recording the names of all 59,408 Turks officially listed as having been killed during the campaign.

A nearby glass plaque chronicles the nine fronts where the Turks fought during the First World War, and the wide range of provinces across the Ottoman Empire from where the dead came. The striking central memorial of blue and white glass spheres in a wooden enclosure represents the Turkish enverieh headgear encased in a pine cone, symbolising the unity of the Turkish people with the landscape of Gallipoli.

Another glass plaque is inscribed with a stirring poem by Mehmet Akif Ersoy, composer of the Turkish national anthem. His poem says:

> Do not ignore the ground on which you have walked,
> It is not ordinary soil.
> Reflect on the thousands of people who lie beneath
> Without a shroud.
> You are the son of a martyr –
> Do not hurt your ancestor,
> Do not give away this beautiful motherland,
> Even if you have the whole world.

Nearby is a statue of Kemal Atatürk in the defiant pose first captured in a photo taken of him at Chunuk Bair, and not far from that is a humble grave, simply marked 'Meçhul Asker' (Unknown Soldier), which commemorates a shameful chapter in Australia's Gallipoli history. In 2003 the mummified head of a Turkish soldier was anonymously handed in at the Echuca police station in Victoria. The macabre trophy, originally collected by an Australian soldier in 1915 and held by his family in a velvet-lined box ever since, was returned to Gallipoli and, appropriately, is now interred here, at the most important Turkish commemorative site on the peninsula.

The main monument on the site is the imposing 40-metre high memorial consisting of four square columns surmounted by a concrete slab. The underside of the slab features the Turkish national symbols of a crescent and star, and a garden next to the memorial is made of 5,000 red and white roses depicting the same image. There is a natural balance in the design as the crescent and star are 'reflected' from the top of the memorial to the garden and back again. The monument also features images in bas-relief of key moments in the campaign, including one depicting the truce at Anzac in May 1915.

The memorial offers sweeping views across the mouth of the Dardanelles to Kumkale on the far shore, the site of a French landing on 25 April 1915 (see page 342). In the other direction is Morto Bay, with the white spire of the French cemetery overlooking it from the hills above. The British Helles Memorial is visible on the skyline. The site of the Turkish memorial couldn't be more appropriate. Today it can be seen from all approaches and guards the entrance to the Dardanelles in the same defiant spirit as the Turkish gunners in March 1915.

As you walk back to your car you will pass a small military museum and a row of artillery pieces and cannons from a range of Turkish wars, some of them quite old, including several made in Liege in 1857.

French soldiers preparing a meal at a field kitchen at Helles. AWM G00478

Return to your car and continue westward along the shore of Morto Bay [15]. During the campaign Morto Bay ('Death Bay' in English) was exposed to Turkish artillery fire from the Asian shore of the Dardanelles, so no major landings were planned here for the morning of 25 April. However, a group of about 750 men from the 2nd South Wales Borderers came ashore at dawn on the day of the landing at S Beach, the tiny cove at the eastern end of the bay. The cove was only lightly defended and the Borderers landed with comparatively light casualties. Once the beachheads at Helles had been secured, Morto Bay became a French sector, and from here the tough fighters of the Corps Expéditionnaire d'Orient pushed the eastern sector of the Allied line steadily forward against tough Turkish opposition. In six months of heavy fighting, French and French colonial troops advanced steadily along the gullies that slash towards Achi Baba and overcame five Turkish redoubts – an advance that didn't even bring them to their first-day objective, but a good effort nonetheless.

After six months of fighting the French had lost more than 27,000 men and their faith in the Gallipoli sideshow was waning. In October they began withdrawing their troops; the last French unit left on New Year's Day 1916. Today the only reminder that they were here is the remnants of a stone pier jutting out into the water at the northern end of S Beach.

In the early hours of 13 May the British battleships *Goliath* and *Cornwallis* were at anchor off Morto Bay when a Turkish destroyer came charging out of the fog and launched three torpedoes at the warships. All three struck *Goliath* and the ship went down in less than two minutes, taking almost 600 sailors with her. The Royal Navy, still smarting from its defeat in the naval battle of 18 March and worried about rumours of German submarines patrolling the Dardanelles, ordered its most valuable ships to return to safe harbours at Imbros and Lemnos Islands. Allied troops watched dismayed as the battleships, their protectors for the past month and their only effective reply to Turkish artillery, disappeared over the horizon. The Royal Navy's fears were well founded, and by the end of May the two largest ships remaining at Gallipoli, *Triumph* and *Majestic*, had both been sunk by submarines, and the navy's role in the Gallipoli fiasco was over.

Continue along the coastal road and turn right towards the French Military Cemetery (Fransız Mezarlığı) **[16]**. Park and climb the stairs to the cemetery entrance. This is the only French cemetery at Gallipoli and the largest on the peninsula.

It was built in the 1920s when several smaller cemeteries were concentrated here, and bodies were brought in from isolated graves or from out in the fields in the French sector of Helles. The current cemetery keeper is the third member of his family to hold the position, following on from his father and grandfather before him.

The bulk of the cemetery consists of 3,236 graves in two plots, east and west of the main path. Each grave is topped by a black cross that looks suspiciously like it has been made from iron garden stakes, flared at the ends into the traditional French *fleur-de-lys*. Graves are laid out according to rank and identified soldiers are named on a diamond-shaped plaque set in the centre of the cross.

The path through the centre of the cemetery leads to a brilliant white obelisk, the centrepiece of the cemetery and a landmark that is visible from all over Helles. The obelisk is built on top of an ossuary containing the remains of Frenchmen who could not be identified. Four other ossuaries, each containing 3,000 unidentified bodies, flank the obelisk. The base of the obelisk declares in Latin *Ave Gallia Immortalis* (Hail Immortal France) and features a stanza from Victor Hugo's *Anthem*, penned 80 years before the Gallipoli campaign but stirringly appropriate nonetheless. It translates as:

Glory to our eternal France!
Glory to those who died for her!
To the martyrs! To the brave! To the strong!
To those who are inspired by their example,
Who wish for a place in the temple,
And who will die as they died!

Memorial tablets on the obelisk commemorate French units and ships, including four French submarines lost during the campaign: *Joule* (sunk 1 May), *Mariotte* (sunk 28 July), *Saphir* (sunk 15 January) and *Turquoise* (sunk 30 October). *Bouvet*, the French battleship sunk during the 18 March naval attack is commemorated nearby. An archway beneath the obelisk features inscriptions from visitors to the cemetery in the post-war years, and a wall facing the cemetery records the names of French officers missing from the campaign.

An ossuary in the southern corner of the cemetery contains the bodies of 22 unknown French soldiers who died while serving with occupation forces in 1918. They were originally buried in a cemetery at Kilitbahir and were moved here in 1929.

The cemetery highlights a curious discrepancy regarding the French dead from the campaign. Official figures estimate the total at around 10,000. But the cemetery contains more than 15,000 bodies, in addition to the hundreds that were repatriated after the war. The disparity has never been explained.

Before you leave the cemetery, spare a thought for the men who lie here, the forgotten warriors of Gallipoli. The French contribution to the campaign was lauded in the years immediately following the war, but today it has slipped through the cracks of history, not least in France. Today the Australians come to Anzac Cove, the New Zealanders come to Chunuk Bair, the British come to Cape Helles, the Turks come to Morto Bay but the French don't come at all.

Leave the cemetery and continue for 3 kilometres to the village of Seddülbahir. Drive through the village, following the signs to Ilk Sehitler Aniti (First Martyrs Memorial). Park next to the memorial [17]. The First Martyrs Memorial commemorates the opening round of the Gallipoli campaign. In late 1914 the British and French fleet was stationed off the mouth of the Dardanelles, attempting to bully Turkey into siding with the Allies in the war. By November negotiations had broken down, Turkey had closed the straits to Allied ships and had begun shelling Russian ports in the Black Sea. On 3 November the Allied fleet was ordered to bombard the forts at the mouth of the Dardanelles in an effort to gauge the Turkish response and soften up the defences in preparation for forcing the straits. The fleet fired on the forts for 20 minutes and got lucky – a shell struck the magazine of the fort at Seddülbahir, causing a catastrophic explosion and killing 86 Turks. The bombardment was a defining moment for both sides. The Allies felt buoyed by their success and from that moment on completely underestimated the ability of the Turks to defend the straits. The results would be disastrous.

The memorial commemorates the men killed in that first bombardment, and is designed as a stylised fort. The men lie in a rather inconspicuous grave beneath a solitary pine tree and surrounded by a white fence at the end of the road on the left of the memorial.

The First Martyrs Memorial overlooks a tiny harbour and jetty known to British troops as the Camber. Small groups of Royal Marines staged a series of daring raids here in early 1915 and destroyed dozens of Turkish guns in preparation for the landings. On 25 April two platoons from the 1st Royal Dublin Fusiliers landed here with orders to help secure the village, but they were cut down by Turkish fire and suffered heavy casualties. Those left alive managed to scramble around the headland to link up with their comrades on V Beach, or were later evacuated from the Camber by lifeboats.

A gate next to the memorial gives access to the ruins of Seddülbahir Fort [18]. Originally constructed in the 17th century, the stone fort was an integral part of the Dardanelles defences, but its exposed position meant that it was never going to fare well against the guns of the Royal Navy. The Turks installed 10 large guns here and strongly garrisoned the fort in expectation of the Allied landings. The fort was badly damaged by the magazine explosion of 3 November 1914, and it was reduced to rubble by the naval bombardment that preceded the landings in April. However, the ruins were used to great effect by Turkish infantry on 25 April, and the fort proved a difficult obstacle for the British troops who came ashore at V Beach. The fort was not captured

A shell hole shaped like Australia in the wall of Seddülbahir Fort

until the next day. Later in the campaign it was used by the French as a hospital.

It was never repaired by the Turks after the evacuation and stood as a derelict reminder of their success at Helles for decades. Until 1993 the fort was part of a Turkish army base and was off limits to visitors, but it is now open to the public and can be explored.

Drive back along the road and veer left, keeping the fort on your left as you drive towards the sea. Follow the road as it curves down to the shore, and park next to the beach. This is V Beach [19], intended to be the main landing beach for British troops and scene of one of the bloodiest sagas of the Gallipoli landings. From an Australian perspective, the landings at Anzac Cove are often visualised like a scene out of *Saving Private Ryan*: thousands of men scrambling ashore against a torrent of machine-gun and artillery fire, the dead and dying piling up on the beach as the survivors crawl grimly forward. In reality, the Australians at Anzac faced relatively light opposition on the beach, and quickly pushed inland. But at V Beach, it was a different story.

Unlike at Anzac, the Turks at V Beach were well armed, well dug-in and well prepared. The cliffs overlooking the beach gave them a perfect platform to pour fire on the landing troops, and the British, in one of the great fiascos of the campaign, gave them easy targets. Perhaps intoxicated by the fables of ancient Troy, British planners devised their own Trojan horse for the landings at V Beach. An old collier, the *River Clyde*, was to surge into the shallows in the early hours of 25 April and beach herself at the eastern end of V Beach. Specially constructed sally ports would open in her sides and 2,000 British troops from the 2nd Hampshire Regiment and the 1st Royal Munster Fusiliers

V Beach and Seddülbahir Fort from the bridge of the *River Clyde* on the morning of the landing. Dead and wounded crowd the bow of the ship, and men can be seen sheltering under the embankment on the beach.
AWM A03076

would stream out of the ship and overwhelm the Turkish defenders. That was the plan, but it went awry from the start. The *River Clyde* hit the beach as planned, but a steamer that was supposed to form a bridge between the ship and the shore ran aground before it could get in position and the troops were stranded. Several men courageously threw themselves into the water and formed a rough bridge out of small wooden boats, but in the confusion the emerging troops bunched up in the sights of the Turkish rifles and machine guns and were mown down. Wave after wave of men was ordered to charge out of the sally ports, down the gangplanks and across the precarious bridge of boats to the shore. Few of them made it alive.

We got it like anything, man after man behind me was shot down but they never wavered. Lieutenant Watts who was wounded in five places and lying on the gangway cheered the men on with cries of 'Follow the Captain.' Captain French of the Dublins told me afterwards that he counted the first 48 men to follow me, and they all fell. I think no finer episode could be found of the men's bravery and discipline than this – of leaving the safety of the *River Clyde* to go to what was practically certain death. (Captain Guy Geddes, in Steel and Hart, p. 93)

Commanders who had witnessed the massacre eventually called a halt and the remaining troops on the *River Clyde* spent a cramped and anxious day in the hold of the ship until they could safely land after nightfall. One can only imagine the terror of being trapped in the ship while the battle raged all around them. They eventually emerged into a scene from hell.

The sight that met our eyes was indescribable. The barges now linked together and more or less reaching the shore were piled high with mutilated bodies – and between the last barge and the shore was a pier formed by piles of dead men. It was impossible to reach the shore without treading on the dead, and the sea round the cove was red with blood. (2nd Lieutenant R. G. Gillett, in Steel and Hart, p. 106)

At the same time the Hampshires and Munsters had been slaughtered trying to land from the *River Clyde*, men from the 1st Royal Dublin Fusiliers had attempted to land in row boats. They fared little better than their comrades. Turkish fire caught them as the boats hit the shore, and casualties were terrible. The survivors charged forward and sheltered behind a low bank that ran the length of the beach – had the Turks thought of levelling the bank during their fortifications of the beach, it is doubtful the British could have landed here at all. The massacre at V Beach prompted the British commanders to divert the bulk of their landing force to W Beach, further along the coast. V Beach was not secured until the fort and town of Seddülbahir were captured the next day.

Nine British men won the VC in the two days of fighting at V Beach:

- **Commander Edward Unwin** of the Royal Navy was on the *River Clyde* and saw that the boats forming the bridge to the shore had come adrift. He jumped into the water and held the boats in place so that the troops could get ashore. He helped rescue several wounded men even though he had been wounded three times himself. Later in the Gallipoli campaign, Unwin served at Suvla Bay and was reportedly the last man to leave there on the day of the evacuation. He survived the war and died in England in 1950.
- **Midshipman George Drewry**, a 20-year-old sailor, worked alongside Unwin to secure the boats, continuing even after he had been shot in the head. He survived the Gallipoli campaign but was killed while serving at the British naval base at Scapa Flow in 1918.
- **Midshipman Wilfred Malleson** was only 18 when he helped Unwin and Drewry secure the boats from the *River Clyde*. Twice he swam between the boats and secured them with ropes, even though he was constantly under rifle and machine-gun fire. He was the youngest VC winner

at Gallipoli and continued to serve in the Royal Navy for most of his life. He died in 1975.

- **Able Seaman William Williams** worked tirelessly in the water alongside Unwin and held a boat in place for over an hour. He was hit in the head by a shell fragment and died in Unwin's arms. Unwin later said that he was 'the man above all others who deserved the VC at the landing'. He was 24.

- **Seaman George Samson** was part of the group that helped secure the boats from the *River Clyde* and later in the day helped rescue several wounded men. In the evening he was hit by machine-gun fire and brought aboard a hospital ship where doctors found he had been wounded 17 times during the day. He was invalided to England and remained there for the rest of the war. He died while serving with the Merchant Navy in Bermuda in 1923.

- **Sub-Lieutenant Arthur Tisdall** witnessed the carnage of the landing from the *River Clyde* and leapt into the water to help the wounded. He assembled a small party of men and led several excursions to the shore to rescue the wounded under extremely heavy fire. Tisdall was killed at Gallipoli on 6 May.

- **Lieutenant-Colonel Charles Doughty-Wylie** of the Royal Welch Fusiliers was the most senior officer to receive the VC at Gallipoli. He was serving on the staff of Sir Ian Hamilton on the morning of the landing, and was on the *River Clyde* as liaison officer. On 26 April he led an attack that helped clear the village of Seddülbahir and Hill 141 beyond it. He is said to have had such respect for the Turks that he refused to carry a weapon against them and led the charge armed only with a stick. Soon after, he was standing on the hill when he was shot and killed by a sniper. He was buried on the spot and his grave is still there today – it is the only solitary Commonwealth gravesite at Gallipoli. For more of the story, including the legend of the woman who visited his grave during the campaign, see page 227.

- **Captain Garth Walford** of the Royal Artillery helped lead the attack on the village of Seddülbahir alongside Doughty-Wylie on 26 April. He was killed late in the battle. He was a career soldier and had served in France and at Ypres in 1914. He was 32 at the time of his death and now lies in V Beach Cemetery.

- **Corporal William Cosgrove** of the Royal Munster Fusiliers was described as an 'Irish Giant' by his commanding officer. During the attack on Seddülbahir on 26 April, the Munsters were held up by a thick barbed wire entanglement. Cosgrove pulled up the stakes with his bare hands and the attack continued. Cosgrove survived the war and died in London in 1936.

Once V Beach had been secured, it was handed over to the French and formed a major support base for the rest of the campaign. It constantly swarmed with men and mules, and mountains of stores were piled on the beach. It was also a major embarkation point during the evacuation, with more than 7,500 men leaving from here. Lieutenant Patrick Shaw-Stewart of the Hood Battalion noted on the last day that even though he was almost sorry to be going, 'It's nothing to be proud of for the British Army or the French either – nine months here, and pretty heavy losses, and now nothing for it but to clear out.' (Knox, p. 158)

V Beach has not changed much since 1915, although in recent years some holiday houses have appeared on the foreshore. Looking inland from the beach, it is obvious how a comparatively small number of Turkish defenders could butcher the landing British troops in this natural amphitheatre. The low bank where the British sheltered from Turkish fire is still there, although it was significantly higher in 1915 than it is today. The *River Clyde* was beached at the furthest rocky spit on the eastern end of the beach. After the landing she was used as a store, field hospital and breakwall for the rest of the campaign and was abandoned during the evacuation. She remained stranded on V Beach until being refloated and repaired in 1919. She was sold to a Spanish shipping company and as the *Maruja y Aurora* she plied the Mediterranean for almost 50 years. In this role she regularly steamed past her old home at V Beach and into the Dardanelles. In 1966 she was broken up for scrap, a decision that outraged many British veterans of the campaign who wanted the ship preserved as an historic relic.

Halfway along the beach is V Beach Cemetery [20], which contains the remains of 696 British soldiers killed in the immediate area. Typical of many of the cemeteries at Gallipoli and a good indicator of the tough fighting in the sector, there are only 20 named headstones in the cemetery – the other 676 bodies are buried in unmarked graves beneath the expanse of lawn. However, special memorials at each end of the cemetery record the names of 196 men known or believed to be buried among them. The cemetery was begun soon after the landing and was used throughout April and May, by which time the front line had moved inland about 3 kilometres. Nearly all the men buried here were killed in the opening weeks of the campaign, with a large proportion killed on the very first day. Thirteen bodies were brought in from isolated graves after the war and were buried in row O.

Look out for the grave of Captain Garth Walford, the officer who won the VC and was killed in the attack on Seddülbahir on 26 April (grave O.1). Also buried here is Lieutenant-Colonel Richard Rooth, commander of the 1st Royal Dublin Fusiliers. He was killed while trying to land with his men on 25 April (joint grave F.4). Buried in the same grave is Reverend William Finn, who was hit at about the same time as Rooth but carried on attending to the wounded until he collapsed and died. He was the first British chaplain killed in the war (joint grave F.4). Another senior officer buried in the cemetery is Major John Costeker of the Royal Warwickshire Regiment, who was killed later the same day (grave F.10). The youngest soldier commemorated here is Private Alfred Verrent of the 1st Royal Dublin Fusiliers. He was only 17 when he was killed during the landing (Special Memorial B.113). Walk behind the cemetery to see the shallow remains of trenches.

Return to your car and follow the track next to the cemetery heading away from the beach. Turn right onto a road. After 200 metres, turn left at a crossroads. Follow this road to the top of the hill and take the track signposted to the Doughty-Wylie grave. Park next to the grave at the top of the hill.

This is the grave of Lieutenant-Colonel Charles Doughty-Wylie VC [21], the only individual Commonwealth gravesite at Gallipoli and one of the few in the world (for details of his death, see page 223). It is situated on a the site known to the British as Hill 141, but now commonly referred to as

Doughty-Wylie Hill. Doughty-Wylie was a graduate from the military college at Sandhurst and had served with distinction in the British Army for 25 years by the time the First World War began. Before Gallipoli he had already served in six campaigns, including the Boer War and the Boxer Rebellion, and had been the British consul in Turkey during the Turkish Revolution in 1909, the uprising that overthrew the Sultan and brought the Young Turks to power. During the revolution he led a group of 50 Turkish soldiers to prevent the massacre of Armenian Christians in the town of Adana, despite being shot in the arm. He was made a Companion of the Order of St Michael and St George for his efforts. In the 1912–13 Balkan Wars he fought with the Turks when the Ottoman Empire was invaded by a united army from Greece, Serbia, Montenegro and Bulgaria. For his good work the Turks awarded him the Imperial Ottoman Order of Medjidieh, 2nd Class. Doughty-Wylie's experience in Turkey made him a natural choice to command at Gallipoli, and he was assigned as an adviser on General Sir Ian Hamilton's staff. During the attack on Seddülbahir village on 26 April, he was killed while standing on this hill and was buried soon after.

This site is associated with one of the most intriguing legends of the Gallipoli campaign. Doughty-Wylie had a devoted wife, Lilian, but had also carried on a lengthy and passionate affair with Gertrude Bell, a British writer, traveller and archaeologist whom he had met in Turkey in 1907. Both women were extremely devoted to him.

One bleak day in November 1915, troops at V Beach were startled by the arrival of a woman, clad in black. She landed from a small boat, walked to the top of the hill, lay some flowers on Doughty-Wylie's grave and stayed briefly, before returning to the beach and re-embarking. Who was the woman? Was it Lilian or Gertrude? It was rare for civilians to be allowed to visit Gallipoli, so common sense suggests that only his wife would stand any chance of being granted permission, but we'll never know for sure. The mystery is heightened by the fact that both Lilian and Gertrude were working in the Mediterranean in November 1915, and neither was far from Gallipoli.

Follow the track back down the hill and turn right on the sealed road. Follow this road for 350 metres and turn left on a road signposted to the Helles Memorial.

The Helles Memorial [22] is both a Commonwealth battle memorial commemorating the Gallipoli campaign and a memorial to missing Commonwealth soldiers who were killed in battles all over the peninsula. The names of all the units and ships that took part in the campaign are recorded on and around the memorial, as are the names of 20,763 Commonwealth soldiers who have no known grave. This is the main memorial to British missing from the campaign, but from an Anzac perspective it's slightly confusing. The main memorial to Australian missing is at Lone Pine, but the Helles Memorial includes the names of 233 Australian soldiers missing from the Second Battle of Krithia, which was fought at Helles in May 1915. As a battle memorial, the Helles Memorial also represents the sacrifice of New Zealand troops in the campaign, but there are no New Zealand names recorded here. New Zealand missing are commemorated at Lone Pine, Chunuk Bair, Hill 60 and Twelve Tree Copse. To make things even more confusing, the memorial also commemorates British men who were lost or buried at sea. Australians who met the same fate are commemorated on the

The Helles Memorial

Lone Pine Memorial, but the Helles Memorial commemorates 15 Australians of the 2nd Division who were lost when the *Southland* transport ship was torpedoed in September while ferrying them to Gallipoli. As one final piece of this confusing jigsaw, no British naval men lost or buried at sea during the Gallipoli campaign are commemorated here. Their names are inscribed on memorials at Portsmouth, Plymouth and Chatham in the UK.

The Helles Memorial records the names of more than 20,000 British and Commonwealth men with no known grave at Gallipoli, including 233 Australians missing from the Second Battle of Krithia.

The Helles Memorial was built in 1924 on a low hill, Guezji Baba, which was captured by the British on the day of the landing and linked their two main landing beaches, W and V. The obelisk is 32.9 metres high and can be seen from all over Helles. More tellingly, it can also be easily seen by ships plying the waters of the Dardanelles. The designers thought that few visitors would actually come to Gallipoli, so the memorial had to be visible from as far away as possible. The names of the men from Anzac divisions who fought at Gallipoli are recorded on the west face of the memorial, and the names of Australians missing from the Second Battle of Krithia are recorded on the outside of the west wall. Missing Australians from the *Southland* are recorded immediately right of the entrance as you enter the memorial.

The most senior Australian soldiers recorded on the memorial are Captains Herbert Hunter of the 7th Battalion and Alfred Possingham of the 8th Battalion. Both were killed on 8 May and were unlucky – Hunter was wounded during the advance and was then hit a second time and killed while trying to return to the Australian line, and Possingham was killed by a stray bullet while the battalion was assembling before the advance.

Fourteen Australian men who fought and died with British units are recorded on the memorial. They are Private Arthur Brown (1/4th King's Own Scottish Borderers, died 12/7/1915), Private Frederick Burr (2nd Battalion Royal Fusiliers, died 16/12/1915), Private Alfred Chester (2nd Battalion Hampshire Regiment, died 4/6/1915), Lieutenant Herbert Debenham (6th Battalion East Lancashire Regiment, died 9/8/1915), Private Bertie Devine (1/7th Battalion Lancashire Fusiliers, died 6/6/1915), Lieutenant Frederick Hurbert (9th Battalion East Yorkshire Regiment, attached 1st Battalion Royal Dublin Fusiliers, died 4/6/1915), Lance Corporal Harold Mountain (5th Battalion Wiltshire Regiment, died 10/8/1915), Private Robert Nelis (1st Battalion Royal Inniskilling Fusiliers, died 14/8/1915), Captain Archibald Scot Skirving (5th Battalion Royal Irish Fusiliers, died 9/8/1915), Lance Corporal Edward Stokes (2nd Battalion Hampshire Regiment, died 6/8/1915), CSM Henry Sunner (1st Battalion Royal Munster Fusiliers, died 2/5/1915), Captain Oscar Walker (12th Battalion Worcester Regiment, attached Royal Fusiliers, died 4/6/1915), Private Frederick Wickham (10th Battalion Hampshire Regiment, died 21/8/1915) and Sergeant Thomas Wooller (9th Battalion West Yorkshire Regiment, died 9/8/1915).

Notable British men recorded on the memorial include 2nd Lieutenant Hamo Sassoon of the Royal Engineers, brother of the English poet Siegfried Sassoon. He was killed on 1 November, only weeks before the evacuation. Also remembered here is Brigadier-General Anthony Baldwin, commander of the 38th Brigade, who was killed at the Farm during the fighting to secure Chunuk Bair on 10 August (see page 174).

There are five British VC winners commemorated on the memorial. Sub-Lieutenant Arthur Tisdall of the Royal Naval Division was awarded the VC for bravery during the landings at V Beach (see page 223). Captain Cuthbert Bromley and Sergeant Frank Stubbs of the 1st Lancashire Fusiliers were both awarded the VC for bravery during the landings at W Beach (see page 238). Captain Gerald O'Sullivan of the 1st Royal Inniskilling Fusiliers was awarded the VC for gallantry during a bombing attack on a Turkish trench on the night of 1–2 July. According to his citation he advanced under very heavy fire and then stood on the parapet of his trench so he could more effectively throw his bombs at the Turkish defenders. He was killed at Suvla on 21 August. Lieutenant-Colonel Sir John Milbanke was the commanding officer of the Sherwood Rangers and had won the VC during the Boer War for rescuing a wounded man under heavy fire in spite of having been wounded himself. He was killed on the same day as Captain O'Sullivan during the advance on Scimitar Hill at Suvla.

Also inscribed here are the names of 167 soldiers from the 1/5th Battalion Norfolk Regiment (the Sandringham Company) who were involved in one of the great mysteries of the Gallipoli campaign. The members of this company were drawn from the staff of the Royal Estate at Sandringham, and were all known personally by the king and other members of the royal family. On 12 August they took part in an attack at Suvla and charged forward into the Turkish positions well ahead of their comrades. They soon became surrounded and about 180 men are reported to have simply disappeared. After the war a number of their bodies were discovered, yet it is still unclear whether the Sandringhams had been captured and executed by the Turks or simply fought to the last. Look for the names of the commander of the battalion, Lieutenant-Colonel Horace Proctor-Beauchamp, his nephew 2nd Lieutenant Montagu Proctor-Beauchamp and Captain Frank Beck, the manager of the King's Estate at Sandringham. For more of the story, see Azmak Cemetery in the Suvla and North of Anzac tour (page 316).

The Helles Memorial serves several purposes and commemorates lots of men, but it is not a symbol of triumph. There's a strange sadness about it, as if the memorial knows the campaign it honours was a shambles but it's trying to put on a brave face nonetheless. It projects an attitude of grim defiance; it wills you to read the thousands of names inscribed on it and find some way of convincing yourself that these men didn't die for nothing.

Before leaving the memorial, spend a minute taking in the excellent views offered from this high point. West of the memorial are the plains above W Beach, which were won at high cost by the attacking British troops on the day of the landing. The small scrub-covered hill north-west of the memorial is Hill 138, which was captured soon after the landing and converted into the headquarters of Lieutenant-General Sir Aylmer Hunter-Weston, commander of the

British 29th Division and the man most responsible for the carnage at Helles. From that point onwards it became known as Hunter-Weston Hill. There is a large Turkish gun embedded in the sand behind the north wall of the memorial. Symbolically it still menaces the landing beaches, long after its adversaries have left. Behind it the flat Helles plains stretch all the way to the innocuous-looking Achi Baba. This is the same view of the hill the British had for the entire campaign, and it seems such an insignificant prize. You can't help but be shocked by the sheer cost in lives of the attempts to obtain it.

Leave the memorial and cross the road to the Ertuğrul Fort [23]. This was one of five forts that made up the outer defences of the Dardanelles and, like the others, it was precariously exposed to the guns of the Royal Navy. It was

Ertuğrul Fort, 1915. AWM H10297

so badly knocked around by the naval bombardments that preceded the landings that it didn't play much of a role on 25 April. It was captured on 26 April and formed a vital link between W and V Beaches. The ruins of the fort were renovated in 2006 and the earth-covered ammunition stores and concrete gun emplacements can be inspected. The barrel of one of its original 24-centimetre guns lies impotently on its smashed base. An excellent diorama in a glass case stands nearby, and gives a good impression of the chaos of the landing at V Beach, with the *River Clyde* the central character in this bloody scene.

Cross the car park to the Yahya Çavuş Şehitliği, a symbolic cemetery dedicated to the Turkish defenders who faced the British at V Beach. There is some confusion about the number of Turkish defenders who opposed the landing. According to legend, only 63 Turks held off the thousands of soldiers trying to get ashore, but this is highly unlikely. There was probably a single company garrisoning the cliffs, which was quickly reinforced by a second. This would mean that about 500 Turks faced the 3,000 British who were attempting to land at V Beach – still an impressively small number considering the carnage they caused as the British came ashore. The British official history credits the resistance of the Turkish defenders at V Beach as the main reason for the failure of the British landings at Helles. The symbolic cemetery and sculpture depicting the heroic defenders was constructed in 1962 and renovated in 1992.

The ruins of the fort offer sweeping views over V Beach and demonstrate what a commanding defensive position the Turks held on the morning of the landing. On the slope

W Beach, 1915. AWM H10391

below you are two small gun emplacements, one with its gun still in place.

Return to your car, drive back along the access road and turn left at the intersection at the end. Follow the road for 500 metres and turn left onto a dirt road at a fork. The scrub-covered hill you will soon pass on your left is Hunter-Weston Hill, which can be seen from the Helles Memorial. Follow the road for 900 metres and turn left onto a track heading downhill. The track is rough but should be passable in fine weather. You will pass the remains of an old army barrier gate and a neglected Turkish cemetery. Veer right at a fork and a rough track will lead you to a wide cove. This is W Beach [24], one of the three main beaches assaulted by the British on the day of the landing. This was a natural defensive position and the Turks had prepared it well. They had laid a thick belt of barbed wire in the water, entrenched most of the high ground around the cove and built machine-gun emplacements in positions that gave them interlocking fields of fire. The Turks had also buried rudimentary land mines in the sand, but the effect of these was negligible on the day of the landing. On 25 April the beach was defended by less than 100 men, but the fury they unleashed on the landing British troops made W Beach one of the most infamous places at Gallipoli.

The 1st Lancashire Fusiliers were tasked with taking W Beach and the entire battalion landed in open boats at 6 a.m. on 25 April. They faced murderous fire and were mown down as they came ashore. Many became entangled in the barbed wire and made easy targets for the Turkish gunners; others drowned under the weight of their heavy packs after jumping overboard before the boats hit the beach.

W Beach, 2008.

The stroke oar of my boat fell forward, to the angry astonishment of his mates. The signal for the massacre had been given: rapid fire, machine-guns and deadly accurate sniping opened from the cliffs above, and soon the casualties included the rest of the crew and many men. The timing of the ambush was perfect: we were completely exposed and helpless in our slow-moving boat, just target practice for the concealed Turks, and within a few minutes only half of the thirty men in my boat were left alive. (Captain Richard Willis VC, 1st Lancashire Fusiliers, in Steel and Hart, p.84)

Eventually the survivors struggled forward and captured the cove, greatly aided by a party who scaled the cliffs north of the beach and silenced the Turkish machine guns. By evening the Lancs had lost 533 men, more than half of the battalion, and had earned six Victoria Crosses. Unusually, the VCs weren't awarded for specific individual acts of bravery but were allocated by ballot. It was considered that the entire battalion had distinguished itself and was worthy of the award. The six recipients were Captain Cuthbert Bromley, Corporal John Grimshaw, Private William Kenealy, Sergeant Alfred Richards, Sergeant Frank Stubbs and Captain Richard Willis, the man whose account of the landing appears above. The press dubbed this unusual arrangement 'six VCs before breakfast', and W Beach came to be known as Lancashire Landing in honour of the battalion.

The six Lancashire VC winners suffered mixed fortunes. Captain Bromley drowned when the troopship *Royal Edward* was torpedoed on 14 August 1915. He is commemorated on the Helles Memorial, as is Sergeant Stubbs, who was killed during the landing. Corporal Grimshaw survived the war and served with distinction in the army for most of his life. He died in London in 1980. Private Kenealy died of wounds on 29 June 1915 during heavy fighting around Gully Ravine, and now lies in Lancashire Landing Cemetery, not far from the beach where he earned the VC (see page 242). Sergeant Richards was later wounded at Gallipoli and had to have his right leg amputated. He died in London in 1953. Captain Willis was also wounded at Gallipoli and later served on the Western Front. He survived the war and died in England in 1966.

After the beaches were secure, W Beach became the main British base in the Helles sector, and V Beach was handed over to the French. Much like Anzac Cove, W Beach soon bustled with activity and was piled high with stores. General Sir Ian Hamilton first set foot on Turkish soil when he landed at W Beach on 29 April and described the scene in his usual delirious tone:

> What a scene! An ants' nest in revolution. Five hundred of our fighting men are running to and fro between cliffs and sea carrying stones wherewith to improve our pier. On to this pier, picket boats, launches, dinghies, barges, all converge through the heavy swell with shouts and curses, bumps and hair's-breadth escapes. Other swarms of half-naked soldiers are sweating, hauling, unloading, loading, road-making; dragging mules up the cliff, pushing mules down the cliff: hundreds more are bathing, and through this pandemonium pass the quiet stretchers bearing pale, blood-stained, smiling burdens.

It is a good indication of Hamilton's uncontainable optimism that he remembered the wounded men on stretchers 'smiling' as they were brought to the beach.

W Beach was the final beach to be evacuated in January 1916. As the last piece of Gallipoli soil touched by Allied troops, it is a worthy spot to remember them, made even more so by the pristine state of the beach today. Until 1993 W Beach was part of a Turkish military base and had therefore been off limits to visitors for decades. It has hardly changed since the campaign and is probably the best place on the peninsula to transport yourself back in time to 1915. The skeletal hulks of stranded barges litter the beach and piles from collapsed piers jut from the water like rusted ribs. Even the tiller from a sunken lighter still skews awkwardly out of the water. On a warm summer evening as the sinking sun paints the Aegean in pinks and purples, this really is a moving place.

In the early hours of 27 May the British battleship *Majestic* was anchored off the southern end of W Beach. The *Goliath* and *Triumph* had both recently been sunk, so the crew of the *Majestic* was on guard. The ship was ringed with protective torpedo nets but in the dawn light the lookouts were distraught to see the wake of a torpedo spearing straight towards the ship. It had been fired from the German submarine *U-21*, whose captain was about to pull off the luckiest shot of his career. The torpedo passed through a gap in the submarine nets, penetrated *Majestic*'s outer hull and exploded in the boiler room. The result was catastrophic. With smoke and steam bellowing from her ruptured side, the *Majestic* keeled over and sank in less than nine minutes. Fortunately she was in very shallow water, and all but 49 sailors were rescued. The ship's keel stuck out of the water until November, a reminder to the troops of how the navy had failed them. The *Majestic* still lies in 16 metres of water.

Return along the track and dirt road. On the left of the road is a flat plain that was home to a makeshift British aerodrome during the campaign. The air war at Gallipoli was insignificant compared to the chaos that was taking place in the skies over France, but Allied aircraft still played a limited role in artillery spotting and enemy observation during the campaign. There were other airfields on the islands of Imbros and Tenedos. Carry on and turn left at the fork with the main road. In 750 metres you will reach Lancashire Landing Cemetery on your left [25].

The cemetery was begun soon after the landing and was used until the evacuation. After the war it was enlarged when remains were brought in from the surrounding area and today it contains 1,237 graves. Surprisingly, the majority are identified, with only 135 of the graves unknowns. Row I contains the graves of more than 80 Lancashire Fusiliers who were killed in the opening two days of the campaign. The cemetery also contains the graves of almost 150 men who were originally buried on the islands of Imbros and Tenedos, and were reinterred here after the war.

Most of the men buried in the cemetery died of wounds received as the British line inched towards Krithia, and a wide range of units and actions are represented. There are also several fliers from the Royal Naval Air Service buried here. One of them is Flight Commander Charles Collet DSO, who was the first British man to carry out a long-range air raid, when he bombed the Zeppelin sheds in Düsseldorf in

September 1914. He was killed when his plane crashed after an engine failure on 19 August 1915 (grave K.49).

Another notable British soldier buried here is Lance-Sergeant William Kenealy, who had won the VC as a private on the day of the landing (grave C.104). Also buried here are several members of the Zion Mule Corps, a unit that comprised mostly Jewish refugees expelled from Palestine by the Turks. It was said to be the first Jewish military unit raised in 2,000 years. Among its members is Private S. Bergman who, at age 60, was probably the oldest Allied soldier killed during the campaign (grave B.74). Twenty-seven Australians and 15 New Zealanders lie among their British comrades, almost all of whom were killed during the Second Battle of Krithia in early May (see page 250). The most senior Australian is Major Richard Wells of the 6th Battalion, who had commanded the right flank of the first Australians to dig in on Lone Pine on 25 April. He was wounded while leading a company of the 6th Battalion during the advance on Krithia on 8 May and died three days later (grave D.1). Another officer buried here is Lieutenant Charles Divine, an Australian who served with the British Royal Naval Reserve as part of the Turkish occupation force in 1918. On 20 January he was killed when his ship, the monitor HMS *M28*, was sunk during a brief battle with the Turkish warships *Yavuz Sultan Selim* (formerly the German battle cruiser SMS *Goeben*) and *Midilli* (formerly the light cruiser SMS *Breslau*) (grave L.32). Many of his shipmates lie nearby. Two other Australians who served in British units are also buried here. They are Private Joseph Gilbert of the 1/6th Manchester Regiment (died 28/5/1915, grave B.5) and Private John Stuart of the 4th Battalion Royal Scots (died 21/6/1915, grave F.7).

Return to your car and continue along the road as it completes a long bend to the right. Drive on for another 750 metres and stop when you reach a rough track cutting into the scrub on the left. Leave your car and continue on foot along the track until you reach the clifftop overlooking a rocky beach. This track was built by British engineers during the campaign to provide access to X Beach [26], the third major British landing beach. Compared to the landings at W and V Beaches, the landing at X Beach was quite successful. The steep cove was only lightly defended by the Turks and two companies (about 500 men) of the 2nd Royal Fusiliers came ashore without major difficulties on the morning of 25 April. The easy landing was mostly due to the supporting fire from the HMS *Implacable* and the HMS *Dublin* which blasted the cliffs from point-blank range and gave the Turkish defenders little hope of resisting.

I have never forgotten the impression which that never to be forgotten run in to the beach made on me, and even more on the soldiers in my boat. They were simply enthralled with the sight of the cliff face being literally blown away by the ship's guns and the spectacle of the ship steaming in firing was magnificent. I think it is no exaggeration to say that the morale of the troops in the boats went up 2 or 3 hundred per cent in that account. I have often felt that if the other landings had been similarly conducted there would have been a very different tale to tell. (Midshipman Stanley Norfolk, Royal Navy, in Steel and Hart, p. 84)

For the rest of the campaign the beach was commonly referred to as Implacable Landing. Once ashore, the fusiliers dug in along the cliff top and repulsed several strong Turkish counterattacks. The 1st Border Regiment and the 1st Royal Inniskilling Fusiliers landed later in the day to reinforce them. The beach and cliffs were now secure and more than 2,000 British troops were embedded behind the main Turkish line of defence, but apart from a foray south to link up with the troops who had landed at W Beach, the troops at X Beach dug in. Had they been ordered to press on, they may have succeeded in outflanking the Turks and capturing the village of Krithia, a vital objective that was never threatened for the rest of the campaign. At the very least they could have supported the troops coming ashore at W and V Beaches and the advance inland could have continued on schedule. The failure to capitalise on the landing at X Beach was just another of the missed opportunities that are the hallmark of the Gallipoli campaign. Today there is nothing there that is connected with the campaign, so if you are short on time there is no need to follow the track all the way down to the beach.

Continue driving for 1.4 kilometres and park just before a sweeping right-hand bend. There is a rough track leading into the fields about 50 metres before a lone tree on the left (there is a much more defined track just after the tree, but this is not the one to follow). Follow the track for about 250 metres until you emerge on Gully Beach [27]. This small beach and the adjacent Gully Ravine were two of the most significant landmarks for British troops who served at Gallipoli. Gully Ravine is probably the only place at Helles that features a landscape as rugged as Anzac, and the fighting here in the early campaign was just as vicious. The beach was

Gully Beach

supposed to be captured during the first day's advance, but it wasn't secured for the best part of a week. Gully Ravine was never entirely secured. A series of violent attacks in May, June and July pushed the British line steadily forward along the gully but by the evacuation in January 1916 the upper reaches still had not been captured.

The most bloody assault along the ravine began on 28 June and later became known as the Battle of Gully Ravine. The plan was for the British left flank to advance and capture Turkish trenches on the high ground west of the ravine known as Gully Spur. With the spur in British hands the Turkish right flank would be untenable and the way to Krithia and Achi Baba would open up. The attack began well, with a heavy artillery bombardment smashing the Turkish trenches. The British attackers took the trenches and held onto them for several days, but the Turks counterattacked in strength. The fighting was at close quarters and bloody. On the night of 1–2 July the Royal Inniskilling Fusiliers recaptured a trench, succeeding in part because of the gallantry of Captain Gerald O'Sullivan and Corporal James Somers, who led a spirited attack with hand grenades. Both men were awarded the VC. O'Sullivan was later killed at Suvla and is remembered on the Helles Memorial (see page 230). The Turks continued to counterattack for three more days but without adequate artillery or machine-gun support their task was hopeless. In just over a week the Turks had lost more than 14,000 men and Gully Ravine was choked with bodies. For days afterwards the sector reeked as the dead were burned on massive funeral pyres.

Gully Beach was an important base for the British, and contemporary photos show it as a twin of Anzac Cove, with stores piled high, men bathing in the ocean and troops advancing into the gully towards the front line. Today the wreck of a transport sits just off the beach and the rotting remnants of piers still line the shore. Just inside the mouth of the ravine is a concrete well dug by British engineers in 1915.

It is possible to walk the entire length of Gully Ravine, following in the footsteps of the British advance, but the return walk will take about four hours and cannot be included in a one-day tour of Helles.

OPTIONAL TOUR: Gully Ravine

Exploring Gully Ravine offers the same challenges as exploring the gullies and valleys at Anzac. Follow the same precautions – ideally don't walk alone, take adequate drinking water and wear sturdy shoes and clothing that will protect you from the sun. The walk up Gully Ravine is only recommended during the warmer months. With winter rains the creek on the gully floor turns into a torrent. Much of the gully is shrouded in low scrub, but it's not as nefarious as the spiky entanglements that choke most of the gullies at Anzac. The walk up the gully is not particularly steep.

Gully Ravine presented a strange paradox to the British in 1915. It was a formidable military obstacle, easily defended by the Turks in its upper reaches and difficult to capture. But at the same time it was one of the few natural features at Helles that afforded a measure of protection to the troops. Its high walls were almost impervious to shell and rifle fire, so the gully became a bustling military base, packed with stores, hospitals, cookhouses, cemeteries and rest areas. A constant parade of men and mules made its way along the gully to the firing line and back again. Shells burst intermittently above its walls and stray bullets whizzed constantly into the sea near its mouth. There is still a lot of evidence of the British presence in 1915 – after heavy rain the gully is often littered with shards of rum jars and the rusty relics of food tins – but in the interest of preserving the site, think twice before souvenir hunting.

Enter the mouth of the ravine and walk past the well. Follow the sandy floor into the gully and carry on for about 1 kilometre (20 minutes' walk) until a small gully cuts into the left bank of the ravine (it is covered in thick scrub and can be difficult to spot). This is Artillery

Row, home to gun batteries throughout the campaign. The 3rd Battery of the New Zealand Field Artillery was briefly stationed here in May, its guns supporting the British infantry advances along the ravine. The shallow remains of trenches snake into Artillery Row and branch out towards the clifftop at its head.

Return to the creek bed and carry on for another 2 kilometres (about 40 minutes' walk). Just before the ravine hooks sharply left you will pass a low shelf on the right bank known to the British as the Football Field. It was at about this point that a British trench known as the Zig-Zag entered the ravine on the right, although there is no trace of it now. Continue along the gully for another 700 metres (about 15 minutes) until you reach a low wall made of rocks and boulders on the western wall of the ravine. This is the remains of a reinforced trench that was part of the old British front line. The wall was built by the 1st Border Regiment in late June and became known as Border Barricade. This marks the furthest point reached by the British in their drive up Gully Ravine. All the ground further up the ravine was Turkish territory.

From this point you can either continue along the ravine, climb its slopes and visit the Turkish memorials at the head of the gully (point [30] in the tour), or return to Gully Beach.

Return to your car and continue driving. After 400 metres you will reach Pink Farm Cemetery [28] on your right. The original Pink Farm was captured on 28 April by British troops, who named it for the distinct red soil of the area. It became a major forward supply base and home to a field ambulance. Men who died while being treated here were buried in three cemeteries, Pink Farm 1, 2 and 3. After the war Pink Farm 1 and 2 were consolidated into Pink Farm 3, on this site, and several smaller cemeteries in the area were closed and their bodies brought here. Isolated graves from the surrounding fields were also relocated here. Today the cemetery contains 602 bodies of which 250 are unidentified. There are 219 special memorials to men known or believed to be buried in the cemetery on a terrace beneath the Stone of Remembrance. Four of the graves are Australian, of which two are identified: Major John Mills (died 30/5/1915, grave IV.A.13) and Captain Robert Crocker (died 12/7/1915, Special Memorial 22), both belonging to the 2nd Australian Field Artillery Brigade.

The British men buried here were killed during actions throughout the Helles campaign and belonged to a wide range of units. Demonstrating what a professional fighting force the British 29th Division was long before it landed at Gallipoli, the cemetery contains a number of men who had led distinguished careers. Among them is Major Charles Vaughan DSO of the 1st Border Regiment, a veteran of the Boer War. He was killed at X Beach on 25 April (Special Memorial 109). A senior officer buried here is Lieutenant-Colonel George Stoney DSO, commander of the 1st King's Own Scottish Borderers. He had just returned with his unit from Suvla when he was killed by a shell on 15 October (Special Memorial 204).

The foundations of the original farm buildings can still be found in the scrub north of the cemetery.

Return to your car and carry on. This road was known during the campaign as West Krithia Road and runs along the backbone of the high ground christened Fir Tree Spur. This spur was the scene of the great British advances between April and August that slogged towards the village of Krithia and the tantalising prize of Achi Baba. For those four months, the fields around you were soaked with British blood. On 28 April the First Battle of Krithia began when British troops surged along Fir Tree Spur while the French held the right of the Allied line. The plan was for the British to swing to the right and take Krithia, before attacking Achi Baba from the west. The attack broke down in the tangle of gullies in front of Krithia and the British suffered more than 3,000 casualties before the attack was called off. On 6 May the British were joined by the Australian 2nd Brigade and the New Zealand Infantry Brigade after the Anzac sector was mistakenly deemed to be secure. Between 6 and 8 May the British and Anzacs, along with the French on their right, threw themselves against the Turkish lines in an attack that became known as the Second Battle of Krithia. Once again Achi Baba was the objective but the advance broke down under extremely heavy Turkish fire, and in three days the Allied line advanced less than a kilometre. More than 6,000 Allied troops were killed or wounded (see page 263 for more about the Australian and New Zealand attack). On 4 June the newly reinforced British launched the Third Battle of Krithia, once again advancing with the French on their right. As before, the attack collapsed under withering fire, with only the 127th Manchester Brigade in the centre making any worthwhile gains. The fighting in the Turkish trenches was brutal.

I sank in almost to my knees in the soft earth, the place was a fearful mess, blood everywhere, arms, legs, entrails lying around. It sounds horrible in cold blood but at this time all that is savage in one seemed to be on top. I remember two things distinctly, one was wanting to cut off a man's ears and keep them as a trophy, the other was jumping on the dead, hacking their faces with my feet or crashing my rifle into them. Men fought with their rifles, their feet, their fists, a pick, a shovel, anything. (Lieutenant Leslie Grant, 1/4th Royal Scots, in Steel and Hart, p. 206)

The British were hard-pressed to hang on to their gains and were eventually pushed back by Turkish counterattacks. By the end of the day the Allied line had only advanced about 250 metres, at a cost of more than 6,000 men. On 6 June the Turks launched a strong attack of their own and almost broke through the British line. Second Lieutenant George Moor of the 3rd Battalion, Hampshire Regiment, won the VC for an action that the army should probably have swept under the carpet. His official citation reads:

For most conspicuous bravery and resource . . . during operations south of Krithia, Dardanelles. When a detachment of a battalion on his left, which had lost all its officers, was rapidly retiring before a heavy Turkish attack, Second Lieutenant Moor, immediately grasping the danger to the remainder of the line, dashed back some 200 yards, stemmed the retirement, led back the men, and recaptured the lost trench. (*London Gazette* (supplement), No. 29240, 23/7/1915)

This rather understates things a bit. Moor 'stemmed the retirement' by shooting four of his own men. In the words of his commanding officer, at the sight of their lieutenant pulling out his revolver and executing four of their panicked comrades, the remainder of the soldiers 'came to their senses' and rejoined the fight (Major-General Beauvoir de Lisle, in Carlyon, p. 309).

When the final tally was done on the advances towards Krithia, the Allies had lost more than 15,000 men in three battles, and the Turks as many again. For all that, the final Allied line still lay 3 kilometres short of the objective for the first day.

Drive for 3 kilometres until you reach Twelve Tree Copse Cemetery [29] on your left. Twelve Tree Copse was a small grove of trees that formed a forward observation post during the fighting at Helles in June. The grove was soon destroyed by shelling but the name lived on, and is today represented by 12 pines that stand in the cemetery. Twelve Tree Copse Cemetery is built on the site of the final British front line and is the largest Commonwealth cemetery at Gallipoli. It was begun just before the evacuation and was greatly enlarged after the war when several cemeteries in the area were closed and their burials concentrated here. Some of these were big plots: Geoghan's Bluff Cemetery contained 925 graves from the fighting in Gully Ravine in June and July 1915 – had it not been closed it alone would be among Gallipoli's largest cemeteries. Clunes Vennel Cemetery was another big one, with 522 burials. Another important cemetery concentrated here was Fir Tree Wood Cemetery, which had been created after the Second Battle of Krithia and contained British and New Zealand burials.

Today Twelve Tree Copse contains the bodies of 3,360 soldiers and, given the cemetery's origins and the tough fighting in the area, it's unsurprising that 2,226 of these are unidentified. There are 189 special memorials to men known or believed to be buried in the cemetery.

Most of the graves are British, but there are also 12 Australians and 80 New Zealanders buried here. There are also some Indian and Ceylonese (Sri Lankan) graves.

There are only three identified Australians buried here. Captain Keith Levi (died 7/8/1915, grave I.E.20) was a doctor from Melbourne who served with the No. 1 Hospital, Australian Army Medical Corps and had been Mentioned in Despatches. In August 1915 he was attached to the 2nd Hampshires as Regimental Medical Officer and was killed in the diversionary attack at Helles that accompanied the August Offensive. Gunner Henry Tueski (died 27/6/1915, Special Memorial C.438) served with the 2nd Brigade Australian Field Artillery and was killed while supporting the British advance in June. Second Lieutenant Neil Campbell (died 8/8/1915, Special Memorial A.52) was born and raised in Geelong and enlisted in the AIF on 17 August 1914, less than two weeks after the declaration of war. He was appointed to the 5th Battalion with the regimental number 15. In April 1915 he applied for a commission in the British Army, and transferred as a 2nd Lieutenant to the 5th Battalion Royal Scots (Queen's Edinburgh Rifles) only six days before the Gallipoli landings. He was killed during the diversionary fighting in August.

There are several notable British soldiers buried here, including 2nd Lieutenant Alfred Smith VC of the 1/5th East Lancashire Regiment (died 22/12/1915, Special Memorial

C.358). Smith was helping to hold a trench at Fusilier Bluff in the closing days of the campaign and:

> . . . was in the act of throwing a grenade when it slipped from his hand and fell to the bottom of the trench, close to several of our officers and men. He immediately shouted out a warning, and himself jumped clear and into safety, but seeing that the officers and men were unable to get into cover, and knowing well that the grenade was due to explode, he returned without any hesitation and flung himself down on it. He was instantly killed by the explosion. His magnificent act of self-sacrifice undoubtedly saved many lives. (*London Gazette*, No. 29496, 3/3/1916)

This was the last VC awarded at Gallipoli. Second Lieutenant Smith was originally buried near Y Beach, his grave marked with a cross bearing the words, 'He gave his life to save others.' He was 24.

Senior British officers buried here include Brigadier-General William Moncrieff, commander of the 156th Brigade and Lieutenant-Colonels Henry Hannan, commander of the 1/8th Cameronians (Scottish Rifles) and John Wilson, commander of the 1/7th Cameronians (Scottish Rifles). All three men were killed in a disastrous advance on 28 June (Special Memorial C.132, grave VII.A.7 and Special Memorial C.406). Lieutenant-Colonel William Law was the commander of the 1/7th Lancashire Fusiliers and was killed on 19 December while helping lay mines as diversions to support the evacuations from Anzac and Suvla (Special Memorial C.305). The family of Lieutenant John Bolton of the 1/5th

East Lancashire Regiment (died 4/6/1915, Special Memorial A.67) chose special words to remember him. The inscription on his headstone reads 'We know that it is well with you, among the very brave, the very true.'

The cemetery also contains the Twelve Tree Copse (New Zealand) Memorial, which commemorates 177 New Zealand missing from the senseless advances along Fir Tree Spur during the Second Battle of Krithia on 8 May (see page 263). Two New Zealand gunners killed while serving with artillery batteries in Helles in July are also remembered here. Other New Zealand missing are commemorated on memorials at Lone Pine, Chunuk Bair and Hill 60. Six of the men recorded on the memorial are Australians who served with the New Zealand forces. They are Private Harold Anderson (Auckland Regiment, died 8/5/1915), Gunner George Fitzsimmons (3rd Battery, New Zealand Field Artillery, died 11/7/1915), Private George McKenna (Auckland Regiment, died 8/5/1915), Private James Mullin (Otago Regiment, died 8/5/1915), Private Charles Rose (Canterbury Regiment, died 9/5/1915) and Lance Sergeant Augustus Rosenfeldt (Wellington Regiment, died 8/5/1915).

Leave the cemetery and drive into the village of Krithia (Alçitepe). As is often the case at Gallipoli, the areas where these monumental battles were fought are very small and in a few minutes of driving you have achieved an advance that the entire Mediterranean Expeditionary Force could only dream about. Enter the village and turn left at a T-junction. After 350 metres you will reach the Son Ok Memorial [30] on the left. The red and white memorial, flanked by shells on either side of the gate, marks the site of an artillery battery that was almost overrun by the Manchesters during their attack in June during the Third Battle of Krithia. It was also from near here that the Turks launched their counterattack that pushed the Manchesters back almost to their start line, thereby snuffing out the British advance. There is a small cemetery next to the memorial.

Drive on for another 650 metres, following the curves in the road as it crosses the head of Gully Ravine, and past a statue of a menacing Turk on the left, advancing bayonet in hand, until you reach a memorial on the right of the road. This is the Ziğindere Field Hospital Memorial [31], a symbolic cemetery that commemorates Turkish soldiers killed in the immediate area. There is a mass grave below the symbolic headstones that was the main burial site for Turks killed in the bloody fighting around Gully Ravine. The number of bodies here is uncertain, but it could be as many as 10,000. Some of the men who lie here were victims of a British naval bombardment that struck the field hospital. The statue near the entrance of the cemetery depicts a Turkish soldier shielding a wounded comrade during the bombardment.

Continue for just over a kilometre and park next to a Turkish memorial. Leave your car here for a walk around the head of Gully Ravine (the walk is about 2 kilometres return and should take an hour to complete). The memorial is known as the Nuri Yamut Memorial [32] and commemorates men killed during the fighting in Gully Ravine. It is located right on the Turkish front line and has as its focal point a small chamber open to the sky which encloses a grave. The simple sentiment on the stone slab translates as 'To the martyrs of 1915'. The memorial was built in 1943 and renovated in 1992.

Leave the memorial and climb over the back fence of the enclosure. Cross the field behind the memorial, walking south-west with the sea on your right. This plateau forms the upper length of Gully Spur, the high ground that runs along the north-west edge of Gully Ravine and was hotly contested during the advances towards Krithia. The ground on your right was known as Fusilier Bluff, and marks the northern limit of the British front line.

After about 800 metres you will cross a field in the footsteps of a Turkish company that advanced towards the British line on 28 April 1915. As they crossed this field they were spotted by the *Queen Elizabeth*, the Royal Navy's flagship at Gallipoli, which fired a single 15-inch shell at them. General Sir Ian Hamilton was aboard the ship and described the action in his diary:

One Turkish Company, about a hundred strong, was making an ugly push within rifle shot of our ship. Its flank rested on the very edge of the cliff, and the men worked forward like German Infantry in a regular line, making a rush of about fifty yards with sloped arms and lying down and firing. They all had their bayonets fixed. Through a glass every move, every signal, could be seen. From where we were our guns exactly enfiladed them. Again they rose and at a heavy sling trot came on with their rifles at the slope; their bayonets glittering and their Officer ten yards ahead of them waving his sword. Someone said they were cheering. Crash! and the [*Queen Elizabeth*] let fly a shrapnel; range 1,200 yards; a lovely shot; we followed it through the air with our eyes. Range and fuse – perfect. The huge projectile exploded fifty yards from the right of the Turkish line, and vomited its contents of 10,000 bullets clean across the stretch whereon the Turkish Company was making its last effort. When the smoke and dust cleared away nothing stirred on the whole of that piece of ground. We looked for a long time, nothing stirred.

Today it's not hard to find the site of this carnage. The bones of the Turkish soldiers still litter the ground.

Bones of Turks killed by a single shrapnel shell fired from the HMS *Queen Elizabeth* on 28 April 1915

Carry on for another 200 metres, veering right into a narrow clearing. Follow a track through the scrub until you can look down over a narrow, rocky cove that opens into a wide and steep gully. This is Y Beach [33], scene of a bold flanking move on the morning of the landing that should have paid dividends and didn't. Late in the planning stages, Hamilton decided that a force of about 2,000 men, drawn from the 1st King's Own Scottish Borderers, the Plymouth Battalion of the Royal Naval Division and a company from the 2nd South Wales Borderers, would land in this narrow cove, well behind the main Turkish defences, and try to outflank them. It was a good plan – the unexpected arrival of 2,000 men behind their lines would have caused chaos among the Turkish defenders and greatly relieved the pressure on the men coming ashore on the toe of the peninsula. The British party at Y Beach came ashore unopposed early on the day of the landing and made short work of the climb up the gully. There they looked out on the gently sloping plains that led directly to Krithia, with hardly a Turk between them and their objective. The British had successfully landed as many men at Y Beach as the Turks had men defending all the other beaches combined. But then things went wrong. Orders were vague, objectives unclear and the commanders of the newly landed battalions began to squabble. Instead of advancing, they dug in on the clifftop and waited for further instructions. At this point strong leadership could have gotten things back on track but Hunter-Weston, the commander at Helles, had never been a fan of the landing at Y Beach and obstinately refused to reply to requests for clear instructions. The Turks weren't as flat-footed. As soon as they realised their flank was under threat they attacked with strength and purpose. The British garrison at Y Beach was soon fighting tooth and nail to hold the clifftop, and was running out of ammunition and men.

> One could see line upon line of Turks advancing against our position. They fought with extraordinary bravery and as each line was swept away by fire another one advanced against us and the survivors collected in some dead ground to our front and came on again. The attack worked up and down our whole front as if they were looking for some weak spot to break through our line. Four times during the night they got right up to my trench before they were shot and one Turk engaged one of my men over the parapet with his bayonet and was then shot. (Captain Robert Whigham, 1st KOSB, in Steel and Hart, p. 108)

Wounded men began to crowd the beach and, in the absence of orders, the local commander called in boats to take them off. Stragglers on the beach took the opportunity to leave with the wounded, and the men on the clifftops took the departing boats as a sign that the order to withdraw had been given. The trickle of men turned into a flood and within hours Y Beach had been abandoned. There ended the best opportunity the British had during the entire campaign to secure Krithia. Y Beach was not held again until two weeks into the campaign, by which stage the advantage had well and truly passed. The strongest result of the debacle at Y Beach was to demonstrate the chronic lack of decisive leadership that would cripple the Gallipoli campaign. General Sir Ian Hamilton was on board the *Queen Elizabeth* just off Y Beach and saw first-hand the men beginning to withdraw. Who had given the order? As commander-in-chief and the man behind the plan to land at Y Beach, surely he would have felt the need to intervene. But he didn't. In his diary he wrote about watching the evacuation of Y Beach and his confusion as to who had ordered it:

> My inclination was to take a hand myself in this affair but the Staff are clear against interference when I have no knowledge of the facts – and I suppose they are right. To see a part of my scheme, from which I had hoped so much, go wrong before my eyes is maddening!

Apparently not maddening enough to prompt him into action. Had Hamilton been more of a general and less of a gentleman, the Gallipoli campaign may well have gone differently.

The point where you are standing is known as Gurkha Bluff, in honour of the 1/6th Gurkha Rifles, who captured it on the night of 12–13 May, allowing British troops to stand on Y Beach for the first time since the day of the landing. Y Beach became a support base for the nearby front line and for the remainder of the campaign was used to evacuate wounded and to land supplies and reinforcements.

Walk back across the fields towards your car. As you look across the flat ground to Krithia village, imagine the damage that 2,000 British troops, heavily armed and unopposed, could have inflicted had they decided to advance instead of digging in. Yet another of the great 'what-ifs' of the Gallipoli campaign.

Return to your car and drive back to Krithia (Alçitepe) village. Go straight on through the T-junction. (There is a

Bodies of Australians killed during the Second Battle of Krithia, May 1915. The photo was taken from the approximate site of Redoubt Cemetery, looking back towards the Australian start line. AWM C01079

small military museum in the centre of town that is worth a brief visit if time allows.) Carry on until you reach an intersection at the end of the road and turn right. Follow this road as it leaves the village, always bearing right and ignoring two roads that join it on the left. 500 metres after the intersection, turn right at a fork, heading south-west.

This long stretch of road takes you through the heart of the British battlefield, across the ground taken at such huge cost during the three savage battles of Krithia (you are driving towards the British line, in the opposite direction of the advance). This road also leads to the ground attacked by the Anzac forces during the Second Battle of Krithia.

Drive for 1.7 kilometres and turn right to Redoubt Cemetery [34]. This stands in the middle of the open plains where Australian and New Zealand troops launched their gallant but hopeless attack on 8 May. This attack is virtually forgotten in the annals of Anzac history, but it really shouldn't be. It was one of the great heroic chapters in an epic of sacrifice and pain.

After the failure of the First Battle of Krithia on 28 April, the British were mounting another push in early May and asked if the Anzacs could spare a few troops to help. The Anzac sector was still a hive of confusion, and the commanders there mistakenly believed that the line was secure enough to spare two brigades, the New Zealand and 2nd Australian, for the attack at Helles. (In reality, the removal of these troops left the Anzac line dangerously undermanned. The commanders on the spot were lucky the Turks didn't attack while the brigades were gone.) The Anzac brigades arrived at Helles on the morning of 6 May and landed at V Beach beside the hulk of the *River Clyde*. Compared to the squalor at Anzac, Helles was 'a fairyland of meadow and scattered trees, busy with bright French uniforms, with the battlefield beyond lying like an open map' (Bean, *Gallipoli Mission*). At 11 a.m. they watched from behind the lines as British and French troops advanced on Krithia. The attack started well but soon broke down under heavy fire, and the New Zealand Brigade was ordered to join the fight on the morning of 8 May and advance along Fir Tree Spur. They crossed a bare plateau known as the Daisy Patch and were badly shot up as they tried to advance. General Hunter-Weston, the commander at Helles, threw them in again at the same spot in the afternoon. Unsurprisingly (except perhaps to Hunter-Weston) the New Zealanders were mown down again, and were withdrawn having suffered 771 casualties.

On the same afternoon the Australian 2nd Brigade was digging in to its support position and preparing its evening meal. At 4.55 p.m. the brigade commanders were astonished to receive an order to attack at 5.30 p.m. It was a big call for the brigade to even advance to its start line in 35 minutes, let alone equip itself and issue orders, but the Australians raced forward as instructed and joined the attack on the right of the New Zealanders. They faced a gently sloping plain that stretched all the way to Achi Baba and as soon as they emerged from cover they came under heavy Turkish fire. They grimly pushed on across no-man's-land, and were surprised to come across a group of English soldiers hunkering down in a well-dug trench. The trench (dubbed 'Tommies' Trench' by the Anzacs) was the only cover on the barren plain and the Australians stopped here awaiting further orders. With a cry of 'come on Australians' their officers led them on, into a storm of Turkish fire. Charles Bean was in the trench with them and said that 'their faces were set, their eyebrows bent, they looked into [the machine-gun fire] for a moment as men would into a dazzling flame. I never saw so many determined faces at once' (*Gallipoli Mission*, p. 291). The fire was so heavy that some men held their shovels in front of their faces as they advanced, like an umbrella against the rain. Unsupported, without cover and in broad daylight the Australians continued to advance, but they weren't even close enough to the Turkish trenches to see where the fire was coming from, let alone to capture them. A British major described the scene in a tone so effusive you suspect he'd been sampling his regiment's rum ration:

> The enemy's shelling was shifted on to them in one great concentration of hell. The machine-guns bellowed and poured on them sheets of flame and of ragged death, buried them alive. They were disembowelled. Their

clothing caught fire, and their flesh hissed and cooked before the burning rags could be torn off or beaten out. But what of it? Why, nothing! . . . They were at home in hell-fire . . . They laughed at it; they sang through it. Their pluck was titanic. They were not men, but gods, demons infuriated. We saw them fall by the score. But what of that? Not for one breath did the great line waver or break. On and up it went, up and on, as steady and as proud as if on parade. A seasoned staff officer watching choked with his own admiration. Our men tore off their helmets and waved them, and poured cheer after cheer after those wonderful Anzacs. (Mure, p. 109)

After advancing 450 metres from Tommies' Trench the Australians could go no further and dug in, on a line that became known as the Redoubt Line and which was only 400 metres short of the furthest point the British would reach in the entire campaign. During the advance the Australians had lost more than 1,000 men from the 2,000 who had gone into battle. The Second Battle of Krithia sputtered out soon after, and the survivors returned to Anzac.

Redoubt Cemetery was built by Australian troops just behind the Redoubt Line soon after the front line had advanced, and was used to bury men who had been killed in the advance and in later battles. It was greatly enlarged after the war when bodies from the surrounding fields were brought in and, along with Twelve Tree Copse Cemetery, now forms the main burial ground where British dead from the Krithia battles lie.

The cemetery contains 2,027 burials but 1,397 of these are unidentified. Special memorials record the names of 349 men known or believed to be buried in the cemetery. There are only 20 identified Australian graves and eight from New Zealand, but the vast majority of Anzacs killed in the Second Battle of Krithia lie here, unidentified and intermingled with their comrades from Britain. Probably the greatest tribute to the British men who lie here is a solitary English oak tree that stands next to the rows on the right of the cemetery. A memorial plaque at its base records that it was planted by the family of 2nd Lieutenant Eric Duckworth of the 1/6th Lancashire Fusiliers. He was killed during fighting at the Vineyard, a small patch of scrub about a kilometre north-east of the cemetery, on 7 August. He has no known grave and is commemorated on the Helles Memorial, but it is probable that his body was buried here in Redoubt Cemetery.

The most senior Australian buried here was the first to arrive. Lieutenant-Colonel Robert Gartside, the stoic commander of the 8th Battalion, was leading the 7th Battalion in their advance on 8 May. According to witnesses, he rose to lead the battalion in one of their final rushes, with the words, 'Come on boys, I know it's deadly but we must get on,' when he was hit in the stomach by machine-gun fire (Bean, Vol. II, p. 31). His grave was used as the starting point for the rest of Redoubt Cemetery (grave I.B.21). Buried nearby is Corporal Mark Wraith (real name Archie Odgers), who was also killed during the 7th Battalion's advance. His headstone touchingly reads 'Still living, still loving, still with us' (grave I.B.13).

All the identified Australians here were killed during the advance towards Krithia on 8 May except for Private Austin McCallum of the 8th Battalion, who is recorded as having been killed on 1 May, but in reality must have died between 6 and 8 May (grave I.C.15). Private James Kitto was an Australian who served with the Auckland Regiment and was also killed on 8 May (Special Memorial B.2).

Private Charles Vose was an Australian who served with the 1st Battalion Essex Regiment. He was killed on 2 January 1916, two weeks after the Anzacs had left the peninsula. Private Vose was the last Australian to be killed at Gallipoli (Special Memorial B.74).

The Second Battle of Krithia deserves a place in Australian military history alongside Lone Pine, Fromelles, El Alamein and Long Tan, but it is usually overlooked. The area immediately surrounding Redoubt Cemetery was soaked in Australian blood, so spend a few minutes wandering the plain and remembering the men who fell here. The approximate location of the two trenches that formed the Redoubt Line can be found about 100 metres behind the cemetery, and reveals itself by the rum jar pieces, rusty bully beef tins and human bone fragments that still litter the ground.

Return to the main road and drive on for 2.5 kilometres. A low hill on your right is a tumulus (ancient burial tomb). To demonstrate that war should not take precedence over culture, the French sent a team of archaeologists to excavate the site during the campaign. Some of them were killed by Turkish shells. The tumulus was also near the site of the Australian camp before the Second Battle of Krithia in May 1915. Australian troops scaled the tumulus and watched the opening stages of the battle unfold on the fields before them.

Continue to Skew Bridge Cemetery [35]. On 27 April British engineers built a wooden 'skew' bridge across a gully just behind their front line, and the name was adopted when a cemetery was started nearby in May (the bridge is long gone but a road still crosses the gully on the site, about 200 metres east of the cemetery). Skew Bridge Cemetery was used until the evacuation and contained only 53 graves at the end of the war. It was greatly enlarged when bodies were concentrated here from other cemeteries and brought in from the surrounding fields. Today it contains 607 burials, of which 351 are unidentified. The ubiquitous special memorials record the names of men known or believed to be buried among them.

There are nine identified Australian graves here and two New Zealanders. All these men were either infantrymen killed during the Second Battle of Krithia (or dying of wounds soon after), or artillerymen killed while supporting the British advances later in the campaign. Quartermaster Sergeant Charles Henman was an Australian who served with the British Royal Marine Engineers. He was killed on 29 July (grave I.B.1).

Notable British soldiers buried here include Lieutenant-Colonel John Quilter, a Boer War veteran who served with the Grenadier Guards but commanded the Hood Battalion of the Royal Naval Division at Gallipoli (English poet Rupert Brooke was also serving with the Hood Battalion when he died of blood poisoning while en route to Gallipoli on 23 April 1915). Quilter was leading the battalion during an advance on 6 May when he was killed. Before the war he had served as the military secretary to the Governor-General of Australia (grave II.B.4).

Lieutenant-Colonel William Maxwell served in the headquarters of the 2nd Brigade, Royal Naval Division and was a shrewd military tactician. He was fond of wearing his staff officer's red-banded cap, even while in the front line, a foible that may have demonstrated courage to his men but didn't do much for his wellbeing: he was killed by a sniper on 9 May (Special Memorial B.19).

There are two other colonels buried in Skew Bridge: Colonel Frank Luard of the Portsmouth Battalion, Royal Naval Division (died 13/07/1915, grave II.B.3) and Lieutenant-Colonel Edmund Evelegh of the Nelson Battalion, Royal Naval Division. Those British battalion commanders certainly could be relied on to go out in a blaze of glory. Colonel Evelegh was last seen alive leaping onto a parapet:

> . . . in advance of any of his men and, standing under a hail of shrapnel, he took off his cap and cheered the men out of the trenches as if he were cheering on a pack of hounds. He was a fine sight. (Aspinall-Oglander, Vol. II, p. 301)

This concludes the tour of Helles and Krithia. From Skew Bridge Cemetery, drive back the way you came to Krithia (Alçitepe) and turn right in the centre of the village. Follow this road north for 1.5 kilometres until you reach a fork. The left fork leads to the village of Gözetleme and eventually Anzac. The right fork is the road that brought you here at the start of the tour and leads to Eceabat via Kilitbahir.

Suvla and North of Anzac

The August Offensive Attacks – North Beach to Kirectepe

The area north of Anzac is often overlooked. Few visitors make the effort to visit this part of the battlefield, and one of the most important chapters of the Gallipoli story – the August Offensive – is left untold.

The vital part of that story is the flanking attack north of Anzac. For the full explanation, see the introduction to the Chunuk Bair and Gun Ridge tour. This tour explores the ground covered by the Anzac and British forces at the start of that advance, and the ground where things started to go wrong. It also explores the other essential component of that grand plan – the oft-maligned campaign at Suvla Bay.

Of all the disasters at Gallipoli, the campaign at Suvla Bay best represents the poor leadership and missed opportunities that so hamstrung the Allies throughout the campaign. The performance of the British commanders here is so derided that Suvla is often held up as one of the all-time great British military disasters, on the scale of the Fall of Singapore in 1942. That's probably taking things a bit far, but it is true to say that Suvla represents a poor plan that was even more poorly carried out.

General Sir Ian Hamilton, commander-in-chief at Gallipoli, had planned a big push for August and asked London for two divisions of reinforcements. He got three. On the cramped fronts at Anzac and Helles there was no room for an additional 30,000 troops, so five brigades were tasked with staging a new landing at Suvla Bay, north of Anzac and really the only place on the peninsula that had enough space to hold them. Originally the plan called for the troops to land on the flat Suvla plain and push on to the heights to help the Anzacs in their advance on the Sari Bair Range. But then the generals watered down the plan to capturing a few guns on the low W Hills and securing the plain as a base for future operations. The high ground would be captured only if the commanders on the spot thought it was a good idea to do so. How all this was going to help in the major offensive taking place at Anzac was not really explained.

The British brigades came ashore on three beaches at Suvla Bay on the night of 6–7 August. The bedraggled Turkish garrison guarding the sector was ill-equipped to oppose a major landing. It had limited artillery and no machine guns, and the British secured the beaches with light casualties. Rocky shoals in the shallow waters of the bay disrupted the landings and the units came ashore mixed up and behind schedule, but by morning the brigades had landed almost 20,000 troops and the Suvla plain lay open before them.

But then things started to go wrong. A critical lack of decisive leadership saw most of the force loitering on the beach for two days with the high ground that was the key to the sector lying virtually undefended. Eventually the British pushed forward in the early hours of 9 August, but they were too late. Turkish reinforcements had been marching for Suvla since hearing of the landing, and they beat the British to the high ground by 30 minutes. Like Anzac and Helles, Suvla became a siege.

For the rest of August the British tried to buy back the advantage they had squandered, with a series of direct assaults against the heights. But the Turks were dug in, and their lack of firepower in the opening days of the Suvla operation had been rectified. The British were mown down in their thousands as they tried to capture the ridges.

The botched job at Suvla spelled the end of offensive operations at Gallipoli, and the careers of several British commanders as well. Lieutenant-General Sir Frederick Stopford was the commander at Suvla. In 1915 his best years were already well behind him and he had been brought out of mothballs to command the Suvla force. His poor leadership during the landings and later advances was probably the main reason the Suvla adventure failed, and he was removed from his post fairly swiftly. But the plan at Suvla was always too vague, it relied too much on everything going right and it skipped a lot of the fine detail that was essential to success for an operation of this size.

What does all this mean for the common soldier who served at Suvla? As in many instances at Gallipoli, he was asked to do too much, and paid for it with his life. At least the soldiers who fought at Anzac and Helles had the promise of victory in their minds (in the early days, anyway). But at Suvla the advance petered out in the first few days, and the soldiers here really did die for nothing.

Suvla is an often forgotten battlefield of Gallipoli. Thousands of visitors go to Anzac and Helles, but not many come north to Suvla. The cemeteries here are isolated, the inscriptions on their headstones fading, the names of the dead seeming to fade from history with them. As Les Carlyon says in his epic *Gallipoli*, while the cemeteries at Anzac and Helles say 'Lest we forget', the cemeteries at Suvla say 'Lest we remember'. Visitors who make the effort to visit Suvla will find it a sad but rewarding experience.

Suvla and North of Anzac Tour

Suvla is the least visited part of the Gallipoli peninsula. Not much occurred here to be proud of, a sentiment that is strongly reflected in the four isolated and lonely Commonwealth cemeteries that hold almost 5,000 dead.

The tour covers a large area – approximately 55 kilometres – so driving is the only option. Allow half a day to complete the tour.

Driving in Suvla can be a challenge. There are few surfaced roads in the area and the minor farm roads and tracks that cross the battlefield offer pot holes large enough to swallow your car. The tour therefore backtracks on a number of occasions to enable travel on the most passable roads. In good weather the whole tour can be driven in a

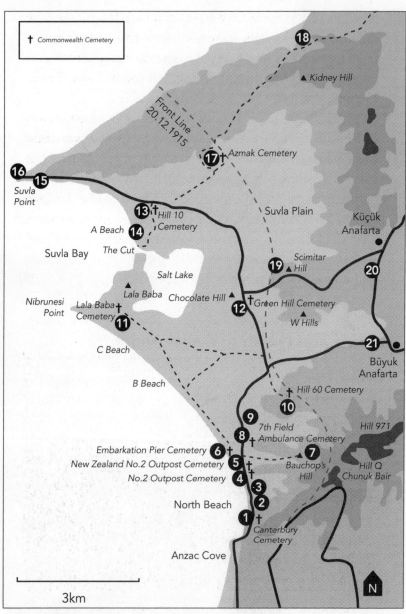

† Commonwealth Cemetery

18

▲ Kidney Hill

Front Line 20.12.1915

17 † Azmak Cemetery

16
15
Suvla
Point

Suvla Plain

Küçük
Anafarta

13 † Hill 10
Cemetery

A Beach 14

The Cut

Suvla Bay

Salt Lake

19 Scimitar
▲ Hill

20

Lala Baba ▲ Chocolate Hill ▲

Nibrunesi
Point

Lala Baba
Cemetery †

11

† Green Hill Cemetery

▲ W Hills

Büyuk
Anafarta

21

C Beach

B Beach

† Hill 60 Cemetery

10

9

8 † 7th Field
Ambulance Cemetery

Hill 971

Embarkation Pier Cemetery 6 †

New Zealand No.2 Outpost Cemetery 5 †

No.2 Outpost Cemetery 4 †

3

2

▲ 7

Bauchop's
Hill

Hill Q

Chunuk Bair

North Beach

1

† Canterbury
Cemetery

Anzac Cove

N

3km

Suvla and North of Anzac tour

regular vehicle, but a four-wheel-drive might be necessary if the weather is poor. Take care, and advise the hosts at your accommodation of your destination before setting out.

The tour begins at the Anzac Commemorative Site at North Beach, where the Anzac Day Dawn Service is held. To reach the site from Eceabat, follow the road to Bigali north out of town, and then turn left at the major intersection after 2 kilometres. Follow this road for about 8 kilometres into the Gallipoli Peace Park, past the Gaba Tepe Museum. Ignore the road leading right to Chunuk Bair (Conkbayiri) and continue with the sea on your left. Three kilometres after the Chunuk Bair turn-off you will reach Anzac Cove, and after a further kilometre the Anzac Commemorative Site. Drive north from the Commemorative Site for 400 metres until you reach Canterbury Cemetery [1]. This is one of the smallest cemeteries at Gallipoli and also a little

Canterbury Cemetery, looking back to the Sphinx

piece of New Zealand. It was built after the war and is named in honour of the Canterbury Mounted Rifles, a unit that operated in this area for most of the campaign. The cemetery contains 27 graves, of which 22 are identified. Sixteen of these men belonged to the Canterbury Mounted Rifles, and four of the five unidentified graves also belong to New Zealanders. The cemetery sits at the base of Walker's Ridge, the main thoroughfare used by the New Zealand Expeditionary Force to reach the front line. On the beach just north of the cemetery is the wreck of a barge. Its ribs stick out of the water at low tide.

Continue driving north and after 350 metres you will pass the entrance to the Commonwealth War Graves Commission compound known as the Anzac Village [2], a group of cottages and workshops home to the maintenance workers who tend the cemeteries and memorials at Anzac and Suvla. The compound also contains an unusual grave. 'Bill' was an Australian Light Horse Waler who sailed from Australia in 1914 and served with the light horse in Egypt. His service during the Gallipoli campaign is unclear. He may have served on the peninsula, or more likely in Palestine from 1916 to 1918. After the war he came to Gallipoli with members of the light horse who helped establish the Commonwealth cemeteries, and he remained here until his death in 1924. He was apparently a well-loved companion – he was buried under a regulation Commonwealth War Graves headstone, the only animal in the world to be so honoured. His inscription reads '"BILL", Australian Light Horse, 1914 to 1924, A waler and one of the best.' Unfortunately the CWGC village is off limits to visitors, but if there are CWGC workers around, ask permission to see the grave.

The small hill behind the village is Outpost No. 1, which formed part of the left flank of the Anzac sector in the days after the landing. The Turks built a memorial near here after the evacuation, but it was removed by Allied troops after the war. An identical memorial at Lone Pine was also destroyed, but another at the Nek was left untouched and still stands there today (see page 143). A concrete bunker in the scrub above the beach in front of the village was built during the Second World War.

Drive on for another 250 metres. The small tumbledown cottage on your right was built after the war on the site of another known as Fisherman's Hut [3]. On 25 April, men from the 7th Battalion were tasked with landing here and capturing the hut to secure the Anzac left flank. They were one of the few units who managed to land in the right spot on the first morning, but even before their boats touched the shore they were caught by extremely heavy fire from Fisherman's Hut. Most of the men in the boats were hit, but the survivors managed to scramble ashore and eventually creep south along the beach to link up with the main Anzac force on Anzac Cove.

> It was found that, of 140 souls in the boats, there were left . . . about thirty-five unhurt or lightly wounded men. The rest lay in the boats or on the beach dead, dying or grievously wounded. (Bean, Vol. I, p. 328)

The next day Lance Corporal Noel Ross, the son of the New Zealand Official War Correspondent, was surveying the boats through a telescope from Walker's Ridge. He noticed that a sailor who lay among the pile of dead men in the boats had changed position since the day before, and realised there must be wounded men still in the boats.

> As Ross watched, he was astonished to see a figure detach itself from the dreadful heap and begin to hobble along the beach. After a few yards it collapsed. A Turkish sniper had opened. The splash of his bullets could be seen in the water just beyond the man. (Bean, Vol. I, p. 331)

Ross and four other men crept out and managed to bring the wounded man to safety. Other men were also rescued from the boats during the day, but several stretcher-bearers were shot and killed in the attempt.

The hill behind Fisherman's Hut was known as Maori Hill during the campaign, after the New Zealand Maori Contingent. The Maori Contingent played an important role in helping to clear the nearby outposts during the August Offensive and, according to legend, did an impromptu *haka* before joining the assault (see page 149 for more about them).

Drive on for another 400 metres and turn right onto a dirt track. This loops back and brings you to No. 2 Outpost Cemetery [4]. Along with No. 1 Outpost, No. 2 Outpost (the hill behind the cemetery) formed the left flank of the Anzac line after the landings. On 30 April both posts were established by the Canterbury Regiment, which also captured a large well from the Turks. This became the most important source of water at Anzac and could supply enough drinking water for 20,000 troops and 4,000 mules each day.

A field hospital was established near the outposts in the early weeks of the campaign and in June this was supplemented by the New Zealand Corps Dental clinic. As was often the case at Gallipoli, the New Zealanders were better organised than the Australians. The Australians had no specialised dental corps and qualified dentists had to be sourced from the ranks. Even then, treatment for dental complaints was rudimentary. Sergeant Cyril Lawrence described visiting a dentist in July, and noted, 'The chair is just a box and I think the dentist only has the one instrument; anyhow I thought that my jaw was broken.' His diary entry four days later reads 'My toothache is still pretty bad. Evidently it was not the one I had pulled.' (East, p. 51)

On 22 June Charles Bean wrote in his diary about an Australians soldier's frustrating attempts to get his teeth fixed:

> A man here had broken his plate, and as we have no dental corps or equipment, he had to be sent away. He was sent to Lemnos or Imbros to be treated by a dentist there. At Lemnos – after being there some days – he found that the dentist had gone, or couldn't fix him, and was sent on to Egypt and told to return in ten days. He came back in ten days and was told the dentist had gone, so he was sent back to Lemnos. He found nothing could be done at Lemnos, and so was sent back here arriving just four weeks after he left, without having the trouble attended to. (Bean in Fewster, p. 132)

Two weeks later Bean described how a shell hit the dental dugout and 'covered the hillside with false teeth'.

No. 2 Outpost Cemetery was started during the campaign and was initially used to bury 28 men of the 7th Battalion who had been killed while landing at Fisherman's Hut on the first day (see page 277). Their bodies could not be retrieved until the area had been secured in early May, so their dates of death are officially recorded as '25 April/2 May'. However, as mentioned on page 277, the men were all killed on the first or second day. The cemetery was used throughout the campaign, and isolated graves were moved here after the war.

Today it contains 152 burials including 32 men from New Zealand, seven from Australia and three from Britain. Special memorials commemorate 48 men known or believed to be buried among them. The rest of the graves are unidentified.

The most senior Australian commemorated here is Captain John Luther, Regimental Medical Officer of the 15th Battalion. He was killed in action on 25 August (Special Memorial 39). Three men who lie here were Australians serving with the New Zealanders: Trooper Robert Bradshaw (Otago Mounted Rifles, died 16/7/1915, grave B.10), Lance Sergeant Harold Fischer (Otago Regiment, died 7/8/1915, grave F.10) and Trooper Neil McMillan (Auckland Mounted Rifles, died 6/8/1915, Special Memorial 34). The inscription on the grave of Private Alfred Baldwin (7th Battalion, died 25/4–2/5/1915, grave C.15) remembers him as 'Just one of the gallant band. A.N.Z.A.C.'

Return along the track to the main road and turn right. Immediately after joining the main road, park next to New Zealand No. 2 Outpost Cemetery [5]. This small cemetery is made up of one long grave that was dug in September 1915, and runs diagonally across the modern cemetery. There are 183 men buried here, but only 33 of them could be identified. Special memorials record the names of 31 men known or believed to be buried in the cemetery. The

New Zealand No. 2 Outpost Cemetery

most notable grave belongs to Colonel Neville Manders of the Royal Army Medical Corps, the Chief Medical Officer of the New Zealand and Australian Division. He had overseen the clearing of wounded from the beaches during the opening days of the campaign, an unenviable task given the inadequate medical preparations that had been made. He performed the same role during the August Offensive, again faced with the overwhelming challenge of treating thousands of wounded with inadequate medical teams and evacuation plans. On both occasions hundreds of men died who might have been saved had the medical arrangements been adequate. On 9 August Manders was killed by a stray bullet while standing outside General Godley's headquarters (Special Memorial 20).

Two men who lie here, Lieutenant Thomas Nisbet and Private William Smith, were Australians who served with the Otago Regiment. They were both killed in August during the advance on Chunuk Bair (Special Memorials 22 and 26). There are eight members of the AIF commemorated here, all except one of them killed in the attack on Hill 971 in August.

A track that roughly follows the New Zealand advance during the August Offensive all the way to Chunuk Bair begins behind the cemetery. The walk up and down takes about half a day, so it can't be included as part of this tour. To find the track, follow the dirt road towards No. 2 Outpost Cemetery and the track begins on the left after about 50 metres. Note that it follows the heights. In August 1915 the New Zealanders advanced along the Chailak Dere (the valley to the north overlooked by the track) and then scaled the slopes of Rhododendron Ridge to reach Chunuk Bair. The track is rough and steep, so only attempt the walk if you are fit and are carrying adequate water and protection from the sun. It can also be followed from the opposite direction, starting on the fire trail leading to the Farm Cemetery at Chunuk Bair.

Drive on for 150 metres and park in front of a large cemetery on the left. This is Embarkation Pier Cemetery [6], named after a pier that was built here to evacuate wounded during the August Offensive. The pier was hopelessly exposed, however, and after coming under a storm of rifle and shell fire it was abandoned after only two days. The cemetery was started when five men were buried next to a casualty clearing station on the site. After the war four small cemeteries were concentrated here, Chailak Dere No. 1 and 2, Mulberry Tree and the Apex. Isolated graves and bodies from the surrounding area were also brought in until the cemetery reached its current size of 944 burials. Of these, 662 are unidentified and there are special memorials to 262 men known or believed to be buried here. In total the cemetery commemorates 64 New Zealanders, 125 Australians and 93 men from Britain. Nearly all these men were killed during the August Offensive in the attacks on Sari Bair.

The most senior Australian commemorated here is Major John Scott of the 10th Light Horse. Major Scott had led the fourth wave in the disastrous charge at the Nek on 7 August, and was lucky to come out of that action unscathed. His luck ran out on 8 October when he was killed by a 'percussion shell' while the regiment was in reserve behind Rhododendron Ridge (Special Memorial C.43). Another notable officer buried here is Captain Clarence Luxton of the 6th Battalion. Luxton had been prominent during the fighting on Pine Ridge on the day of the landing. Pine Ridge was on the far right of the Anzac line, and the 6th Battalion stayed in that area for the first few days of the campaign. Captain Luxton was killed on 26 April, so how he came to be buried here, at the opposite end of the Anzac line, is a mystery.

Also commemorated here is Lieutenant Archibald Auchterlonie of the 25th Battalion (Special Memorial A.31). Auchterlonie, a sportsman, had captained the 25th Battalion rugby team in a charity match against Woolloongabba in Brisbane in May 1915. In a tight match the soldiers triumphed 6–3. Five of the starting 15 would not survive the war. On 20 October the 25th Battalion was holding the front line on Cheshire Ridge, below the summit of Chunuk Bair, when Auchterlonie was shot in the head and killed. His younger brother Bert had been killed during the attack on Hill 971 on 8 August. Bert's body was never found and he is commemorated on the Lone Pine Memorial. Another brother, Cecil, later served with distinction on the Western Front and won the Military Cross twice in two weeks in July 1918. On 10 August 1918 Cecil was leading a company near Harbonnieres in the Somme when he was killed by machine-gun fire. He is buried in the Heath Cemetery, Harbonnieres.

Another officer who lies here was prominent during the fighting at Quinn's Post on 29 May, the action in which Major Hugh Quinn was killed. Lieutenant Hubert Hartnell-Sinclair had helped hold the front line against the attacking Turks until he was wounded. He was killed on 9 August during the attack on Hill 971 (Special Memorial B.67).

Several Australians buried in this cemetery served with New Zealand forces. They are Private Ivan Armstrong (grave I.A.1), Second Lieutenant Valentine Blake (Special Memorial A.12), Sergeant Ernest Cohen (Special Memorial B.53), Private William Haddock (grave I.A.9), Lance Corporal George Ilsley (grave I.A.6) and Gunner John Mills (Special Memorial C.22). Private C. Sharpe, originally from Coogee in Sydney, served with the 1/4th Norfolk Regiment in the British Army (Special Memorial D.2).

Trooper George Johnston was one of four men hit when the bivouacs of the 2nd Light Horse were shelled on 10 November. As he lay dying he told his comrades, 'Never mind me boys, save Sergeant Beaton,' a statement inscribed on his headstone (Special Memorial B.39). The Sergeant Beaton in question was Sergeant Edward Beaton, who later served in Palestine and won the Distinguished Flying Cross as a pilot in the Australian Flying Corps.

The inscription on the grave of Trooper William Baker of the 9th Light Horse, reads 'Brother Bill a sniping fell, we miss him still, we ever will.' Trooper Baker was killed on 28 November, only three weeks before the evacuation (grave I.A.12).

The wide valley opposite the cemetery is Chailak Dere, the gully that the New Zealanders followed in their advance to Chunuk Bair on the night of 6 August. The Australian 4th Brigade lost heavily at the mouth of the gully as they followed the road north to the next valley, Aghyl Dere.

Embarkation Pier Cemetery marks the northern boundary of the Anzac battlefield. All the ground north of here is designated as the Suvla sector.

Drive north for 100 metres, and turn right onto a rough dirt track. This track follows the beginning of the New Zealand advance up Chailak Dere towards the heights of Chunuk Bair. Follow the road for 1.5 kilometres and it will get very rough and steep, before eventually reaching the top of a prominent hill. Park beside the small white building on the summit. This is Bauchop's Hill [7], named after Lieutenant-Colonel Arthur Bauchop, commander of the Otago Mounted Rifles. On the night of 6 August this was one of the foothills that had to be seized early in the New Zealand advance, to open up the route to the high ground of Chunuk Bair and Hill 971. The seizure of the foothills by the Mounted Rifles was one of the few successes of the August Offensive, and one of the most daring and well-executed feats of the entire campaign. The New Zealanders were aided by a cunning ruse. Every night for six weeks before the attack, British destroyers would shine their searchlights on the foothills and pound them with gunfire. The searchlights were then turned off. The pattern was repeated at the same time every night and the Turks gradually became used to the schedule, and would take shelter as soon as the searchlights came on.

On the night of 6 August, the Mounted Rifles crept forward under the cover of the barrage, and charged the hills the moment the searchlights were turned off. The Turks were caught completely off guard, and more than 100 were killed at the first post alone. At Bauchop's Hill the Turks resisted more strongly, but the Otago and Canterbury Mounted Rifles eventually pushed up the slope and captured the post.

> A Turkish machine gun on the spur leading to Walden's Point was responsible for many casualties, and this section of the attack was momentarily held up. 'Tap, tap, tap' went the gun, exacting a heavy toll; but a subaltern, named Davidson, who gained the ridge higher up, collected a few ardent spirits, and with fixed bayonets charged straight down the slope. The dirt thrown up by the angry bullets flicked in their faces as they ran straight for the gun. Down tumbled the subaltern, killed leading his men, but the remnants of the party fell upon the gun crew. The keen bayonets did their silent work, and the gun ceased its death-dealing tapping. (Waite, p. 211)

Colonel Bauchop was wounded during the assault and died four days later. He has no known grave and is commemorated on the Lone Pine Memorial.

Bauchop's Hill provides a vantage point to try and make some sense of the opening phase of the August advances. Walk behind the white building and climb onto its roof. Face east, towards the white memorials on the skyline, which mark the summit of Chunuk Bair. The hill to the left of Chunuk Bair is Hill Q, and the hill to the left of that is Hill 971 (marked by an antenna), with the bare slope of Abdel

Rahman Bair, the ridge the Australians were supposed to climb to reach the summit, leading to it.

The eroded hillock directly in front (below Chunuk Bair) is Little Table Top and the ridge behind it is Cheshire Ridge, which formed part of the left flank of the Anzac position after the failure of the August Offensive. To your right (south) are three ridge lines. The farthest on the skyline is Second Ridge at Anzac, extending from the sea to Chunuk Bair. The middle ridge is Rhododendron Ridge, the spur that the New Zealanders followed in their advance towards Chunuk. The prominent flat-topped hill on the nearer ridge, with its side washed away by erosion, is Table Top, the foothill captured by the Mounted Rifles immediately after Bauchop's on the night of 6 August.

The ground to your left (north) is broken by three gullies. The nearest gully is the southern fork of Aghyl Dere, the route taken by the Gurkhas in their attack on Hill Q. The next gully is the northern fork of Aghyl Dere, the valley that the Australian 4th Brigade was supposed to follow during its advance on Hill 971. The furthest fork is the valley it actually did follow, after taking a wrong turn when leaving a narrow pass known as Taylor's Gap. From that moment on it became known as Australia Valley. The flat-topped hill overlooking Australia Valley is Hill 80, and the next height to the right is Hill 100. These two hills and the ground behind them roughly mark the furthest position reached by the Australians in their failed attempt to capture Hill 971.

Drive back down the track, turn right at the main road and continue north (past the intersection with a road on your left). After 650 metres, turn right onto a track that leads to 7th Field Ambulance Cemetery [8]. The cemetery was begun

Taylor's Gap. More than 3,000 men of the Australian 4th Brigade had to squeeze through this narrow pass in single file during the night of 6 August 1915.

in September 1915 when men who died while being treated at the 7th Australian Field Ambulance were buried nearby. After the war several small cemeteries in the surrounding area were concentrated here and the cemetery grew to its current size of 640 graves. Of these, 276 are unidentified and there are special memorials commemorating 207 men known or believed to be buried here. Headstones commemorate 290 men from Britain, 68 from Australia and 20 from New Zealand. The cemetery is located in the ground between the August Offensive jumping off points and the later phases of the campaign, and the burials reflect this. You'll find many graves of men killed in the August Offensive (particularly of British soldiers killed in the Turkish counterattack at

Chunuk Bair on 10 August, Australians killed in the advance towards Hill 971 on 6–10 August and New Zealanders killed clearing the foothills on 6–7 August), but also during the attack on Hill 60 in late August and the period leading up to the evacuation, September to December.

A notable soldier buried here is Major Percy Overton of the Canterbury Mounted Rifles, commander of the left assaulting column on 6 August. Overton had scouted the ground before the attack, but on 6 August was convinced by a Greek guide to head inland via Taylor's Gap. This was a fatal decision that tied the column up for hours as it hacked its way through thick scrub in the narrow pass. Overton then compounded the problem by misjudging several important landmarks and directing his troops into the wrong valley during the advance on the heights. This mistake was the major contributing factor in the failure to capture Hill 971. Overton was shot and killed early on 7 August (grave II.A.5).

Buried nearby is Second Lieutenant Charles Pulling of the 13th Battalion, who had fought bravely during the Turkish attack at Quinn's Post on 29 May. During the advance on 7 August he was killed by fire from a Turkish field gun (grave II.C.4).

A late Australian burial is Private Frank Dyer of the 16th Battalion, who was killed on 9 December, just 11 days before the evacuation (Special Memorial A.7). Lieutenant Grant Michaelis was an Australian who served with the 1/2nd East Anglian Field Company, Royal Engineers. He was killed on 23 September (grave II.C.II).

OPTIONAL TOUR: Taylor's Gap

From 7th Field Ambulance Cemetery it is possible to follow in the footsteps of Monash's 4th Australian Brigade at the beginning of its journey into the Aghyl Dere valley and, most crucially, the point where they got lost. The return walk takes about an hour and involves a steep scramble up a hillside through the scrub.

Leave the cemetery and walk south across the fields for 250 metres (with the road on your right) until you reach the opening to a wide valley on your left. Follow the valley inland. You are now walking in the footsteps of the 4th Brigade during their disastrous shortcut on the night of 6 August. The plan called for the brigade to continue following the road north past the site of the modern 7th Field Ambulance Cemetery and then turn inland at the mouth of the Aghyl Dere valley. But the Greek guide escorting the column convinced its commander, Major Percy Overton, that a shortcut into the valley where you are now walking would save considerable time. Follow the valley inland for about 250 metres until the open fields give way to scrub. Climb the slope on the left of the valley and, after a short but tough climb, follow the height inland until you can look down over the valley to your right. The scrub-choked, narrow cutting below you is Taylor's Gap. Imagine the scene that played out here on 6 August 1915: 3,000 Australian troops, exhausted, sick and heavily laden, trying to squeeze through the narrow gap in single file in the pitch dark, their leaders urging them on, anxious to get the troops into their starting position for the attack on Hill 971 before dawn.

> As the troops climbed, the pass narrowed. The gully-bed, choked with prickly undergrowth, would permit only of movement in single file. Soon even that became almost impossible, and the pioneers of the 13th were accordingly sent forward to hack a passage. (Bean, Vol. II, p. 587)

The delays caused by the shortcut were fatal to the advance. Even if the brigade had not gotten lost in the later stages, the time spent hacking through Taylor's Gap destroyed any chance of them attacking Hill 971 before daybreak. This episode was typical of the frustrating failures so common at Gallipoli.

Follow the ridge further inland until you can look out on the valley at the head of Taylor's Gap. As the troops emerged from the gap, they were caught by Turkish fire from the ridge on your left, and casualties were heavy. Their advance was again delayed while the ridge was cleared. The leaders of the 4th Brigade, now hopelessly behind schedule, then sealed the brigade's fate. After clearing Taylor's Gap, they should have led the men into the valley and turned hard right into the northern fork of the Aghyl Dere. Instead, they went straight on, into Australia Valley and lost any chance of successfully attacking Hill 971. From where you are standing, Australia

Valley starts to the left of the red earth bank in the middle distance (to the north-east).

The brigade's advance that night through unfamiliar country was terrifying, and its encounters with the Turks were brutal.

> We charged 3 hills that night. On the first hill I bayoneted a Turk who was feigning death, with a few extra thrusts. He was an oldish man & on the first thrust which did not go right home he tried to get his revolver out at me, but failed . . . coming up the third hill, a gigantic Turk . . . grabbed me round the chest . . . he was a veritable Samson . . . [and] slowly began to crush the life out of me, I was almost gone when a mate of mine called Tippen came up and bayoneted him . . . We made sure of him then continued up the hill. Poor Tippen got shot just in front of their trench in the stomach with two bullets, he died groaning horribly. I killed his assailant however by giving him five rounds in the head. I . . . let him have it full in the face. It was unrecognisable. (Sergeant Harry Jackson, 13th Battalion, in Gammage, p. 97) [Sergeant Jackson later served on the Western Front and died of wounds as a prisoner of the Germans in August 1916. No record of a soldier named Tippen serving with the AIF can be found.]

To relive the difficulties of the 4th Brigade's advance first hand, climb down the slope and hack your way back

the way you have come along Taylor's Gap. But be warned
– it was tough going in 1915 and hasn't changed since.
Walk back to 7th Field Ambulance Cemetery.

Return to your car and continue north on the main road.
After 650 metres, you will pass a white memorial on a low hill
on the right. This is the Damakçilik Memorial [9], a Turkish
monument that commemorates the counterattack that drove
the Allies off Chunuk Bair and effectively ended the August
Offensive. It stands on the western end of Damakçilik Spur,
the ridge from which the Turks were firing on the Australians
as they emerged from Taylor's Gap. The inscription on the
memorial translates as:

Colonel Mustafa Kemal, commander of the Anafarta
[Anzac and Suvla] Group, ordered the 7th Division to
attack towards the Damakçilik Slope on 9 August 1915,
thus preventing the Anzac Corps from linking up with
the British 9th Army Corps and eliminating the threat to
Kocaçimen Tepe [Hill 971].

Damakçilik Spur was also the start line for the Anzac
attack on Hill 60 on 21 August (see below).

Continue north for 1.3 kilometres, until you reach the
intersection of the main road with a number of dirt tracks.
Follow the track heading south, signposted to Hill 60, for
650 metres (the track is passable in fine weather but may
only be suitable for four-wheel drives in the wet). Park next
to the cemetery at the top of the hill.

An Australian recruitment poster, most likely depicting the capture of Hill 60 in August 1915. *NSW Government, WA Gullick, Government Printer, Weston, Harry J, "We took the Hill, come and help us keep it", 1915, lithograph, 91.2x59cm, Australian War Memorial (ARTV00140)*

Hill 60 **[10]** is a low rise that, in August 1915, lay between the Allied fronts at Anzac and Suvla. While it remained in Turkish hands the two sectors could not be effectively linked, so in late August an attack was planned to wrest it from the Turks and consolidate the British line.

Hill 60 is a fairly inconspicuous bump – it is hardly worthy of being called a hill – but it completely dominates the surrounding plains. On 21 August a composite force of New Zealand, Australian and British soldiers left their

Hill 60 Cemetery

hard-won positions on Damakçilik Spur and charged at the hill. Turkish machine guns opened fire and casualties were heavy, but some men managed to claw their way up the slope and gain a foothold in the Turkish trenches. A panicked call for reinforcements went out and the Australian 18th Battalion was ordered into the attack on the morning of the 22nd. The 18th was part of the newly arrived 2nd Division and had only been at Gallipoli for three days. Even as it was ordered forward its men had no idea they were about to attack, and assumed they were simply being sent to garrison part of the front line. The 18th was sent through some scrub that formed a rough 'hedge' at the base of the hill, and despite their inexperience they fought their way onto the lower slopes. But the full weight of Turkish counterattacks descended on them, and over the next 24 hours the fighting was at close quarters and extremely brutal.

Again and again the Turks attacked, mad with fanaticism, shrieking at the top of their voices and calling on Allah. The merciless bombing continued and the trenches slowly became encumbered with dead. At last about 10.30 p.m., after the fight had lasted five hours, a crowd of Turks succeeded in entering the Rangers' trench near its northern extremity. This northern end was held by a small party of men who died where they stood. The remainder of the trench was, however, blocked and further progress by the enemy arrested. Still the fight raged and bombs and ammunition were running short, while the losses became so heavy. Fresh Turkish attacks kept coming on, and for every assailant that was struck down, two more sprang up in his place. (Captain Bryan Cooper, 5th Connaught Rangers, in Steel and Hart, p. 297)

After this fight, the Turks dubbed the hill Bomba Tepe (Bomb Hill), and the name was well chosen. The 18th Battalion lost more than 300 of the 750 men who went into battle. The Allies had gained a foothold on the southern slopes of the hill, but the Turks still held the rest and over the next week each side launched violent attacks that were met by a hail of machine-gun and rifle fire.

On 29 August the 9th and 10th Light Horse had been sent into the line and ordered to charge the Turkish positions on the crest. The light horsemen were in a bad way. The 10th was still recovering from the mauling it had taken at the Nek only three weeks before, but it managed to capture the Turkish trench and hold it against three ferocious attacks. Throughout the fighting Second Lieutenant Hugo Throssell was seen charging at the Turks and rallying his men, in spite of being wounded several times. Apparently he kept a smile on his face the whole time, and his men were greatly inspired by his 'fiery valour and witty sallies' (Wigmore, p. 49). Throssell refused to leave the line until the Turks were beaten back, and only sought treatment after a direct order from his commanding officer. He was so knocked around by grenade explosions that one of his brass 'Australia' badges had been smashed and driven into his shoulder. For his gallant display he received the VC, the only one awarded to a light horseman during the war.

Hugo Throssell was part of a distinguished family. His father George was the Western Australian premier in 1901. Hugo was working as a farmer when war broke out and he enlisted in October 1914. He was assigned to the 10th Light Horse and joined them at Gallipoli in August. He survived the attack at the Nek, but was so badly wounded in the fight at Hill 60 that he was sent to recover in England. In 1916 he was invalided back to Australia but lobbied to return to the front line, and eventually rejoined his unit in Palestine in 1917. He served there until the end of the war, being wounded again and joining the attack that captured Jerusalem in 1918.

After the war Throssell returned to farming in Western Australia, but never really recovered from his wounds or the grief of losing his brother during the war. On 19 November 1933 Hugo Throssell sat down on the verandah of his Greenmount property and shot himself. He was 49.

By the end of the attack in which Throssell won the VC, both sides were exhausted and the fighting petered out. The Allies contented themselves with the tenuous link they had forged with Suvla, and the lines wouldn't move for the rest of the campaign. The Allied advance at Gallipoli was over.

Hill 60 Cemetery was started soon after the fighting died down in August, and was greatly enlarged after the war when bodies were brought in from the nearby Norfolk Trench Cemetery and from isolated graves in the surrounding fields. Today it contains 788 burials, of which 712 are unidentified. Special memorials commemorate 34 men known or believed to be buried among them.

The most senior Australian commemorated here is Lieutenant-Colonel Carew Reynell, commander of the 9th Light Horse. In July he had led a counterattack against a group of Turks who had broken through the Australian lines at the Nek. On 28 August he led a small group of men to try to capture a Turkish trench on Hill 60 – his party disappeared into the gloom and never returned. Reynell's body and those of several other men from the group were later recovered from the trench among the bodies of dozens of Turks, but exactly how the Australians died remains unclear (Special Memorial 4). The body of Captain Alfred Jaffray was found near the colonel's, and he is also commemorated nearby (Special Memorial 27). Trooper James Wood was from Gloucester in New South Wales but served with the Wellington Mounted Rifles. He was killed on 27 August (Special Memorial 33).

The cemetery also contains the Hill 60 (New Zealand) Memorial, which records the names of 183 New Zealanders missing from the fighting here in August. Other New Zealand missing are commemorated at Lone Pine, Chunuk Bair and Twelve Tree Copse. Nearly all the men commemorated here served with the New Zealand Mounted Rifles, one of the toughest Anzac brigades, so Hill 60 has become a de facto memorial for the entire brigade.

One of the names on the memorial is Trooper Frank Clark of the Auckland Mounted Rifles, great uncle of former New Zealand Prime Minister Helen Clark. On 21 August he wrote:

> There are stray bullets flying everywhere and one stands a chance of 'stopping one' at any time. Our sergeant was standing in our trench yesterday and he got one in the right breast. The big guns from land and sea make an awful row and this is accompanied always with machine guns and rifle fire. We can hear the shells screaming overhead and shrapnel bursting all day long. (Quoted in Anzac Day speech given by Helen Clark, Rockefeller Centre, New York, 26/4/2009)

He was killed a week later.

Also commemorated on the memorial are Trooper Edward and Lance Corporal Henry Brittan, brothers serving with the Canterbury Mounted Rifles who were killed on 28 August. Also look out for the name of 56-year-old Reverend William Grant who, against all orders, began treating the wounded in the front line during the thick of the fighting. He was moving along the trench trying to reach some wounded Turks when he was shot and killed.

Five of the men named on the memorial were Australians serving with the New Zealanders: 18-year-old Trooper Murdock Campbell, Trooper James McMenamin, Trooper George Pinch, Trooper George Pugh and Trooper Eric Thompson.

Leave the cemetery and drive back along the access track. Note the rows of scrub on your left. These are the remains of the hedges through which the 18th Battalion attacked on 22 August. They moved from here, across the access track and up the slope towards the site of the cemetery.

Continue until you reach the intersection and follow the rough road heading north, signposted to Hill 10, Azmak and Green Hill Cemeteries. After 300 metres, turn left at a crossroads onto a rough dirt track, signposted to Lala Baba Cemetery. Follow this west for 1 kilometre, then turn right at an intersection. Turn left at a T-junction shortly afterwards. Follow this track west for 3 kilometres and park beside Lala Baba Cemetery [11]. Lala Baba is the hill north-east of the cemetery. Even before the Suvla landings it was prominent in the campaign. The hill offers views of the southern end of Anzac Cove and, after the landings on 25 April, the Turks built an observation post here and used it to direct artillery fire onto the Anzac positions. Before dawn on 2 May, a group of about 60 New Zealanders staged a daring raid on the observation post.

They crept in three groups up the side of Lala Baba. In a trench immediately below the crest they surprised twenty-one Turks asleep. These, on being disturbed, fired a few shots. Several were killed and 15 captured. The New Zealanders searched the hill. They found a machine-gun emplacement, blew up several huts, destroyed the telephone wire, and embarked before midday without interference from the enemy. (Bean, Vol. I, p. 566)

On the night of 6–7 August Lala Baba was the first height captured by British troops during the Suvla landing. The hill was attacked by the 6th Yorkshire Regiment, the first unit of Kitchener's New Army to go into action in the First World War. The Yorkshires were enthusiastic but inexperienced and they suffered extremely heavy casualties securing the hill. More than a third of the unit became casualties and all but two of its officers were killed or wounded. After the landing Lala Baba offered good protection from Turkish shells. Artillery batteries, stores, headquarters and hospitals were established in its shadow.

The cemetery sits on a low knoll known as Little Lala Baba, and was started after the war when several smaller cemeteries in the area were concentrated here. Isolated graves were also brought in from the surrounding fields. Today the cemetery contains 216 burials, of which 53 are unidentified. Special memorials record the names of 16 men known or believed to be buried among them. All the men buried here served with British units.

An inscription next to the gate records that 'Near this spot the IX Army Corps landed on the night of 6–7 August 1915.'

One notable grave belongs to Brigadier-General Paul Kenna VC, commander of the 3rd (Nottinghamshire and Derbyshire) Mounted Brigade. Kenna had served in the Sudan and at Omdurman in 1898 was awarded the VC for this act of gallantry:

On 2 September 1898, at the Battle of Omdurman, Sudan, when a major of the 21st Lancers was in danger, as his horse had been shot in the charge, Captain Kenna took the major up on his own horse, to a place of safety. After the charge Captain Kenna returned to help Lieutenant De Montmorency who was trying to recover the body of an officer who had been killed. (*London Gazette*, No. 27023, 15/11/1898)

On 21 August Kenna was killed by a sniper (grave II.A.1).

A number of very young soldiers are buried in Lala Baba, perhaps indicative of the wave of patriotism that drove many men to enlist in the New Army in 1915. Private Thomas Parkinson of the West Yorkshire Regiment was only 16 when he was killed on 7 August (grave II.D.4). Private Bruce Rae of the Essex Regiment was killed on 30 August aged 17. Private T. Downing of the South Wales Borderers was also 17, and he was also unlucky: he died on 19 December, the last day at Suvla. Private Angus Sutherland of the Lovat Scouts was the same age when he was killed on 11 October. There are also several graves of men aged 18 and 19.

After viewing the headstones, climb onto the back wall of the cemetery and face south. You are now looking directly across the plains that formed the heart of the British sector at Suvla. In the distance the ground at Anzac rises from Ari Burnu point to the heights of Hill 971. Anzac Cove is unfortunately all too easy to spot, thanks to the ugly scar of the cliff face gouged by bulldozers in 2005. An original Turkish trench cuts through the hillside a few metres in front of you.

The long sweep of beach directly in front of you is where the British first came ashore at Suvla on the night of 6–7 August. The beach was divided by an imaginary line into two sectors, B and C Beach, with C Beach closest to you (the concrete bunkers on the beach were built during the Second World War). On the night of 6 August 1915 infantry from the British 32nd and 33rd Brigades landed in three waves on both beaches. The planners had learned some valuable lessons from the landings of 25 April, and at Suvla abandoned the idea of landing the troops in open boats in favour of motorised landing craft known as 'beetles' (similar to the landing craft used so successfully on D-Day 29 years later). The tides were so favourable at Suvla that most of the beetles were able to pull directly in to the beach and drop their ramps on the sand – many of the troops landed without getting their feet wet. B and C Beaches were undefended and the only casualty as the troops came ashore was a sailor who was killed by a stray bullet.

> The run-in took less than 10 minutes. But how different from Anzac! The landing was a complete surprise. There was no opposition and not a single casualty. A few rockets were fired, and one or two rifle shots rang out in the darkness, but that was all. Our motor lighter grounded rather far out, making it necessary for the men to wade in about three feet of water. They made a poor showing – no dash and a certain amount of talking. Indeed a handful, who obviously had had the wind up, looked as if they were afraid to land. Petty Officer Main sang out and told them to get a move on. They went ashore after that. (Bush, p. 243)

From your vantage point it is obvious that Suvla is a natural amphitheatre, the flat plain dominated by a semicircle of hills, and how securing the high ground was vital as soon as the troops were ashore. But a strange malaise seemed to permeate through all levels of the Suvla force. The men were reluctant to move forward and their leaders were reluctant

GALLIPOLI: THE BATTLEFIELD GUIDE

to make them. Complicating things further, the landing plan didn't call for the men to charge straight at the high ground, but instead to advance north along the shore, circle around the Salt Lake and then move inland. This caused unnecessary confusion. Several battalions got lost and the schedule for the landing, so dependent on precise timing, went off the rails.

However, one thing the British had achieved was getting a large number of men ashore with light casualties. Major-General Hans Kannengiesser, the German officer who faced the New Zealanders in their advance on Chunuk Bair described the view of Suvla from the Anzac heights on the morning of 7 August:

> Suvla Bay lay full of ships. We counted ten transports, six warships and seven hospital ships. On land we saw a confused mass of troops like a disturbed ant-heap, and across the blinding white surface of the dried salt sea we saw a battery marching in a southerly direction. I saw English troops on the Lala Baba and, on the flat, in certain places, entrenching. Nowhere was there fighting in progress. (Kannengiesser, p. 205)

Had the men in this 'disturbed ant-heap' been ordered to advance on the hills rather than wasting time on the beach, the Gallipoli story may well have ended differently.

Return to your car and follow the rough track all the way back to the intersection with the main road. Turn left at the intersection and follow the road heading north. After 2 kilometres park beside Green Hill Cemetery [12]. Green Hill and the adjacent Chocolate Hill (on the other side of the road) lie roughly on the site of the final front line at Suvla. The hills were prominent landmarks from both the Suvla plain and the Anzac sector and a confusing assortment of names was applied to them. Officially the hills were known collectively as Yilghin Burnu (or sometimes Mastantepe) but to the troops at Anzac, the western hill with its dry scrub and brown earth was Chocolate Hill, and its scrub-covered cousin was Green Hill. Confusingly, the troops at Suvla also referred to several other hills as Green Hill, and when fire swept through here soon after the landing, the two hills (and several others) were sometimes referred to as Burnt Hill. Not until long after the evacuation was the issue resolved, with the two hills officially dubbed Chocolate and Green.

Immediately after the landing, the British troops should have been pushing towards these hills, and then on to the higher ground further east. But a chronic lack of decisive leadership meant that the battalions were simply marched from one place to another without any cohesive plan or, worse still, ordered to dig in near the beach. By 7 August almost 20,000 British troops were ashore, and they faced less than 1,500 Turks who had little artillery and no machine guns. But the British commanders dithered and their numerical advantage soon fizzled as Turkish reinforcements poured onto the heights. Eventually the British began inching timidly inland.

In their retirement the Turks had artfully concealed a whole army of snipers in a thousand and one different places. What an effect these pests had on our progress is best described by the casualties which were mostly the victims of some fiendish snipers. Already we have lost the majority of our commissioned officers, to say nothing

of a good few NCOs and men. Parties would go out –
voluntarily – in search of these fiends, but all to no good,
for generally they would return with the majority of them
missing – victims to the snipers. (Private G. Handford, 8th
Duke of Wellington's Regiment, in Steel and Hart, p. 258)

Chocolate Hill was supposed to have been captured before
dawn on 7 August, but it was not until after dark that it was
finally taken. Even then, the British could have exploited
their success by pushing further inland to the prominent W
Hills, but instead they dug in. Some battalions were even
ordered back to the beach. Green Hill was captured at about
the same time, and both positions formed part of the new
British front line. Stores, dumps, hospitals and wells were
built on the leeward side of Chocolate Hill, and the remains
of trenches still snake through the scrub on its western and
southern slopes.

Green Hill Cemetery was built after the war when remains
were brought in from smaller cemeteries in the area or the
nearby battlefields of August 1915. It is one of the largest
Commonwealth cemeteries at Gallipoli and contains 2,971
burials. Considering the tough fighting in the area, it is
not surprising that 2,472 of these are unidentified. The
ubiquitous special memorials record the names of men
known or believed to be buried in the cemetery.

Notable burials include Lieutenant William Niven of the
Berkshire Yeomanry, the father of actor David Niven (Special
Memorial F.10). He was reported missing during the advance
on Scimitar Hill on 21 August, but a letter to Mrs Niven later
advised that Lieutenant Niven had been shot in the head
(and rather optimistically added that this 'does not exclude

the possibility of your husband having been taken prisoner by the Turks'). (Lord, p. 4)

David Niven wrote about his father in his autobiography *The Moon's a Balloon*:

> My sister and I were swapping cigarette cards on an old tree trunk in the paddock when a red-eyed maid came and told us our mother wanted to see us and that we were not to stay too long. After a rather incoherent interview with my mother, who displayed a telegram and tried to explain what 'missing' meant, we returned to the swapping of cigarette cards and resumed our perusal of endless trains lumbering along a distant embankment loaded with guns and cheering young men. (Niven, p. 12)

Also buried here is Private Harry Salter of the 6th Battalion, East Lancashire Regiment, who was executed on 11 December (grave I.G.26). A comrade described his unfortunate end:

> This youth barely 19 years of age was shot by twelve of his comrades for taking 'French Leave' from his Regiment on two occasions and attaching himself to the Anzacs. Not by any stretch of imagination could my comrades or I catalogue it as desertion, as 'twas impossible to desert from the Peninsula even had he so desired. I was one of the firing party; he was marched from a dugout about 80 yards away, to a kind of disused quarry where the final scene was enacted. A clergyman preceded the doomed youth and his escort, reading prayers for the dying (the mockery of it all). The doomed youth was

tied up to a stake, his grave already dug. His last request was, 'Don't blindfold me.' What followed I'll leave to the reader's imagination, in other words, I'll pull the pall of oblivion over the ghastly scene – if I can ever forget it. I only wish that the distinguished person who signed the death warrant, without taking into consideration extenuating circumstances, would leave his comfortable island residence and visit the men under his command who were going through it. Well, we'd have a bit more faith in our leaders and confidence in ourselves. (Private Edward Roe, in Downham, p. 131)

Lieutenant-Colonel Henry Moore was the commander of the 6th Battalion, East Yorkshire Regiment. On 9 August he and a small group of his men were surrounded by the Turks during an attack on Tekketepe Hill. They surrendered, but as Moore went to sit down a Turk stepped forward and bayoneted him (grave II.B.13). This prompted a killing spree among the Turks and several other men were bayoneted, including Major Francis Brunner of the Royal Engineers (Special Memorial A.8). Two other British officers were lined up to be shot, but a Turkish officer intervened and ordered that the survivors be marched to the rear as prisoners. They spent the rest of the war in the squalor of a Turkish POW camp.

In 1971 former Sergeant George Dale returned to Gallipoli for the first time since the war and visited the grave of Gunner Charles Chrisp of the Royal Field Artillery (grave II.C.15).

The most impressive cemeteries were Lancashire Landing (Helles), Lone Pine (Anzac) and Green Hill (Suvla). In the latter I paused over a name. For there lies quiet, decent

Charlie – moved from where we laid him below Chocolate Hill. Charlie never knew our brave new world of strikes and demos. He missed the Slump, another World War, and several cold ones. Charlie never watched 'telly' nor saw an honest 'bob' become five new pence. All that trouble and strife he missed. Ah, but life is sweet. Rest in peace, old pal. (Bush, p. 131)

Green Hill is one of the few Gallipoli cemeteries that is laid out in a similar design to the Commonwealth cemeteries on the Western Front. The large freestanding Stone of Remembrance in particular invites comparisons to the cemeteries in France and Belgium. And like many of those cemeteries, Green Hill should be a lovely place to visit, to

A large Turkish shell explodes in the water beside the pier built by the Royal Australian Bridging Train, Suvla. AWM P01326.006

stand in isolation and ponder the glorious deeds of the fallen. But it isn't. Even on warm days a cool breeze can spring up from nowhere, and the whispering of the pines seems sinister. Even the graves themselves seem to have something to hide. The weathered inscriptions are slowly fading, and soon the dead really will become nameless. There's no glory to be found at Suvla.

Leave the cemetery, continue driving north for 2 kilometres and turn left at an intersection. Follow this track roughly west for just over 2 kilometres, and turn left on a minor track towards Hill 10 Cemetery [13]. The cemetery is 100 metres along the track on your left.

Hill 10 was a Turkish forward strongpoint that was intended to be captured soon after the landing. But confusion during the landing at nearby A Beach caused so many delays that the Turks had abandoned the hill by the time the British arrived. Once the Suvla beachhead was secure, Hill 10 became an artillery battery position.

Hill 10 Cemetery was created after the war when six small cemeteries in the immediate area were closed and isolated graves were moved from the surrounding fields. Today the cemetery contains 699 burials, of which 150 are unidentified. Special memorials commemorate men known or believed to be buried in the cemetery.

The most senior soldier buried here is Lieutenant-Colonel Harry Welstead, commander of the 9th Battalion, Lancashire Fusiliers. Prior to the First World War he had led a distinguished career through several wars and retired from the Army in 1908. He was recalled in 1915 and landed with his battalion at A Beach in the early hours of 7 August. He was wounded by a sniper soon after coming ashore and later in the day was shot a second time and killed. His headstone incorrectly records his date of death as 17 August (grave V.D.1).

There are three Australians commemorated in this cemetery. Chief Petty Officer Edward Perkins served with the Royal Australian Naval Bridging Train, a unit that was sent to Suvla to build piers and harbour facilities soon after the British landing. On 9 August it constructed its first pier at Suvla, and the British began using it to evacuate their wounded within five minutes of its completion. The Bridging Train lost more than 60 men at Gallipoli, but only four of these were killed. The others were wounded or evacuated due to injuries or illness. Perkins is the only member of the unit buried on the peninsula, and was the last to be killed when his dugout received a direct hit from a Turkish shell on 6 September (Special Memorial 47).

Lance Corporal Herbert Peters served with the 8th Australian Light Horse. He had survived the disastrous charge at the Nek on 7 August, and later in the month was sent to Suvla as a scout attached to the British 161st Brigade. He was killed by shrapnel fire at Jephson's Post on 30 August.

Second Corporal Hubert Govett was born in Geelong and studied at Geelong College. After school he moved to England to study engineering and joined the Royal Engineers in 1914. He was killed on 19 December during the evacuation, and was one of the last men to die at Suvla (grave I.I.7).

Look out for graves from the Newfoundland Regiment, a famous unit that served briefly at Suvla before transferring to the Western Front and being all but wiped out on the first day of the battle of the Somme, 1 July 1916. Also pause at the grave of Lieutenant Leslie Osborne of the 9th

Battalion, Lancashire Fusiliers, who died on 7 August. His inscription reads 'Lt. W. J. Osborne (brother) wounded same day. Died on 9th. Buried at sea.' The brother in question was Second Lieutenant William Osborne, who served in the same battalion and is commemorated on the Helles Memorial.

Continue driving south past the cemetery all the way to the end of the road. Turn right and drive until you reach a beach. In 1915 the channel on your left was known as the Cut and drained the Salt Lake into Suvla Bay. On the night of the Suvla landing, British troops came ashore all along the sandbar south of the Cut. The Turks had good observation of this area, and blasted the troops with high explosive and shrapnel shells from the moment they came ashore. This was also a happy hunting ground for snipers, who picked off officers and men as they moved between Lala Baba and Hill 10. It was near here that the Bridging Train built their pier that was used to remove wounded to hospital ships.

The sweeping white beach in front of you is A Beach [14], another of the landing beaches on the night of 6–7 August 1915. The navy had grave concerns about landing troops here, due to the rocky shoals that choke much of Suvla Bay. Their fears were brushed aside, but turned out to be well-founded, and the landing at A Beach was a shambles. Things started badly when the ships carrying the troops anchored too far south, and then got a whole lot worse when the landing craft started grounding on the shoals before they got anywhere near the beach.

> When we got about 150 yards from the shore the lighter
> ran aground and we were stuck. We could not get out
> and walk ashore because it was too deep and of course

impossible to swim with all our equipment on, rifles, etc. Eventually we got help from a beach party about 2.30, and they took us in small rowing boats to within 40 yards of the shore, where we got out and walked ashore. Then it was quite a job collecting the company. (Captain Montie Carlisle, 8th Northumberland Fusiliers, in Steel and Hart, p. 252)

Many of the troops who were supposed to land on A Beach actually came ashore south of the Cut, and their orders to capture Hill 10 were almost impossible to carry out in the dark. Other landing craft were forced to veer north to dodge the shoals and ended up landing their troops in the narrow coves on the north side of the bay. From the moment they came ashore the troops were badly disorganised and the attack was soon hours behind schedule. The rusted remains of a landing boat lie on the water's edge a couple of hundred metres along the sand.

Drive back past Hill 10 Cemetery and turn left at the intersection. Continue west for 3 kilometres and turn left towards a small cottage (the first of three in a group just before the point). Park near the cottage and follow a track past the outhouse towards the rocky headland on your left. Scale the headland and look down on the rusty skeleton of a 'beetle' landing craft in the water below [15]. This beetle had brought troops ashore during the landing in August but then sunk during the winter storms that lashed the peninsula in November. It was abandoned at the evacuation. The beetles were revolutionary.

They were bullet-proof, could carry 500 men each, and had long ramps at the bows down which the troops could disembark in a matter of minutes when the boats grounded. This removed the nightmare of April 25th; this time there would be not pathetic gaggles of rowing-boats toiling ashore under fire, but fast, armoured landing-craft, capable of landing a division in a few hours. The arrival of the lighters at Mudros in July – at once called 'beetles' by the sailors on account of long projecting arms of the landing ramps, which resembled antennae, and their black paint – removed G.H.Q.'s greatest anxiety about a new landing. (James, p. 239)

The design of landing craft has not changed much since 1915.

The wreck of the beetle lies in the small cove known during the war as West Beach. From August to December 1915 the shoreline teemed with men. This was Suvla Base, a network of offices, workshops, stores, ammunition dumps, mess halls, post offices, reservoirs, piers and dugouts, all connected by light tram. Some rough concrete foundations are all that remain of the base today. A cove further east is known as Kangaroo Beach, named in honour of the Royal Naval Bridging Train, the only Australian unit to be stationed continuously at Suvla.

Return to your car, continue driving west on the track and park beside the white Turkish monument on the point. This is Suvla Point, the northern finger of Suvla Bay [16]. The Turkish memorial is sited to commemorate the evacuation of Suvla on 20 December (the last British troops to leave the sector embarked at the nearby Suvla Base). The inscription translates as:

Troops disembarking from a 'beetle' landing craft at Suvla Base. AWM H10334

The wreck of a 'beetle' near Suvla Point

> The enemy forces which landed at Ari Burnu [Anzac Cove] on the morning of 25 April 1915 and Anafarta Harbour [Suvla Bay] on the night of 6/7 August 1915 realised after months of bloody fighting that they could not break through the Turkish defences on the Gallipoli Peninsula. They therefore abandoned these fronts on 20 December.

The high ground behind the memorial offers excellent views of the west coast of the peninsula, all the way to Helles. On a clear day the twin humps of Achi Baba and the Kilitbahir Plateau can be spotted in the distance.

Drive back along the track, past the turn-off to Hill 10 Cemetery. After another 400 metres, turn left at a fork signposted to Azmak Cemetery. Follow a rough and narrow track for 1.3 kilometres and veer right at an intersection. Follow an even rougher and narrower track for 400 metres and park beside the cemetery (this track may be impassable in poor weather).

Azmak Cemetery **[17]** is named after the Azmak Dere, the often dry watercourse that runs past it. The cemetery was built after the war in the shadow of the Kirectepe Ridge, the long sweep of hills that forms the dress circle to the amphitheatre of Suvla Bay. Thousands of British men were killed in a series of bloody advances to capture the ridge, and the cemetery stands on roughly the line of the furthest British advance. Today it contains 1,074 graves, mostly brought in when 16 small cemeteries in the surrounding area were closed. Unidentified graves number 684, and the usual special memorials record the names of men known or believed to be buried in the cemetery. Twelve graves and three special memorials commemorate men from the

Newfoundland Regiment. All the other graves and special memorials record the names of men from Britain. This is the northernmost and probably least visited Allied cemetery at Gallipoli. When Australian historian John Laffin visited it in the 1970s, a Commonwealth War Graves gardener told him that he was the first visitor the gardener had seen in three years. Visitor numbers have improved since then, but not by much. In October 2008 I visited the cemetery with Kenan Çelik, who leads daily tours of the peninsula, and this was only his second visit to Azmak for the year.

This is the final resting place of 114 men from the Sandringham Company of the 1/5th Norfolks. These men were volunteers from the Royal Estate at Sandringham, the household staff of King George V's Norfolk residence. On 12 August they joined a general advance across the Suvla plain and were last seen advancing well ahead of their comrades. A wounded sergeant from a neighbouring company described their dire predicament:

[The Turks] had surrounded us. Most of the battalion went through the Turkish line unknowingly. We were intermixed with the Turks, they were scattered around us. My only hope was to get back, I was finished as far as Gallipoli was concerned. It was then that I noticed the Sandringham Platoon, part of E Company, about 40 men, under Sergeant Aymers sheltering in a barn. The scrub was on fire, the snipers, more or less surrounded by the Turks, a hopeless position for them to be in. They were undoubtedly killed or wounded where they were. (Sergeant Tom Williamson, 1/5th Norfolk Regiment, in Steel and Hart, p. 280)

Sergeant Williamson's assessment was unfortunately accurate. Not a single man of the 180 or so Sandringhams who went into battle ever returned. In 1919 the remains of many of them were found in a mass grave and reinterred in Azmak Cemetery. One of the burial party later claimed that every man he buried had been shot in the head, giving weight to rumours that the Turks had shot the Sandringhams after taking them prisoner, but this account is difficult to substantiate. The strange circumstances of their disappearance and their personal connection to the King lent an air of mystery to the Sandringhams' demise that has persisted to this day. Theories abound about their unfortunate end, from a heroic last stand to abduction by aliens. The mass grave indicates that the Sandringhams were disposed of by the Turks, either after a fight to the death or while trying to surrender. The only conclusion that should be drawn from this is that Gallipoli was a savage conflict and prisoners were rarely taken by either side. Only two of the men exhumed from the mass grave could be identified. The rest, including the battalion commander Lieutenant-Colonel Sir Horace Proctor-Beauchamp, are recorded on the Helles Memorial. The last advance of the Sandringham Company took place in the valley in front of the cemetery.

A senior officer commemorated at Azmak Cemetery is Lieutenant-Colonel Edward Chapman, commander of the 6th Yorkshire Regiment, who was killed in the attack on Lala Baba in the opening hours of the landing. How he came to lie here, 4 kilometres from where he was killed, is a mystery (Special Memorial 5).

Major Algernon Wood had landed with the 1st Battalion, Essex Regiment at Helles on 25 April and fought with the unit for the next six months. He had been awarded the Distinguished Service Order for his outstanding leadership in October. Two weeks later he was standing in a trench at Suvla watching an aeroplane fly overhead when he was hit in the throat by a sniper. Witnesses reported that he made a gesture of 'extreme annoyance' and muttered 'Damn it!' before collapsing into the arms of his sergeant-major and dying. He was well liked by his men, and one of them wrote in his diary 'Cruel, cruel luck! At least Algy Wood, one of the most gallant officers of that pick of Divisions – the 29th – should have been spared' (grave II.A.14). (Gillam, diary entry 3/11/1915)

Captain Arthur Preston of the 6th Battalion, Royal Dublin Fusiliers is remembered with the proud inscription 'Sans Touche', French for 'Unblemished'. He was killed on 15 August (Special Memorial 50).

Because Azmak Cemetery is isolated and rarely visited, the headstones in this cemetery have not been maintained as well as the ones in the more 'popular' cemeteries at Anzac and Helles. Some of the inscriptions have faded almost beyond recognition. In stark contrast to the noble words inscribed on the special memorials, at Azmak the glory of the dead is in danger of being blotted out.

Return along the access track for 400 metres and turn right at the intersection. Follow an extremely rough, winding track as it climbs the ridge. Ignore the intersection with several other tracks and after about 6 kilometres (15 minutes' driving), you will reach a memorial. This is the Turkish Jandarma Memorial [18] and when it comes to Gallipoli this is as isolated as it gets. The memorial commemorates the three companies from the Gelibolu and Bursa Jandarma (military

The Turkish Jandarma Memorial, probably the most isolated at Gallipoli.

police) who stopped an attack by two British Brigades near here in the opening days of the Suvla campaign. A tower made from painted artillery shells overlooks a cemetery containing the lavender-covered graves of Jandarma killed in the area. There is a famous photograph of Kemal Atatürk taken here during the closing stages of the campaign. On clear days the memorial offers a spectacular view northwards across the Gulf of Saros to the northern Turkish provinces and the Greek shore.

The memorial is not far from two features known to the British as Kidney Hill and the Pimple. An attack here by the 31st and 162nd Brigades on 15 August almost broke through the Turkish line and threatened the entire left flank, but it was stopped by a determined Turkish defence. A stretcher-bearer arrived to ghastly scenes:

That hillside was a shambles: evidently there had been fierce hand to hand fighting there a few hours ago, rifles, kits, water-bottles, khaki, Turkish tunics and headgear were strewn everywhere among the scrub. While we were following a phantom-like voice we came suddenly on a half dug trench which an RAMC officer had made into a combined mortuary and first-aid station; there we set furiously to work sorting out the dead from the living; there reeled among us out of the darkness an officer raving, 'My men have taken that bloody hill but they're dying of thirst.' He passed on and we continued our ghastly work. (Private Harold Thomas, 3rd East Anglian Field Ambulance, in Steel and Hart, p. 285)

Soon after the battle the Turks counterattacked, and the British were driven back to their start lines. The fighting reverted to trench warfare and the line would not advance again for the rest of the campaign.

Drive back down the track, turn right at the intersection that leads to Azmak Cemetery and return along the track for 1.3 kilometres. Turn left at the intersection and follow this track for 3.5 kilometres back towards Green Hill Cemetery. Just before the cemetery, turn left at an intersection. As you drive along this stretch of road, you are following the route of a murderous advance made by the British 29th Division on 21 August on a feature known as Scimitar Hill, the largest Allied attack of the Gallipoli campaign. You will reach the hill after driving 1.3 kilometres. Park beside the three memorials on the summit [19]. Scimitar Hill had been captured by the British on 8 August, but in one of the farcical episodes common at Gallipoli, the occupying troops were ordered to relinquish the hill and return to the beach.

By August 1915 the 29th Division was famous, having made the original landing at Helles on 25 April. Private Ernest Lye of the 8th Duke of Wellington's Regiment, a newly arrived unit, watched the 29th marching to their start line at Chocolate Hill before the attack:

> From early morning, troops were to be seen going towards Chocolate Hill in batches of threes and fours. We were told they were men of the 29th Division who made the landing at Cape Helles. We looked at them with something akin to awe, as they were 'old sweats', while we were just 'rookies' and we had read about their deeds before leaving England. (Steel and Hart, p. 289)

Of course after the mauling they had received in the great battles at Helles, most of the original men of the 29th Division were long gone, replaced by new recruits not much more experienced than Lye.

The 29th's advance on Scimitar Hill was to be made in conjunction with a British attack on the nearby W Hills (named after the w-shaped patterns formed by scrub on their southern slopes) and the Anzac attack at Hill 60 (see page 294).

The attack was a disaster. Launched in broad daylight and without adequate artillery support, the men of the 29th were mown down by machine-gun and artillery fire. They eventually clawed their way to the summit, but were driven off with heavy loss. Thousands of them were killed or wounded within a few metres of where you are standing.

At 3pm the Battalion shoved off 700 strong. The furthest any got was 500 yards and none came back from there. They all got mown down by machine-gun fire. We lost 9 officers and 400 men. The Turks shelled us very heavily and the whole country, which is covered with gorse, caught fire. This split up the attack and parties got cut up. Many of our wounded were burnt alive and it was as nasty a sight as I ever want to see. (Captain Guy Nightingale, 1st Royal Munster Fusiliers, in Steel and Hart, p. 29)

The only two Victoria Crosses awarded at Suvla were both earned by acts of bravery at Scimitar Hill. On 9 August Captain Percy Hansen of the 6th Lincolnshires rescued six wounded men after the scrub on Scimitar Hill caught fire. On 21 August Trooper Frederick Potts of the 1/1st Berkshire Yeomanry rescued a wounded comrade even though he had been shot in the thigh. He eventually dragged his mate back over 500 metres of fire-swept ground using a shovel as a sled.

The three memorials on the hill were built by the Turks to commemorate their victory here. The inscription on the southern monument records how the British landed at Suvla on 6–7 August and advanced as far as Scimitar Hill in an effort to surround the Turkish garrison at Anzac (a rather curious interpretation of the Allied plan). The middle panel details the defence of the Turkish forces between 9 and 12 August, and their success at driving the British back to Chocolate Hill. The third panel records how the Turks defeated the attack of 21 and 22 August, and how the British suffered almost 20,000 casualties compared to the Turks' 8,000, one of the few occasions at Gallipoli where the ledger of death favoured the Turks.

Winston Churchill neatly summed up the final attack on Scimitar Hill: 'It was the largest action fought upon the Peninsula, and it was destined to be the last.' (Holt, p. 228) No major British offensives took place at Gallipoli again.

Return to your car and continue for 3 kilometres. Turn right at the T-junction at the end of the road. After 250 metres, park beside the two large guns on the right of the road.

These two 210-millimetre Krupp guns, one damaged and one mostly intact, are known as the Anafarta Guns [20]. They shelled the British positions at Anzac and Suvla for much of the campaign. This may well be the battery frequently referred to by the Allies as 'Anafarta Annie'.

The first thing one hears is a noise like the rending of linen, or perhaps the rush of steam describes it better. This gets louder and louder, and then, as the projectile nears the end of its journey, one hears a whine, half-whistle, half-scream, and then the explosion. If it is very near there is an acrid smell in the air. One's feelings are difficult to describe. You duck your head instinctively – you feel absolutely helpless, wondering where the thing will burst, and as you hear the explosion a quick wave of feeling sweeps over you as you murmur, 'Thank Heaven, not this time!' (Unidentified officer, in James, p. 156)

The guns were manufactured in 1876 and still point due west towards the Suvla front of the British, as they did at the end of the campaign in December 1915. The gun pits have been reconstructed.

Continue along the road for 2.5 kilometres and turn right at a crossroads, on the outskirts of the village of Büyük

One of two heavy Turkish guns near the town of Anafarta

Anafarta. Soon after the intersection there is a Turkish cemetery on both sides of the road [21], which contains the graves of several Turkish officers killed at Suvla in August. The cemetery is neglected and many of the headstones are worn and unreadable.

Continue driving westwards for 3.5 kilometres, ignoring the intersection with several minor tracks, until you reach the road that brought you to Suvla at the start of the tour. This is the conclusion of the Suvla tour.

Follow the road south to reach the Anzac sector.

The Asian Shore

The 'Other' Side of the Dardanelles – Çanakkale to Kumkale

The story of Gallipoli centres around the Gallipoli peninsula. This was the key geographic feature that needed to be captured to secure the Dardanelles, at least according to the British plan. But one aspect of the plan was never fully explained. Even if the British managed to capture the entire peninsula and knock out the guns on the European shore of the Dardanelles, how were they going to deal with the hundreds of guns that lined the Asian shore? It seems fairly obvious that the straits would not be safe for shipping until both shores had been captured, but a land campaign on the Asian shore was never really part of the Allied plan. It's yet another of the big questions that the Allies never quite got around to answering.

Today the Asian shore of the Dardanelles does not hold nearly as many attractions for Australian and New Zealand battlefield visitors as the peninsula. The area is quite developed and there are few memorials on this side of the straits. It's an interesting area for exploring the naval battles, however, and is near Ancient Troy, one of the must-see sites in the Gallipoli area. From the Asian side of the Dardanelles, the magnitude of the obstacles faced by the Allies becomes truly apparent. For a complete description of the naval battle, see the Helles and Krithia tour.

The Asian Shore Tour

This tour of the Asian side of the Dardanelles begins in Çanakkale and leads south along the coast, visiting key sites associated with the naval campaign. The route is about 70 kilometres long and takes about half a day. The tour ends near the site of Ancient Troy, so this is a natural add-on if you would like to make a day of it.

Begin the tour at the Cimenlik Fort Naval Museum [1] on the Çanakkale waterfront, south of the two ferry ports (follow signs to the Deniz Müzesi). As is the case with many Turkish museums, it often closes for a lunch break at midday. The museum is on the site of the former headquarters that controlled the defences of the straits. An impressive collection of artefacts, uniforms, equipment, relics and artworks relating to the Gallipoli campaign is displayed over two floors. Outside, mine rails lead to the water's edge. During the naval battle of 18 March, the Turks launched floating mines from these rails which drifted down the Dardanelles towards the

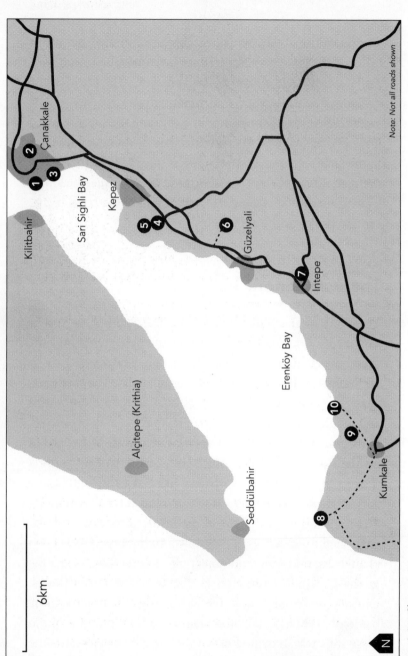

The Asian Shore tour

6km

N

Note: Not all roads shown

Kilitbahir

Çanakkale

Sari Sighli Bay

Kepez

Alçitepe (Krithia)

Seddülbahir

Güzelyali

Intepe

Erenköy Bay

Kumkale

1
2
3
4
5
6
7
8
9
10

An assortment of sea mines outside the Cimenlik Fort Naval Museum in Çanakkale. The rails were used during the campaign to launch drifting mines towards the Allied fleet.

Allied fleet. A floating mine may have been responsible for sinking the French battleship *Bouvet*. There is no doubt the ship was sunk by a mine, but it is unclear whether the mine was part of a static minefield or was drifting in the current. Deactivated mines and a large range of artillery guns are displayed in the park outside the museum.

From the water's edge there are good views across the straits to the rear of the Anzac sector, with the New Zealand and Turkish memorials on Chunuk Bair standing out on the skyline. Two Turkish memorials built into hillsides can also be seen from here. On the opposite shore is the Dur Yolcu Memorial above the village of Kilitbahir. It features a depiction of a Turkish soldier and a stanza from a famous poem by Necmettin Halil Onan which is commonly translated as:

A replica of the minelayer *Nusrat*. During the naval battle in March 1915, a secret minefield laid by the *Nusrat* sank three Allied ships and changed the course of the Gallipoli campaign.

Traveller halt!
The soil you tread
Once witnessed the end of an era.

This translation is misleading. As far as modern Turkey is concerned the Gallipoli campaign marked the beginning of a proud new era, not the lamentable end of an old one. The complete poem urges that visitors to Gallipoli remember the huge number of Turkish soldiers who gave their lives to preserve the freedom of Turkey, so the last line is probably more accurately translated as 'The soil on which you tread once witnessed the death of a generation.'

To your right on the near shore is a hillside memorial above Çanakkale, which simply commemorates the date of the great naval victory over the Allied fleet: '18 Mart [March] 1915.'

Near the mine rails is a replica of the Turkish minelayer *Nusrat*, the real hero of the naval battle. Early in March the Turks had noticed the Allied fleet was using the wide Erenköy Bay as a turning circle, so on 8 March the *Nusrat* crept out and laid a line of mines parallel to the shore in the bay. On 18 March the fleet sailed right into them and several ships were lost. Inside the *Nusrat* replica is an excellent small museum of the naval battles, which includes an interesting assortment of relics from ships that fought in the Dardanelles in 1915.

The bulk of the museum is housed in the imposing Cimenlik Fort, which was originally built by the Ottomans in 1462, a decade after its sister fort at Kilitbahir. In 1915 the fort bristled with heavy guns and it came under ferocious fire from the Allied fleet. A large shell most likely fired from the HMS *Queen Elizabeth* is embedded in the wall opposite the entrance to the keep.

Return to the main ferry port and drive east on the main road through the centre of town. You will soon pass Republic Square on the left, which features an imposing statue of Kemal Atatürk. Continue through two intersections until you reach a T-junction at the end of the road. Turn left, then turn immediately hard left and park.

On the left is the Chanak Consular Cemetery [2], an intriguing cemetery with a number of interesting tales to tell. (The cemetery is often locked. To have it opened, contact the Commonwealth War Graves Office in Çanakkale on +90 286 217 1010.) The cemetery was begun in the mid 1800s when the British established a consulate in Çanakkale, and civilians associated with the consulate were buried here. The first military burials were made during the Crimean War (1854–56) when Britain and Turkey were allies and British soldiers were stationed at Gallipoli.

The cemetery was used again in 1915 to bury the bodies of three sailors from the Royal Navy who were killed when their submarine, *E-15*, was run aground and sunk in the Dardanelles in April. The submarine's commander, Lieutenant-Commander Theo Brodie (grave I.A.3), was killed when a shell struck the conning tower and two of his men, Able Seaman Fred Cornish and Engine Room Artificer Ernest Hindman (graves I.C.6 and I.A.7) died later of wounds. Six other men were killed when chlorine gas filled the submarine after her batteries were exposed to sea water. The rest of the crew was taken prisoner, and six of them later died in an Istanbul POW camp. *E-15* still lies in 8 metres of water near Kephez Point.

Two Australian soldiers and 11 New Zealanders also lie here, all of whom died while serving in the occupation forces after the Armistice. The cemetery also contains Russian nurses, Russian labourers and two Greek soldiers.

Buried nearby is Basil Bourne, an Australian veteran who had served in the 3rd Field Artillery Brigade at Gallipoli and on the Western Front. In 1965, aged 82, he joined a group of British veterans on a pilgrimage to Gallipoli. His travelling companions called him 'the Anzac'.

We crossed the Narrows to Eceabat and went by coaches across to Anzac Cove. It was noticed by those in his coach that the Anzac became more and more excited as we approached. The guide with the first coach, in which was the Anzac, arranged for the stop to be a little beyond the Cove for traffic reasons. Friends noted that the Anzac worried over this; he would rather have stopped right at the Cove. But it was only a short walk back to the Cove and the party left the coach at the Anzac cemetery by the roadside. The Anzac stepped forward too but fell immediately. Later on, when we had time to adjust ourselves to the situation, it was agreed that this was a fine way to go out. (*The Gallipolian*, December 1969)

Return the way you came on the main road towards the ferry port, and turn left in the direction of 18 Mart University at the first set of traffic lights. Follow this road for 1.5 kilometres, cross a bridge and turn right at the third

Members of the Australian 7th Light Horse Regiment inspect a 14-inch gun in a Turkish fort, December 1918. The light horsemen were sent to garrison the Gallipoli peninsula immediately after the end of the war, and to begin construction work on the Commonwealth cemeteries from the campaign. AWM P05460.003

set of traffic lights, in front of the Çanakkale Archaeological Museum (well worth a visit if time allows). At the end of this road on the shore of the straits is the Hamidiye Fort [3]. Park where you have a view of the fort. It is well preserved but sits on military ground so cannot be visited. The fort was the largest and most heavily armed fort on the Dardanelles. The American Ambassador to the Ottoman Empire, Henry Morgenthau, toured the Dardanelles forts in March 1915, just before the naval battle.

> The location of Anadolu Hamidié seemed ideal. It stands right at the water's edge, and consists of ten guns, every one completely sweeping the Dardanelles. Walking upon the parapet, I had a clear view of the strait, and Kumkale, at the entrance, about fifteen miles away, stood out. No warships could enter these waters without immediately coming within complete sight of her gunners. This was the most important fortification in the Dardanelles. Throughout the whole bombardment it attracted more of the Allied fire than any other position, and it inflicted at least 60 percent of all the damage that was done to the attacking ships. (Morgenthau, p. 147)

How Morgenthau came up with these figures is anyone's guess, but he was right about it being a major target for the guns of the Royal Navy. It was blasted throughout the naval battle and its 10 guns were badly damaged.

Return to the main road and turn right at the traffic lights. Continue for 1.7 kilometres and veer right at an intersection towards Kepez (do not take the road to Izmir). As you follow this road, the water to your right is Sari Sighli

Bay, where British submarine *B-11* attacked Turkish shipping in December 1914. After dodging several lines of mines and coming under heavy fire from shore batteries and Turkish ships, *B-11* fired two torpedoes which sank the Turkish ironclad *Mesudiye*. The submarine then successfully evaded capture and returned to port. Her commander, Lieutenant Norman Holbrook, received the first VC ever awarded to a submariner. For more information about this exploit, see the *Mesudiye* Gun (page 155) in the Second Ridge tour.

Drive on for 4 kilometres, through a crossroads and across a creek. A kilometre after the creek, turn right at the white memorial topped by a shell, and a sign to 18 Mart 1915 Hasan Mevsuf Şehitliği.

After a short distance, park next to a cemetery on the right. This is the Hasan-Mevsuf Memorial and Cemetery [4], the final resting place of six Turkish gunners who were killed during the naval battle of 18 March. Their commander, Lieutenant Hasan, had engaged the British warships during attacks in February 1915 from the nearby Dardanos Battery. The British fired more than 4,000 shells at the battery, but its gun crews kept firing throughout. A few days later a senior Turkish general visited the battery to commend Hasan for his good work.

He was a little fellow, with jet-black hair, black eyes, extremely modest and almost shrinking in the presence of these great generals. 'It is men like you of whom great heroes are made,' said General Djevad. He asked Hassan to describe the attack and the way it had been met. The embarrassed Lieutenant quickly told his story, though he was moved almost to tears by the appreciation of his

A Turkish memorial commemorating Lieutenant Hasan, commander of the Dardanos Battery, who was killed during the naval battle of March 1915.

exalted chiefs. 'There is a great future for you in the army,' said General Djevad, as we parted from this hero. Poor Hassan's 'future' came two days afterwards when the Allied fleet made its greatest attack. One of the shells struck his dugout, which caved in, killing the young man. Yet his behaviour on the day I visited his battery showed that he regarded the praise of his general sufficient compensation for all that he had suffered or all that he might suffer. (Morgenthau, p. 149)

Today Hasan lies alongside his men in the small and peaceful cemetery.

After visiting the cemetery, continue driving uphill and park next to the Dardanos Battery [5]. Its five guns are still in situ, although in various states of disrepair. In 1915 they were enclosed in metal turrets. The battery sits on top of Kephez Point and offers sweeping views of the Dardanelles. The British submarine *E-15* ran aground on the shore immediately below the battery (see page 332). The white communications tower on the hilltop is the one you saw from the opposite side of the straits early in the Helles and Krithia tour.

The site of the battery is named after Dardanus, who in Greek mythology was the son of Zeus and Electra. According to legend he founded the city of Dardania on nearby Mount Ida, and his descendants later founded the city of Troy. Another prominent mythological figure associated with the

The Dardanos Battery

site is Helle, twin sister of Phrixus, who was rescued along with her brother from certain death at the hands of their stepmother by a flying ram with a fleece made of gold. Helle fell off the ram and drowned in the sea, but Phrixus reached safety and was taken in by King Aeetes. In gratitude Phrixus slaughtered the ram and gave Aeetes the golden fleece, which Aeetes hung from an oak guarded by a dragon, where it remained until taken by Jason. The straits where Helle drowned were named the Hellespont, and are now known by a contraction of the words Dardanus and Helle: the Dardanelles. Helles is also named after Helle.

Return to the main road, turn right and drive for 3 kilometres until the road joins the highway. Continue for 2 kilometres and turn left at a sign to Turgutreis Tabyasi. Follow a rough road for 2 kilometres uphill and park next to a gun battery.

This is the *Turget Reis* battery [6], made up of guns which originally formed part of the armament of the Turkish cruisers *Barbaros Hayrettin* and *Turget Reis*. On 25 April 1915, both ships were stationed in the Dardanelles and shelled the landing beaches at Anzac from across the peninsula. The guns were removed from the ships in the 1930s and installed in this battery to bolster the Dardanelles defences in the lead-up to the Second World War. By this time the guns were close to obsolete – the ships from which they came had been constructed in 1891 – but as a shore-based battery they would have been a formidable defensive weapon for the straits. Fortunately they were not needed. Turkey remained neutral during the Second World War and the Dardanelles were not threatened. The battery is one of the most impressive remaining on the Asian shore. The guns

The *Turget Reis* Battery

are housed in metal cupolas and stare menacingly over the straits. There is another battery higher up the hill.

Return to the main road and turn left. After 3 kilometres, turn left to Intepe and follow the road until you reach a cemetery on the right. This is the Erenköy Turkish Cemetery and Memorial [7], which commemorates Lieutenant Ali Riza of the Turkish Air Force. On 30 November 1915 Ali Riza was piloting an Albatros AK1 near the Anzac line at Gaba Tepe when he was engaged by a French Farman aircraft. After a brief dogfight the French plane hurtled to the ground in flames after its fuel tank was hit. This was the first Turkish aerial victory of the war.

The cemetery is near the site of the Erenköy Battery which was typical of the dozens of mobile batteries that dotted the Dardanelles shore and caused havoc with the Allied fleet in March 1915. The Erenköy Battery was commanded by a

German officer, Lieutenant-Colonel Heinrich Wehrle, who constantly kept his guns on the move to confuse Allied air reconnaissance and to deny the Allied warships a clear target. During the 18 March naval battle, Wehrle's battery maintained a devastating fire on the Allied fleet and scored 139 direct hits from the 1,600 rounds fired. HMS *Ocean* and HMS *Irresistible* were particularly badly damaged by Wehrle's well-directed fire, and both eventually sank. In response the fleet fired thousands of shells at Wherle's position, but his guns were so well concealed that he lost only 14 men.

The cemetery offers sweeping views over the entrance to the Dardanelles and the scene of the naval battle. The British Memorial at Cape Helles, the Turkish Memorial at Morto Bay and the low hump of Achi Baba can all be seen clearly.

Return to the main road and turn left. Continue for 2 kilometres and turn right to Kumkale. Follow the road for 6 kilometres until you reach the village. Drive straight through (noting the smashed guns from the campaign in the centre of town) and continue into the fields beyond the village, following a cobbled road. After crossing several bridges, drive straight through a crossroads and turn left at the intersection with a farm track, always following the cobbled road. Veer right soon after and stop at a red Forbidden Zone sign.

From this position you have a good view of the ruins of Kumkale Fort near the shore [8]. The fort is in a restricted military area, so do not go further than the Forbidden Zone sign and be careful about taking photographs in this area.

In 1915 Kumkale Fort was surrounded by Kumkale village. The village was abandoned after the war and 'New' Kumkale was built 4 kilometres inland. The fort had been

Rusted relics from the campaign in the village of Kumkale

A warning sign on the road to Kumkale Fort

built in the 17th century by Sultan Mehmet IV and in 1915 it was the primary defence on the Asian side of the mouth of the straits. As such it was a major target for British guns and was almost completely destroyed by shellfire in the naval battles of March and in the bombardments before the landings of 25 April. A correspondent for the *New York Times* described the bombardment that descended on the fort and village on the day of the landing:

> About 2:30 o'clock the bombardment became still more intense. The great warships sent forth shattering salvos of sound, and new fires could be seen at several points along the Asiatic shore. The pall of smoke grew thicker, and for a time obscured my vision up the strait. An English warship, evidently one of the Lord Nelson type, and the *Jeanne d'Arc* kept up a continuous cannonade. Bright flashes of flame spurted from the mouths of the guns, and the roars which followed were almost deafening at times. Several shots from the French warship seemed directed against the batteries in and near Kum Kale, and one shell I saw took a huge mass of masonry and rock out of the cliffside there. (*New York Times*, 30/4/1915)

The actions at Kumkale really are the forgotten chapters of the Gallipoli story. On the day of the landing the plan called for the French to launch a diversionary landing at Kumkale and then evacuate to Helles once the British had secured the beachheads. On 25 April a force of French Senegalese troops came ashore here at about 9.30 a.m. and cleared the fort and village within 90 minutes. Turkish reinforcements arrived and boxed the French in, and fierce fighting persisted until the French withdrew to Helles on 27 April, taking 800 Turkish prisoners with them.

Kumkale had also been prominent in the early stages of the campaign. On 26 February a group of British marines landed here with orders to destroy the guns in the fort. The Turks saw the marines come ashore and defended fiercely. Several marines were hit and it seemed likely that they would have to withdraw. At that moment a solitary figure in a white uniform was seen 'strolling around under heavy rifle fire, like a sparrow enjoying a bath from a garden hose' (Snelling, p. 20) and planting explosives on the Turkish guns. The man was identified as Lieutenant-Commander Eric Robinson of the Royal Navy, the leader of the party. After the guns were destroyed, Robinson oversaw the loading of the wounded into boats and the marines successfully evacuated the beach. He then directed gunfire from the fleet onto the Turkish positions, inflicting heavy casualties on the Turks. Robinson was awarded the VC, the first given for an action on land at Gallipoli. Robinson served in the navy for the remainder of the war, then in the Russian Civil War. During the Second World War he was promoted to Admiral and commanded convoys across the Atlantic. He died in 1965 and was buried in his local churchyard in Langrish, Hampshire. His grave was unmarked until the Commonwealth War Graves Commission erected a headstone over it in 1998.

Commander Robinson's heroic action occurred on the low mound to the left of the fort. According to ancient legend, the mound is the tomb of Achilles, hero of the Trojan War. Achilles is supposedly buried alongside his inseparable comrade Patroclus, who was killed by the Trojans. Alexander

HMS *Cornwallis* fires a salvo at Turkish positions during the campaign.
AWM H10388

The Intepe Battery Cemetery is the resting place of Turks killed fighting the French in the early days of the campaign.

the Great purportedly visited the tomb in about 334BC, during his rampage across Asia.

Return along the cobbled road for 250 metres, turn right onto a dirt road and veer right at a fork. You will soon pass some Second World War bunkers on a small hill on the left of the road. Park nearby and climb up beside the bunkers. From here you have outstanding views across the Dardanelles to Cape Helles and directly into the rear of V Beach. This position demonstrates how the Turkish gunners on the Asian shore completely dominated the Allied positions at Helles. From here they could lob shells into the British positions from directly behind them.

Drive back to Kumkale and turn left in the village on a road signposted to the Kumkale Şehitliği. Follow the road out of the village until you reach a cemetery on the left. This is the Intepe Battery Cemetery [9], the final resting place of Turks killed in the battle with the French at Kumkale and members of a nearby battery who were killed by British shells in the days following the landing. The gate is decorated with painted shells and cannonballs, a common feature of Turkish military cemeteries.

Continue along the road to the coast, and you will reach the Çakaltepe Battery [10] next to a picturesque small harbour. The incongruous scenes of fishermen peacefully unloading their catch in the shadow of a rusted artillery gun neatly sum up the Gallipoli of today. Life goes on, but the war is never far away.

This is the end of The Asian Shore tour. Return to Kumkale, turn left and drive back to the main road. Turn right to visit Ancient Troy, or left to return to Çanakkale.

Gallipoli Timeline

1914

1 August   As a result of rapidly escalating tensions following the assassination of Archduke Franz Ferdinand, heir to the Austro-Hungarian throne, Germany declares war on Russia.

2 August   Turkey signs a secret alliance with Germany against Russia, its old rival.

3 August   France rejects Germany's ultimatum to remain neutral. Germany declares war on France.

4 August   Germany invades neutral Belgium, prompting Britain to declare war on Germany. British dominions, including Australia and New Zealand, pledge their support and begin raising troops.

10 August   Germany delivers two battle cruisers to the Turkish navy, the *Goeben* and the *Breslau*, to replace two Turkish warships that had been confiscated by Britain.

15 August   The Australian Imperial Force is formed under the command of Major-General William Bridges.

27 September	Turkey closes the Dardanelles, the narrow straits that separate Asia from Europe and control access to the Black Sea. Russia is now cut off from its allies, France and Britain.
28 October	Relations between Turkey and Russia deteriorate. The Turkish navy bombards Russian ports in the Black Sea.
1 November	The first contingent of Australian and New Zealand troops departs from Albany, Western Australia, bound for Egypt. The troops are intended to garrison the Suez Canal and guard it against Turkish attack.
2 November	Russia declares war on Turkey.
3 November	British and French warships bombard the Turkish forts guarding the entrance to the Dardanelles. A shell hits the magazine in the Seddülbahir fort, causing a massive explosion and killing 86 Turks.
4 November	Britain declares war on Turkey and immediately begins looking at options to capture the Dardanelles and open up a supply route to Russia.
3 December	The first contingent of Australian and New Zealand troops arrives in Egypt.
13 December	British submarine *B-11* sinks the Turkish battleship *Mesudiye* in the straits. *B-11*'s commander, Lieutenant Norman Holbrook, becomes the first submariner to receive the VC.
21 December	Lieutenant-General William Birdwood arrives in Egypt to take command of the newly formed Australian and New Zealand Army Corps (ANZAC). Initially the corps comprises two divisions, the 1st Australian Division (under the command of Major-General William Bridges) and the New Zealand and Australian Division (under the command of Major-General Alexander Godley). In August 1915 the corps is supplemented by the arrival of the 2nd Australian Division at Gallipoli.

1915

13 January   The British War Council approves a plan put forward by
a young Winston Churchill, First Lord of the Admiralty, to
force the Dardanelles using a fleet of obsolete battleships.
The plan is to subdue the forts that guard the straits, clear
the waterway of mines and steam through the Sea of
Marmara to Constantinople (now Istanbul).

February   The Royal Navy launches several preliminary attacks against
the forts guarding the straits.

12 March   Lord Kitchener, the Secretary of State for War, appoints
General Sir Ian Hamilton commander of the newly formed
Mediterranean Expeditionary Force, the branch of the
British Army that will be responsible for military actions
against Turkey. Originally dubbed the Constantinople
Expeditionary Force, it is hastily renamed in order to
disguise its intentions from the Turks.

18 March   Dardanelles Naval Battle. A British and French fleet of 18
warships attempts to force the straits. Although successful
in damaging the forts on both shores of the Dardanelles,
many of the ships are damaged by Turkish mobile artillery
batteries. Disaster strikes when three ships are sunk by a
hidden minefield and several others are badly damaged.
The Royal Navy retreats and refuses to attempt to force the
straits again unless supported by the army.

22 March   Hamilton agrees to land troops on the Gallipoli peninsula.
His plan calls for British, French, Australian and New
Zealand infantry to land on several beaches and capture the
forts that guard the Dardanelles. The navy will then steam
through the straits and capture Constantinople.

25 April	Gallipoli Landings. British forces land at five beaches at Cape Helles, on the southern toe of the Gallipoli peninsula, while Australian and New Zealand troops land at Anzac Cove and the French stage a diversionary landing on the Asian shore at Kumkale. The Royal Naval Division also stages a diversion at Bulair, in the far north of the peninsula. At first the Turkish defenders are caught off guard, but soon rally and send reinforcements streaming towards the beaches. The Allies secure the beachheads but are unable to advance inland. Fifteen Victoria Crosses are awarded to British soldiers for gallantry during the landings and in the days immediately after.
26 April	The Australian submarine *AE-2* becomes the first Allied ship to pass through the Dardanelles and reach the Sea of Marmara. Her instructions are to 'generally run amok' as a diversion to support the landings. After five days she suffers trim problems and surfaces uncontrollably in front of a Turkish ship. After receiving three direct hits to her engine room, her crew abandons ship and scuttles the sub. All crew members survive, but three later die as prisoners of the Turks. *AE-2*'s brief incursion in the straits gives heart to the beleaguered troops who have come ashore and helps silence murmurings that the peninsula should be evacuated.
28 April	First Battle of Krithia. British and French troops try to advance at Helles and capture the village of Krithia and Achi Baba hill. The attack is repulsed at a cost of more than 3,000 casualties.
30 April – 1 May	Lance Corporal Walter Parker of the Royal Naval Division wins the first VC at Anzac.
4 May	An Australian party under Major Ray Leane raids the Gaba Tepe promontory south of Anzac. They are beaten off by heavy fire and lose 25 men.
6–8 May	Second Battle of Krithia. British, French, Australian and New Zealand troops attack Krithia and Achi Baba. They make some ground, but lose more than 6,000 men in three days' fighting.

13 May	HMS *Goliath* sunk by a Turkish torpedo boat in Morto Bay, Helles.
15 May	Major-General William Bridges, commander of the AIF, is mortally wounded by a sniper in Monash Valley. Three days later he dies on a hospital ship.
19 May	Almost 50,000 Turkish troops launch suicidal attacks along most of the Anzac front. They are mown down by machine-gun and rifle fire and lose 10,000 men without capturing a single Anzac trench.
19 May	Corporal Albert Jacka wins Australia's first VC of the war at Courtney's Post.
24 May	A formal truce is held at Anzac to bury the decomposing bodies in no-man's-land. Anzac and Turkish soldiers fraternise.
25 May	HMS *Triumph* sunk by a German submarine off Anzac.
27 May	HMS *Majestic* torpedoed and sunk off W Beach at Helles.
4 June	Third Battle of Krithia. British and French troops advance against Krithia and Achi Baba again, gaining little ground and losing more than 6,000 men.
4–5 July	The Turks attack in force at Helles. They fail to capture the British line and lose more than 6,000 men. A request for a truce to bury the dead is refused by British commanders.
12–13 July	British attack at Helles pushes the line slightly forward but costs 4,000 men.
6 August	August Offensive begins. Buoyed by the arrival of three divisions of reinforcements, the Allies launch a major attack against Turkish positions throughout the peninsula. Diversionary attacks at Anzac and Helles distract the Turks from the main assault, a flanking manoeuvre north of Anzac against the Sari Bair Range. Five British brigades also stage a new landing at Suvla Bay.

6–13 August	British troops launch a diversionary attack at Helles that achieves little but results in more than 3,500 casualties.
6–9 August	Battle of Lone Pine. The Australian 1st Brigade attacks the strong Turkish positions at Lone Pine, as a diversion from the advance taking place on Sari Bair. The Australians take the Turkish trenches in the first hour, but then struggle to hold them through some of the most vicious close-quarter fighting of the campaign. After four days the new positions are secure, but the Australians have lost 2,000 men. Seven Victoria Crosses are awarded to Australians during the battle.
6–7 August	Suvla Landing. The British IX Army Corps lands at Suvla Bay under the cover of darkness. The sector is only lightly defended but confusion among the landing troops and ineffective leadership leads to delays and missed opportunities. The vital high ground is not attacked and the troops dig in near the beach.
6 August	After the foothills north of Anzac have been cleared by the New Zealand Mounted Rifles, two columns of Anzac and British troops advance on Hill 971, Hill Q and Chunuk Bair, the three prominent heights on the Sari Bair Range.
7 August	Chunuk Bair. After a lengthy delay, the New Zealand Infantry Brigade launches an attack on the heights of Chunuk Bair but is beaten back with heavy loss.
7 August	Charge at the Nek. The 8th and 10th Australian Light Horse Regiments launch suicidal attacks against the Turkish trenches at the Nek, a narrow saddle on the left of the Anzac line. The attack is intended to support the New Zealand advance on Chunuk Bair, but the failure of the New Zealand attack means the light horsemen must advance on their own, and more than 350 of them are killed or wounded as they attack in four waves.
8 August	The New Zealanders attack Chunuk Bair again and gain a tenuous hold on the crest.

9 August   Fighting intensifies on the heights of Sari Bair. The Australian 4th Brigade under General John Monash gets lost in its advance on Hill 971 and suffers heavy casualties from Turkish machine guns. A Gurkha attack on Hill Q briefly succeeds but is then broken up by friendly artillery fire. The New Zealanders on Chunuk Bair face ferocious counterattacks from the Turks and lose most of their men. At Suvla the British defer attacking the heights, in spite of reports that Turkish reinforcements will soon arrive.

10 August   The exhausted New Zealanders are relieved by British units at Chunuk Bair. The Turks, commanded by Mustafa Kemal (later Kemal Atatürk), launch a massive counterattack that overwhelms the British defenders and drives them off the hill. At Suvla, the British belatedly advance on the heights but are beaten back by Turkish reinforcements who have arrived 30 minutes earlier. With the Turks on the high ground, Suvla becomes a siege.

15 August   Sir Frederick Stopford, the bumbling commander of the Suvla force, is sacked.

21–29 August   The Allies attempt to link the Anzac and Suvla sectors by launching attacks on Scimitar Hill and Hill 60. The attack on Scimitar Hill is the largest launched by the British at Gallipoli, but is shattered under murderous Turkish fire. The scrub on the hillside catches fire and many wounded men are burnt to death. At Hill 60, the Anzacs launch a brave but costly attack which gives them a toehold on the hill. Over the next week both sides attack relentlessly and the Anzacs eventually secure most of the hill. Second Lieutenant Hugo Throssell of the 10th Australian Light Horse wins the VC on 29 August.

19 September   The Newfoundland Regiment arrives as reinforcements at Suvla Bay. Although seeing little action at Gallipoli, the regiment would be decimated less than a year later on the first day of the Battle of the Somme in France.

15 October	General Sir Ian Hamilton is sacked as commander of the Mediterranean Expeditionary Force. He is replaced by General Sir Charles Munro, who announces that Gallipoli should be evacuated soon after he arrives. Winston Churchill would later say, 'He came, he saw, he capitulated.'
15 November	Lord Kitchener visits Gallipoli and determines that further operations on the peninsula are unlikely to succeed. A week later he recommends evacuation.
27 November	A furious blizzard envelopes the peninsula. It lasts for three days and floods the trench systems of both sides. Hundreds of men drown or die of exposure. This is the final straw that convinces the Allies that Gallipoli will be untenable during the winter.
7 December	The British Cabinet gives the official order to evacuate Anzac and Suvla. The front at Helles will be maintained for the time being.
18 December	The evacuation of Anzac and Suvla begins.
20 December	The last troops leave Anzac and Suvla before dawn.
28 December	Cabinet orders the evacuation of Helles.

1916

1 January	French troops evacuate Helles.
7 January	British evacuation of Helles begins. Heavy Turkish fire rains down on the British lines and it appears the Turks are about to attack. No attack comes.
9 January	The last British troops evacuate Helles. The Gallipoli campaign is over.

Who's Who at Gallipoli

Name	Unit/role	Historical notes
Allanson, Major Cecil	Commander, 1/6th Gurkha Rifles	Led the Gurkhas in an attack on Hill 971 during the August Offensive. They briefly held the summit but were hit by friendly artillery fire and forced to retreat.
Antill, Lieutenant-Colonel John	Brigade major, 3rd Australian Light Horse Brigade	As acting commander of the 3rd Light Horse Brigade, he gave the order for the charge at the Nek to continue, even after the first wave had been wiped out by Turkish fire.
Ashmead-Bartlett, Ellis	British war correspondent	His early reports about the Anzac landing were partly responsible for the birth of the Anzac legend. Later he was a vocal critic of the campaign.

Name	Unit/role	Historical notes
Aspinall, Captain Cecil	General Headquarters	Staff officer during the Gallipoli campaign. After the war (as Aspinall-Oglander) he became the British official historian.
Asquith, Herbert	British prime minister	His support for the Gallipoli debacle contributed to his political downfall in 1916.
Atatürk, Mustafa Kemal	Commander, Turkish 19th Division and XVI Corps	Credited as the saviour of Turkey during the Gallipoli campaign. His decisive leadership during the landings and the August Offensive was vital in halting the Allied attacks, although other Turkish and German commanders also played important roles. After the war he founded the Turkish Republic and became its first president. He remains the most revered leader in modern Turkish history. 'Atatürk' means 'Father of the Turks'.
Baldwin, Brigadier-General Anthony	Commander, British 38th Brigade	Commanded British troops at the Farm during the attack on Chunuk Bair during the August Offensive. He was killed during the Turkish counterattack on 10 August and is commemorated on the Helles Memorial.
Bassett, Lance Corporal Cyril, VC	New Zealand Divisional Signal Company	Awarded the VC for laying and maintaining telephone lines during the attack on Chunuk Bair, 7 August. He was the only New Zealander to win the VC at Gallipoli.

Name	Unit/role	Historical notes
Bauchop, Lieutenant-Colonel Arthur	Commander, Otago Mounted Rifles	Led his regiment in an attack on the outposts north of Anzac at the beginning of the August Offensive. He was killed in the capture of Bauchop's Hill and is commemorated on the Lone Pine Memorial.
Bean, Charles	Australian official war correspondent	The person most responsible for the birth of the Anzac legend. He landed at Anzac Cove on 25 April and served throughout the Gallipoli campaign and the remainder of the war on the Western Front. In 1919 he returned to Gallipoli as the leader of the Australian Historical Mission, and answered many questions still remaining about the campaign. After the war he wrote and edited the Australian *Official History* and founded the Australian War Memorial.
Bell, Gertrude	British writer and archaeologist	Carried on a long affair with Lieutenant-Colonel Charles Doughty-Wylie, a distinguished British Army officer. After he was killed at Gallipoli, a mysterious woman visited his grave. It is unknown whether it was Bell or his wife Lilian.

Name	Unit/role	Historical notes
Birdwood, Lieutenant-General William	Commander, Australian and New Zealand Army Corps	The much-admired commander of the Australians and New Zealanders at Gallipoli was the man who planned the landings at Anzac and the most important components of the August Offensive. Both attacks went badly, and Birdwood probably came out of the campaign looking better than he should have. He later commanded the Australians on the Western Front.
Blackburn, Private Arthur	10th Battalion, AIF	On the day of the landing he and a companion advanced further than any other Australian in the campaign, reaching the inland slopes of Scrubby Knoll. In 1916 he won the VC at Pozieres in France.
Blamey, Major Thomas	General Staff, 1st Division, AIF	Served as a staff officer to General Bridges. In 1950 he became Australia's first and only field marshal.
Bolton, Lieutenant-Colonel William	Commander, 8th Battalion, AIF	Bolton's Ridge, the high ground above Shell Green, is named after him. The 8th Battalion held the ridge in the days after the landing.
Braund, Lieutenant-Colonel George	Commander, 2nd Battalion, AIF	Braund's Hill, in the centre of the Anzac sector, is named after him.

Name	Unit/role	Historical notes
Bridges, Major-General William	Commander, Australian Imperial Force and 1st Division, AIF	Founder of the Australian Imperial Force. His division was the first ashore at Gallipoli and in the opening weeks of the campaign he led from the front, often with a complete disregard for his own safety. He was shot by a sniper in Monash Valley on 15 May and died on a hospital ship three days later. His body was returned to Australia and buried at the military college at Duntroon – the only body of an Australian soldier to be repatriated during the war.
Brooke, Rupert	British poet	Early in the war he penned idealistic poems about glory and sacrifice. In 1914 he enlisted in the Royal Naval Division and died of blood poisoning two days before the Gallipoli landings, probably as the result of a mosquito bite. Brooke's innocent sonnets are often seen as the antithesis of later, more gritty and realistic war poetry by the likes of Wilfred Owen and Siegfried Sassoon.
Burton, Corporal Alexander, VC	7th Battalion, AIF	Awarded a posthumous VC for gallantry during the fighting at Lone Pine on 9 August.
Carden, Vice Admiral Sackville	Royal Navy	Commander of the British fleet during the attacks on the Dardanelles forts in February and early March.

Name	Unit/role	Historical notes
Casey, Major Richard	1st Division Headquarters	At Gallipoli he served as aide-de-camp to General Bridges and was standing beside him when he was shot. After the war he had a distinguished political career and became Governor-General of Australia in 1965.
Chauvel, Lieutenant-Colonel Harry	Commander, 1st Light Horse Brigade	At Gallipoli he commanded his brigade from May until September, when he was promoted to divisional commander. He later led the light horse in Palestine and in 1917 was given command of the Desert Mounted Corps, becoming Australia's highest ranking soldier of the war.
Churchill, Winston	First Lord of the Admiralty	One of the chief architects of the Gallipoli campaign. The failure of his plan to capture the Dardanelles by naval attack alone led directly to the land campaign. After Gallipoli was evacuated, Churchill bore much of the blame for the fiasco, and eventually resigned from parliament to command a battalion on the Western Front. During the Second World War he became the most beloved prime minister in British history.
Clarke, Lieutenant-Colonel Lancelot	Commander, 12th Battalion, AIF	Landed with his battalion on the first morning and led them in a climb up to Second Ridge near the Sphinx. He was killed later in the morning at the Nek.

Name	Unit/role	Historical notes
Courtney, Lieutenant-Colonel Richard	Commander, 14th Battalion, AIF	Courtney's Post at Anzac is named after him. Men from his battalion consolidated this position on 27 April.
Cox, Brigadier-General Vaughan	Commander, 29th Indian Infantry Brigade	Commanded the left assaulting column of Australians and Gurkhas in the attack on Hill 971 during the August Offensive.
d'Amande, General Albert	Commander, Corps Expéditionnaire d'Orient	Commander of the French forces at Gallipoli.
Davies, Lieutenant-General Sir Francis	Commander, British VIII Corps	Assumed command at Helles in August when Hunter-Weston fell ill.
de Lisle, Major-General Beauvoir	Commander, British 29th Division	Assumed command of the 29th Division at Helles in June, and later took over command of Suvla when General Stopford was sacked.
de Robeck, Vice Admiral John	Royal Navy	Succeeded Admiral Carden as commander of the Allied fleet and led the naval attack on the Dardanelles forts on 18 March.
Dix, Commander Charles	Royal Navy	Commanded the landing of the covering force at Anzac on 25 April. After hitting the beach, he famously declared: 'Tell the Colonel that the damn fools have taken us a mile too far north!'

Name	Unit/role	Historical notes
Doughty-Wylie, Lieutenant-Colonel Charles, VC	General Headquarters	Awarded a posthumous VC for gallantry during the landings at V Beach, Helles and during the capture of Seddülbahir village the following day.
Dunstan, Corporal William, VC	7th Battalion, AIF	Awarded the VC for gallantry during the fighting at Lone Pine on 9 August.
Elliott, Lieutenant-Colonel Harold 'Pompey'	Commander, 7th Battalion, AIF	Landed with his battalion at Anzac on 25 April and was shot in the foot the same day. After Gallipoli he commanded the 15th Brigade on the Western Front.
Enver Pasha	Turkish Minister of War	One of the Young Turks who led the Ottoman Empire during the First World War.
Essad Pasha	Turkish General	Commander of Turkish forces in the Anzac sector.
Fisher, John	First Sea Lord	As a senior member of the British War Cabinet, he gave his support to the Gallipoli plan while secretly working to undermine it.

Name	Unit/role	Historical notes
Freyburg, Lieutenant-Commander Bernard	Hood Battalion, Royal Naval Division	Responsible for a one-man diversionary landing at Bulair on 25 April. After Freyburg had swum ashore and lit beacons on the beach, the Turks held reserve troops in the Bulair area in anticipation of a British landing (which never came). Freyburg later won the VC on the Western Front and served as Governor-General of New Zealand from 1946–52.
Godley, Major-General Alexander	Commander, New Zealand Expeditionary Force and New Zealand and Australian Division	Founded the New Zealand Expeditionary Force at the beginning of the war and later commanded the New Zealand and Australian Division at Gallipoli. Godley lacked imagination and was loathed by his men. He commanded the ill-fated attack on the Sari Bair Range during the August Offensive.
Hamilton, General Sir Ian	Commander-in-Chief, Mediterranean Expeditionary Force	Commander of the Commonwealth forces at Gallipoli. Hamilton was a fine thinker, but was not able to impose his authority on his subordinates. His subservience to Lord Kitchener meant that he was afraid to ask for the tools he needed to get the job done. After overseeing one disaster after another at Gallipoli, he was unceremoniously dumped as commander in October.

Name	Unit/role	Historical notes
Hamilton, Private John, VC	3rd Battalion, AIF	Awarded the VC for gallantry during the attack at Lone Pine on 9 August.
Hammersley, Major-General Frederick	Commander, British 11th Division	Commander of the first troops ashore at Suvla. His ineffective leadership during the first few days of the Suvla campaign greatly contributed to its failure. He was sacked on 15 August.
Harper, Trooper Gresley and Private Wilfred	10th Australian Light Horse	Brothers who were killed in the charge at the Nek on 7 August. Wilfred was last seen 'running forward like a schoolboy in a foot-race', and became the inspiration for the character of Archy Hamilton in Peter Weir's 1981 film, *Gallipoli*.
Herbert, Captain Aubrey	British writer and diplomat	Served as an intelligence officer at Anzac, and penned some of the most insightful accounts of the campaign ever written.
Hunter-Weston, Major-General Aylmer	Commander, British 29th Division and VIII Corps	Commanded the British forces at Helles and oversaw a series of costly and futile attacks early in the campaign. His leadership improved as time went on, but he was evacuated sick in August and never returned.
Idriess, Trooper Ion	5th Australian Light Horse	Australian author who served at Gallipoli and wrote prolifically about his experiences during the campaign.

Name	Unit/role	Historical notes
Jacka, Lance Corporal Albert, VC	14th Battalion, AIF	Awarded Australia's first VC of the war for gallantry at Courtney's Post on 19 May.
James, Robert Rhodes	British historian	Author of *Gallipoli*, one of the most influential histories of the campaign.
Johnston, Colonel Francis	Commander, New Zealand Infantry Brigade	Commanded his New Zealand troops with varying degrees of incompetence, especially during the attack on Chunuk Bair in August. Mentally frail and not well liked by his men, his dithering during the advance led to fatal delays.
Johnston, Colonel George	Commander, 2nd Australian Field Artillery Brigade	Early in the campaign it was said that his guns did a good job 'jollying up' the Turks. A prominent sector in the Anzac line was named 'Johnston's Jolly' after him.
Kannengiesser, Colonel Hans	Commander, Turkish 9th Division	German officer who led with great skill throughout the campaign. History has not remembered him adequately for his achievements.
Keyes, Commodore Roger	Royal Navy	Chief of Staff to Admiral de Robeck during the naval battle of 18 March. He lobbied for the naval attack to be resumed during the campaign.
Keysor, Lance Corporal Leonard, VC	1st Battalion, AIF	Awarded the VC for gallantry during the attack on Lone Pine, 7 August.

Name	Unit/role	Historical notes
Kitchener, Lord Herbert Horatio	British Secretary of State for War	British field marshal who, in 1915, was in charge of the armed forces of Britain. He was adored by the public and his 1914 'Lord Kitchener Wants You' recruitment drive led to a flood of volunteers. He oversaw the Gallipoli fiasco with a mixture of bluster and impulsiveness. In November 1915 he came to Gallipoli and recommended the peninsula be evacuated. His reputation was severely dented by the failure of the campaign, but his death in 1916 arrested his fall from grace.
Lalor, Captain Joseph	12th Battalion, AIF	Grandson of Peter Lalor, the leader of the Eureka Stockade. On the day of the landing at Gallipoli, Joseph led a small group of men forward to the Nek. He was killed there late in the afternoon.
Liman von Sanders, General Otto	Commander, Turkish Fifth Army	German commander of the Turkish troops at Gallipoli. His astute planning and steady leadership during the campaign greatly contributed to the Turkish victory.

Name	Unit/role	Historical notes
Lloyd George, David	British Cabinet Minister	As a member of the War Council, Lloyd George initially gave his qualified approval to an attack on the Dardanelles, but became an outspoken critic of the campaign in its later stages. Succeeded Kitchener as secretary of state for war in 1916 and later that year became prime minister.
MacLaurin, Colonel Henry	Commander, 1st Australian Brigade	MacLaurin's Hill, in the centre of the Anzac line, was named after him. He was killed there by a sniper on 27 April.
Mahon, Lieutenant-General Sir Bryan	Commander, British 10th Division	One of the British generals responsible for the debacle at Suvla. On 15 August he was outraged when a lower-ranked general inherited the Suvla command and resigned, abandoning his men while they were fighting for their lives on the heights.
Malone, Lieutenant-Colonel William	Commander, Wellington Battalion, NZEF	One of the unsung heroes of the campaign, he led his men with bravery and skill during the attack on Chunuk Bair. He was killed on 8 August and is commemorated on the Chunuk Bair Memorial.
Martin, Private James	21st Battalion, AIF	Australia's youngest casualty at Gallipoli. He died of enteric fever on 25 October, aged 14.

Name	Unit/role	Historical notes
M'Cay, Colonel James	Commander, 2nd Australian Brigade	M'Cay's Hill, behind Lone Pine, is named after him. He coolly led his brigade during the landing and the Second Battle of Krithia in May.
Monash, Colonel John	Commander, 4th Australian Brigade	In 1918 he commanded the Australian Corps in France and became one of Australia's greatest generals, but in 1915 his leadership abilities left a bit to be desired. His shortcomings during the August Offensive contributed to the costly failure of his brigade in its attack on Hill 971. Monash Valley, the main thoroughfare to the front line at Anzac, is named after him.
Monroe, General Sir Charles	Commander-in-Chief, Mediterranean Expeditionary Force	Replaced Hamilton as commander of the MEF in October and immediately called for Gallipoli to be abandoned. He oversaw the successful evacuation in December and January.
Moorehead, Alan	Australian war correspondent and historian	His 1956 book *Gallipoli* was widely acclaimed. His uncle had been killed during the campaign.
Morgenthau, Henry	American Ambassador to the Ottoman Empire	Morgenthau toured the Turkish defences in the lead-up to the naval battle, and his accounts provide a useful insight into the Turkish preparations for the campaign.

Name	Unit/role	Historical notes
Morshead, Captain Leslie	2nd Battalion, AIF	Landed on the first day and fought throughout the campaign. Later fought on the Western Front and in the Second World War won fame as the defender of Tobruk. Remains one of Australia's most respected military commanders.
Murdoch, Keith	Australian journalist	Father of Rupert Murdoch. At the start of the war he unsuccessfully lobbied to become Australia's Official War Correspondent. He visited Gallipoli in August and later wrote a letter to the British prime minister that was highly critical of the conduct of the campaign and its commander, General Hamilton. The letter helped crystallise the Cabinet's failing faith in the campaign and contributed to Hamilton's eventual sacking.
Onslow Thompson, Lieutenant-Colonel Astley	Commander, 4th Battalion, AIF	Led his men in the misguided charge across the Daisy Patch on 26 April. He was killed late in the day.
Owen, Lieutenant-Colonel Robert	Commander, 3rd Battalion, AIF	Owen's Gully near Lone Pine is named after him.
Parker, Lance Corporal Walter, VC	Portsmouth Battalion, Royal Naval Division	British soldier who won the first VC at Anzac, for rescuing wounded on the night of 28–29 April.

Name	Unit/role	Historical notes
Plugge, Colonel Arthur	Commander, Auckland Battalion, NZEF	Established his headquarters on Plugge's Plateau, the first significant height at captured at Anzac, on 25 April.
Pope, Lieutenant-Colonel Howard	Commander, 16th Battalion, AIF	Pope's Hill, the dominant hill at the head of Monash Valley, is named after him. Men from the 16th Battalion dug in here on the evening of 25 April.
Quinn, Major Hugh	15th Battalion, AIF	Quinn's Post, probably the most deadly spot at Anzac, was named after him. He was killed there on 29 May.
Russell, Brigadier-General Andrew	Commander, New Zealand Mounted Rifles Brigade	Russell's Top, on the left of the Anzac line, was named after him.
Schuler, Phillip	Australian journalist	Correspondent for the Melbourne *Age*. His observations about the campaign were astute. He joined the army in 1916 and was killed on the Western Front the following year.
Shout, Captain Alfred, VC	1st Battalion, AIF	Awarded a posthumous VC for gallantry during the attack at Lone Pine on 9 August.
Simpson, Private John	3rd Field Ambulance	The 'man with the donkey'. Early in the campaign he commandeered a donkey which he used to carry men with leg wounds from the front line to the dressing station on the beach. He was killed in Shrapnel Gully on 19 May.

Name	Unit/role	Historical notes
Sinclair-MacLagan, Lieutenant-Colonel Ewan	Commander, Australian 3rd Brigade	MacLagan's Hill, above Anzac Cove, is named after him. His brigade was the first ashore on the day of the landing.
Steel, Major Thomas	14th Battalion, AIF	Steele's Post at Anzac is named after him.
Stopford, Lieutenant-General Sir Frederick	Commander, British IX Corps	The bumbling commander of the Suvla force. His inaction and pessimism during the landing was the key contributing factor to the failure of the Suvla campaign. He was sacked on 15 August.
Symons, Lieutenant William, VC	7th Battalion, AIF	Awarded the VC for gallantry at Lone Pine on 9 August.
Talat Bey	Turkish Minister of the Interior	One of the Young Turks who led the Ottoman Empire during the First World War. He was assassinated in Berlin in 1921.
Temperley, Lieutenant-Colonel Arthur	Brigade major, New Zealand Infantry Brigade	Partly responsible for the failure of the attack on Chunuk Bair. On 10 August he ordered 'with deep regret' his machine-gunners to fire on British troops who were attempting to surrender to the Turks.
Throssell, Second Lieutenant Hugo, VC	10th Australian Light Horse	Awarded the VC for gallantry at Hill 60 on 29 August.
Tubb, Lieutenant Frederick, VC	7th Battalion, AIF	Awarded the VC for gallantry at Lone Pine, 9 August. He was killed in 1917 in Belgium.
Tulloch, Captain Eric	11th Battalion, AIF	Led a group of 60 men further inland than just about any other group of Australians on the day of the landing.

Name	Unit/role	Historical notes
Walker, Brigadier-General Harold 'Hooky'	Commander, Australian 1st Brigade	Walker's Ridge, on the left of the Anzac line, is named after him.
White, Major Cyril Brudnell	1st Australian Division Headquarters	Chief of Staff of the 1st Division. He was the chief architect of the successful evacuation of Anzac.
Zeki Bey	Commander, Turkish 21st Regiment	Commanded his regiment during the Australian attack at Lone Pine. In 1919 he returned to Gallipoli with Charles Bean and answered many questions about the campaign from the Turkish perspective.

Casualties of the Gallipoli Campaign

	Killed	Wounded	Total
Britain	26,054	44,721	70,775
France (estimated)	10,000	17,000	27,000
India	1,682	3,796	5,478
Australia	8,141	17,970	26,111
New Zealand	2,445	4,752	7,197
Turkey (estimated)	59,500	110,500	170,000
Total	**107,822**	**198,739**	**306,561**

The above figures are battle casualties only. When non-battle casualties (due to such things as disease and accidental injury) are considered, the total casualties for both sides probably exceed 900,000. France and Turkey did not produce official casualty figures for the campaign, so casualties for these two countries are estimates based on a number of sources.

References and Sources

Aspinall-Oglander, C. F., *Military Operations, Gallipoli*, Volumes I–II, W. Heinemann, London, 1929–1932.

Bean, Charles, *Official History of Australia in the War of 1914–18*, Volumes I–II: The Story of Anzac, Angus & Robertson, Sydney, 1921–1924.

Bean, Charles, *Gallipoli Mission*, ABC Books, Sydney, 1991.

Bean, Charles, *Anzac to Amiens*, Australian War Memorial, Canberra, 1961.

Bush, Eric, *Gallipoli*, Allen & Unwin, London, 1975.

Carlyon, Les, *Gallipoli*, Macmillan, Sydney, 2004.

Cutlack, F.M., *Official History of Australia in the War of 1914–18*, Volume VIII: The Australian Flying Corps, Angus & Robertson, Sydney, 1923.

Downham, Peter, *Diary of an Old Contemptible*, Leo Cooper, London, 2004.

East, Ronald (ed.), *The Gallipoli Diary of Sergeant Lawrence of the Australian Engineers – 1st A.I.F. 1915*, Melbourne University Press, Carlton, 1981.

Facey, Albert, *A Fortunate Life*, Viking, Ringwood, 1984.

Fewster, Kevin (ed.), *Gallipoli Correspondent: The Frontline Diary of C. E. W. Bean*, Allen & Unwin, Sydney, 1985.

Frame, Tom, *The Shores of Gallipoli*, Hale & Iremonger, Sydney, 2000.

Gammage, Bill, *The Broken Years*, Australian National University Press, Canberra, 1974.

Gillam, John, *Gallipoli Diary*, George Allen & Unwin, London, 1918.

Grant, Ian, *Jacka VC*, Macmillan, Sydney, 1989.

Hamilton, Sir Ian, *Gallipoli Diary*, Volumes I–II, George H. Doran, New York, 1920.

Herbert, Alan, *The Secret Battle*, Knopf, New York, 1920.

Herbert, Captain Aubrey, *Mons, Anzac and Kut*, Hutchison & Co., London, 1930.

Holt, Tonie and Valmai, *Major & Mrs Holt's Battlefield Guide to Gallipoli*, Leo Cooper, London, 2000.

Idriess, Ion, *The Desert Column*, Angus & Robertson, Sydney, 1941.

James, Robert Rhodes, *Gallipoli*, Papermac, London, 1989.

Kannengiesser, Hans, *The Campaign in Gallipoli*, Hutchinson & Co., London, 1928.

Kemal, Mustafa, *Atatürk's Memoirs of the Anafartalar Battles*, Istanbul, 2005.

Knox, Ronald, *Patrick Shaw-Stewart,* W. Collins, Glasgow, 1920.

Lord, Graham, *Niv: The Authorized Biography of David Niven*, St Martin's Press, New York, 2004.

Mackenzie, Sir Compton, *Gallipoli Memories*, Cassell, London, 1929.

McLachlan, Mat, *Walking with the Anzacs*, Hachette, Sydney, 2007.

Morgenthau, Henry, *Ambassador Morgenthau's Story*, Doubleday, Page & Co, New York, 1919.

Mure, Major A. H., *With the Incomparable 29th*, Chambers, Edinburgh, 1918.

Niven, David, *The Moon's a Balloon*, Dell, New York, 1976.

Pedersen, Peter, *Monash as Military Commander*, Melbourne University Press, Carlton, 1985.

Prior, Robin, *Gallipoli: The End of the Myth*, UNSW Press, Sydney, 2009.

Rule, Edgar, *Jacka's Mob*, Angus & Robertson, Sydney, 1933.

Shadbolt, Maurice, *Voices of Gallipoli*, David Ling, Auckland, 2001.

Snelling, Stephen, *VCs of the First World War: Gallipoli 1915*, Sutton, Gloucestershire, 1995.

Stanley, Peter, *Quinn's Post*, Allen & Unwin, Sydney, 2005.

Steel, Nigel and Hart, Peter, *Defeat at Gallipoli*, Papermac, London, 1995.

Taylor, Phil and Cupper, Pam, *Gallipoli: A Battlefield Guide*, Kangaroo Press, Sydney, 2000.

Waite, Fred, *The New Zealanders at Gallipoli*, Whitcombe and Tombs, Christchurch, 1919.

Wigmore, Lionel (ed.), *They Dared Mightily*, Australian War Memorial, Canberra, 1963.

Index